# BLACK ALCOHOL ABUSE AND ALCOHOLISM

# BLACK ALCOHOL ABUSE AND ALCOHOLISM

## An Annotated Bibliography

Thomas D. Watts, D.S.W.
Roosevelt Wright, Jr., Ph.D.

PRAEGER

PRAEGER SPECIAL STUDIES • PRAEGER SCIENTIFIC

New York • Westport, Connecticut • London

Library of Congress Cataloging-in-Publication Data

Watts, Thomas D.
Black alcohol abuse and alcoholism.

Includes indexes.
1. Afro-Americans--Alcohol use--Bibliography.
2. Alcoholism--Treatment--United States--Bibliography.
3. Alcoholism--United States--Prevention--Bibliography.
I. Wright, Roosevelt. II. Title.
Z7721.W37 1986 016.3622'92'08996073 85-28245
[HV5292]
ISBN 0-275-92083-6 (alk. paper)



Library of Congress Catalog Card Number: 85-28245
ISBN: 0-275-92083-6

First published in 1986

Praeger Publishers, 521 Fifth Avenue, New York, NY 10175
A division of Greenwood Press, Inc.

Printed in the United States of America

The paper used in this book complies with the Permanent Paper Standards issued by the National Information Standards Organization (Z39.48-1984)

10 9 8 7 6 5 4 3 2 1

Dedicated to

The memory of my mother, Martina C. Watts,
and to my father, Dale Watts

My dear wife and friend, Elaine Wright

## Foreword

Drinking, alcoholism, and alcohol abuse are subjects that hold deep personal meaning for many people. Scholars in many disciplines including psychology, medicine, law, politics, sociology and social work, religion and literature have long been fascinated by the use and effects of alcohol. It remains a difficult area to study.

While alcohol abuse and alcoholism are recognized as significant and growing problems among the general population, the focus on these problems among black Americans is yet in the development stage. Dr. Frances Larry Brisbane has observed: "There is no such thing as 'black alcoholism,' however--there are black people with alcoholism." Nonetheless, despite lingering concern by some over the characteristics and needs of black Americans, less focused information has been published that is devoted to the unique problems of alcohol abuse and alcoholism within this population. Also, the problem is further compounded by the interdisciplinary nature of the subject. Information on black drinking, alcohol abuse and alcoholism is scattered throughout the literature of many disciplines, and in a variety of formats. Needless to say, searching this literature can be a very difficult and tedious task.

In response, Drs. Watts and Wright have developed in book form a bibliography that presents annotations of articles, books, and other published material concerned with various aspects of drinking, alcohol abuse and alcoholism among black people. The result is a book that brings together a substantial amount of literature on this group, a book that will serve as a reference for those who wish to learn more about this important subject. It should serve as a seminal resource for anyone wishing to pursue a scholarly examination of this topic.

Fulton Caldwell
National Institute on Alcohol Abuse and Alcoholism
Rockville, Maryland

## Acknowledgments

We have many people to thank in the preparation of this book. We wish to thank William Day, Medical/Life Science Editor, Praeger Publishing Co., for his valued assistance, and as well Fulton Caldwell and Paula Pachon of the National Institute on Alcohol Abuse and Alcoholism, Rockville, Maryland and Ms. Billie D. Starr, Head, Minority Cultures Collection, The University of Texas at Arlington Library. We wish to thank the bibliographers who have gone before us in this area, and wish to express special thanks to Donna Turner, and thanks also to Carol Davis, Joy Crow and Joanne Tenery for their work on the manuscript itself. We wish to thank anyone who has been of any assistance to us in this effort, and we know that it has all been worthwhile if we can say that we have learned more about black alcoholism and in turn have helped to prevent or helped to treat in more effective ways the many-sided problem of black alcoholism.

## CONTENTS


Foreword vii

Acknowledgments ix

Introduction xiii

References xvii

Bibliography 1

Appendix 237

Directory of State and Territorial Alcoholism Program Directors 240

## Introduction

Black alcoholism is a severe health and mental health problem. Yet, historically there has been relatively little research done on black alcoholism (U.S. NIAAA, 1981:7). The authoritative _Fifth Special Report to the U.S. Congress on Alcohol and Health_ (U.S. NIAAA, 1984:129) states:

> For many years, accurate data on the nature and extent of alcoholism among ethnic and racial minorities within this country were unavailable, making the task of prevention efforts within and between these groups difficult. Now, however, better data are available on alcoholism and problem drinking among Black, Asian, Hispanic, and Native Americans.

More and better research has begun to appear in recent years on this problem. Admittedly, much of the earlier published material was descriptive. But more substantive research has begun to appear (both quantitative and qualitative) and has reached such a size that a reasonably large bibliographical compilation is now possible.

Our aim here is to bring together in one volume most of the written literature in the English language on the seminal subject of black alcoholism. We hope that this book bibliography on black alcoholism will be of help in coming to grips with this problem, and in launching further research into the causes, prevention and treatment of black alcoholism. We want this book to have utility throughout the human services, among a variety of practitioners and professionals, in the social and behavioral sciences, the biological sciences, and with anyone who in any way is interested in black alcohol abuse and alcoholism.

Defining "alcohol abuse" and "alcoholism" is a difficult task:

> When the term "alcoholic," "alcohol abuser," or "problem drinker" is used to designate an alcohol abuser, it must be kept in mind that these designations are somewhat less than precise. What is usually meant by an alcoholic is an individual who has been formally diagnosed as such or has (or has had) serious alcohol problems that meet implicit or explicit criteria of alcoholism, whether or not these have ever been formally diagnosed.... the term "heavy use" sometimes means use that is statistically

> more frequent than is true of American users generally.... it is used to indicate a level at which pathological (or adverse behavioral) changes occur more frequently. Some types of episodic or binge drinking may fit neither definition of heavy use, but may nevertheless have serious implications (e.g., drunk driving) (U.S. NIAAA, 1984: xiii).

Alcoholism is a "complex, chronic psychological and physiological disorder associated with excessive drinking" (U.S. NIAAA, 1981: 125). Our concern here is with alcohol abuse and alcoholism in the black community. By "black" we mean a person "belonging to a dark-skinned race or one stemming in part from such a race; esp... Afro-American" (Webster's Ninth New Collegiate Dictionary, 1983: 155). Our concern here is primarily that of alcohol abuse and alcoholism among American blacks. However, there are several references to African blacks. There is recognition here that blacks as a population group are quite varied, speaking different languages, and living in various areas of the globe. Still, our primary concern here, in reiteration, is with blacks in the United States. We are primarily behavioral science oriented here. Many references to blacks and alcohol in history (Prohibition period, etc.) are not included.

Bell and Evans (1981:1) state that alcoholism can be treated and prevented most effectively when cultural contexts are taken into account. The cultural and environmental contexts of black alcoholism are of much importance. Blacks in the U.S. (and in other parts of the world, as well) have been an oppressed people. Racism, classism and inequality have been and still are very much part of the black experience (Wright, Jr., et. al., 1983). Alcohol abuse and alcoholism cannot be separated from that context. Social thinking and social thought on alcoholism are important (Watts, 1982, 1986) in respect to the total context of alcoholism. Black alcohol abuse and alcoholism in the U.S. must be considered in the context of black social thought on alcohol abuse and alcoholism and as well in the context of American social thought in general on alcohol abuse and alcoholism.

Dorothy B. Porter (1984) has remarked that "no bibliography is ever completed," and this one is no exception. Some references (not many) were deliberately left out for purposes of space, and others were simply either unavailable, or unknown to us. We did try to include nearly every reference on black alcoholism from the 1940s to the present. We gave more weight to current pieces, and to research based studies over descriptive ones. We followed a chronological order by year (and within year by alphabetical arrangement) with the subject and author index in the back of the book. We could have followed a subject format (for example, putting all studies on black youth in one section, etc.) but we decided against doing so. One reason for not doing so is that "everything is related to everything else." Subject groupings in the text itself pose a number of other problems. One problem here is that older pieces are grouped together alongside more recent research. But a chronological grouping such as is followed in this book is not without its problems as well. There is no one approach to bibliographic organization that is completely satisfactory to everyone, and there is no totally comprehensive bibliography on any topic (as has already been mentioned).

Bibliographers (or those who attempt to put together bibliographies) must labor under many burdens, not the least of which is the fact there does not exist a comprehensive information policy in the U.S. (Henry, 1974) or at the international level. Information is generated by a wide range of people and institutions, on a wide range of subjects, and often with no understanding in common of the meaning of key words or phrases.

We would recommend that readers approach this bibliography with a holistic perspective. Other bibliographies on the black family (Davis, 1978), the black aged (Davis, 1980), black child development (Myers, Rana, et. al., 1979), black mental health and bibliographies on a host of other areas are helpful for studying black alcoholism. Black alcoholism is such a wide-ranging problem (Watts and Wright, Jr., 1983; Wright, Jr, and Watts, 1985) affecting so many areas of life, that to confine a bibliographic search to references specifically on "black alcoholism" may miss other important aspects that need to be examined. The reader here is specifically referred to a bibliography of black bibliographies, compiled by Richard Newman (1984).

The following guide should be helpful for utilizing this book bibliography:

Book

## FORMAT: SAMPLE ENTRIES

Authors

Book Title

Bell, Peter and Evans, Jimmy, Counseling the Black Client: Alcohol Use and Abuse in Black America. Center City, Minnesota: Hazelden Foundation, 1981, pp.

Publisher

Year Published

Publisher Location

Pages (if known)

Abstract would go here.

Article

Author

Title of Article

Dawkins, Marvin P., "Alcohol Information on Black Americans: Current Status and Future Needs," Journal of Alcohol and Drug Education, 25(3): 28-40, 1980.

Volume number

Issue number

Page numbers

Year

Journal Title

Abstract would go here.

## References


The American Heritage Dictionary of the English Language, ed. by William Morris. New York: American Heritage Publishing Co., Inc., and Houghton Mifflin Co., 1970.

Bell, Peter and Evans, Jimmy Counseling the Black Client: Alcohol Use and Abuse in Black America. Center City, Minnesota: Hazelden Educational Services, 1981.

Davis, Lenwood, G., The Black Aged in the United States: An Annotated Bibliography. Westport, Connecticut: Greenwood Press, 1980.

Davis, Lenwood G. (with the assistance of Janet Sims), The Black in the United States: A Selected Bibliography of Annotated Books, Articles, and Dissertations on Black Families in America. Westport, Connecticut: Greenwood Press, 1978.

Henry, Nicholas L., "Knowledge Management: A New Concern for Public Administration," Public Administration Review 34(3): 189-196, 1974.

Myers, Hector F., Rana, Phyllis G., and others., Black Child Development in America 1927-1977: An Annotated Bibliography. Westport, Connecticut: Greenwood Press, 1979.

Newman, Richard, comp., Black Access: A Bibliography of Afro-American Bibliographies. Westport, Connecticut: Greenwood Press, 1984.

Porter, Dorothy B. "Introduction: Fifty Years of Collecting." In Richard Newman, comp., Black Access: A Bibliography of Afro-American Bibliographies. Westport, Connecticut: Greenwood Press, 1984, pp. xvii-xxviii.

United States. National Institute on Alcohol Abuse and Alcoholism. A Guidebook for Planning Alcohol Prevention Programs with Black Youth. Rockville, Maryland, 1981.

United States. National Institute on Alcohol Abuse and Alcoholism. Fifth Special Report to the U.S. Congress on Alcohol and Health. Rockville, Maryland, 1984.

Watts, Thomas D., ed., Social Thought on Alcoholism. Melbourne, Florida: Krieger Publ. Co., 1986.

Watts, Thomas D., "Three Traditions in Social Thought on Alcoholism," International Journal of the Addictions 17(7): 1231-1239, 1982.

Watts, Thomas D., and Wright, Jr., Roosevelt, eds., Black Alcoholism: Toward a Comprehensive Understanding. Springfield, Illinois: Charles C. Thomas Publ., 1983.

Webster's Ninth New Collegiate Dictionary, ed. by Frederick C. Mish. Springfield, Mass: Merriam Webster Inc., Publishers, 1983.

Wright, Jr., Roosevelt; Saleebey, Dennis; Watts, Thomas D.; Lecca, Pedro J., Transcultural Perspectives in the Human Services: Organizational Issues and Trends. Springfield, Illinois: Charles C. Thomas, Publ., 1983.

Wright, Jr., Roosevelt and Watts, Thomas D., eds., Prevention of Black Alcoholism: Issues and Strategies. Springfield, Illinois: Charles C. Thomas, Publ., 1985.

On each Saturday night it is quite common in Maryland (the slave state from which I escaped) for masters to give their slaves a considerable quantity of whiskey to keep them during the Sabbath in a state of stupidity. At the time when they would be apt to think--at a time when they would be apt to devise means for their freedom--their masters give them of the stupefying draught which paralyzes their intellect, and in this way prevents their seeking emancipation.

----------Frederick Douglass (1846)

The above from: Frederick Douglass, "Intemperance Viewed in Connection with Slavery: An Address Delivered in Glasgow, Scotland, on 18 February 1846." Reported in the Glasgow *Saturday Post*, 21 February 1846, and in the Glasgow *Examiner*, 21 February 1846. In *The Frederick Douglass Papers, Series One: Speeches, Debates, and Interviews*. Volume 1: 1841-46, ed. by John W. Blassingame. New Haven, Connecticut: Yale University Press, 1979.

# 1943 - 1964

## 1943

1
Winston, S. and Butler, M., "Negro Bootleggers in Eastern North Carolina," American Sociological Review, 8(6): 692-697, 1943.

The pattern of rural crime covered by the expression "bootlegging" is studied in terms of black youth on probation for violations of the Federal Revenue Act. Two hundred Eastern North Carolina black males on probation between the ages of 16 and 24 (mean age 20.7) years) were studied. Data was obtained by interview over a period of six years (1934-1940)... The authors conclude here that "the problem of probation goes beyond that of the individual. The institutional, agricultural and rural-industrial resources of the rural South need to be developed as to provide opportunities for all youth, only then will it be possible to effectively counteract the forces which have produced youthful Negro bootleggers."

## 1954

2
Skolnick, J.H. "A Study of the Relations of Ethnic Background to Arrests for Inebriety," Quarterly Journal of Studies on Alcohol, 15(2): 622-630, 1954.

This study is based on the police records of all male residents of the city of New Haven, totalling 1,169, with 47% being booked on charges of inebriety. Working from an assumption that there are marked differences in arrest rates along ethnic lines, this study found a disproportionately high rate of black arrests. However, when controls for ecological social class areas were instituted, the black rates dropped considerably. The data suggested that factors from at least two different settings--subcultural ethnic groups and social stratification groups--operate to determine the differences in arrest rates.

## 1955

3
Lewis, H. Blackways of Kent. Chapel Hill, N.C.: University of North Carolina, 1955.

This was a four month long demographic study of the customs of the black population in a bi-racial community in the Piedmont South, a region bordering the Appalachian Mountains. The town studied had a population of 4,000 and was given a pseudonym, "Kent". Cultural aspects such as religion, family, marriage, government, education and social control were studied, using a participant observation approach. The social effects of drinking and drunkenness are considered in regard to both public drinking (in the town's seven "colored" taverns) and private drinking. In "Kent" the frequency with which alcohol appears as a factor in non-marital sex-play, "touchy" behavior, and "having a good time," and the lack of extensive rationalizations for its use or abuse point to near successful integration of alcohol with other aspects of the culture. In "Kent", whiskey tends to be more of an individual or family problem than a social problem.

## 1961

4
Maddox, G.L., and Allen, B. "A Comparative Study of Social Definitions of Alcohol and its Uses Among Selected Male Negro and White Undergraduates," Quarterly Journal of Studies on Alcohol, 22: 418-427, 1961.

This study considers some applications of symbolic interaction theory to the understanding of drinking practices in certain groups (selected black and white undergraduates). The study focuses on the establishment, by means of an adapted Thematic Apperception Test (TAT), of modalities in social expectations associated with alcohol as they appeared in the fantasies of comparable groups of white and black male college undergraduates. 48 male volunteers, 24 white and 24 black, predominantly Protestant, from families of middle class background, were included (abstainers as well). White and black respondents did not differ reliably in the content of their TAT projections about alcohol: black respondents reflected even more ambivalence and a more negative emphasis than whites. The researchers attribute the observed responses of the black sample to the ambiguous social position of the "black bourgeoisie," as described by Frazier, and to different modes of communication among persons placed differently in the social structure, as discussed by Schatzman and Strauss in their hypothesis.

5
Strayer, R., "A Study of the Negro Alcoholic," Quarterly Journal of Studies on Alcohol, 22: 111-123, 1961.

This study examined how the black alcoholic differs from the Anglo alcoholic, especially in regard to factors relating to treatment success. All black alcoholics admitted to the Bridgeport Clinic of the Connecticut Commission on Alcoholism for a nine and one-half year period ending in 1958 were studied (44 blacks and 1264 anglos). These numbers were proportionate to the distribution of the population in the area, but black women were over-represented. Black women responded more favorably to treatment than black men or Anglo women (Anglo men were not included in the comparison). The author maintains that cultural features set the black alcoholic apart from Anglos (i.e., attempting to achieve respectability, the treatment relationship being viewed as an unwritten contract, matriarchial family). Individual therapy is advocated for all patients, but the therapist should recognize cultural differences in respect to blacks.

## 1962

6
Roebuck, J. and Johnson, R. "The Negro Drinker and Assaulter as a Criminal Type," Crime and Delinquency, 8(1): 21-33, 1962.

A sample of 40 black offenders with an arrest pattern composed largely of simultaneous "drunk and assault" charges was compared according to 34 sociopsychological characteristics with a sample of 360 black offenders who had one or more of a large number of other arrest patterns. In 24 of the 34 comparisons, the drunk-and-assault group were different (p * .01) from the larger sample. Its members were raised far more often in homes with a rigid, fundamentalist background, which was enforced by strict, dominating fathers. Their primary group ties were close in childhood, and in adulthood. Their general social milieu was less criminogenic. Parental efforts at character development were to some degree successful, so that this group could manifest hostility only after alcohol had weakened inhibitions, and then a rather explosive outburst of violence generally occurred. Sociopsychological and not strictly sociological factors are the significant variables which dispose this drunk-and-assault group to law violation. Alcohol problems in the ghetto, as in a previously researched white sample, are predicted by being raised in families that are broken, and irresponsible, and containing adults with drinking problems. Alcohol problems are predicted by early school problems, drug use, and delinquency. If an attack on early school problems can reduce the amount of problem drinking, a host of other ghetto problems may well decline as a result.

## 1964

7
Globetti, G. and McReynolds, M. *Comparative Study of the White and the Negro High School Students' Use of Alcohol in Two Mississippi Communities*. State College, Miss.: Mississippi State University, Report, 1964.

This study attempted to identify the sociocultural factors associated with alcohol consumption of teenagers in the white culture and black subculture of two Mississippi communities, and was based on the assumption that a cultural system defines the functions of an object within that system, determining the types of responses which an individual may take toward that object. A correlation analysis was done in which frequency of alcohol use was studied in relation to three broad groups of sociocultural factors.

8
Maddox, G.L. and Borinski, E. "Drinking Behavior of Negro Collegians; a Study of Selected Men," *Quarterly Journal of Studies on Alcohol*, 25(4): 651-668, 1964.

Three themes were extracted here: (1) drinking is prevalent among blacks; (2) drinking among blacks is associated with a high incidence of personal and social complications; and (3) Middle-status blacks are characterized by self-disparagement as a prominent component of the complications associated with drinking. A probability sample of 49 black male collegians in a southern Protestant coeducational college was sued to assess the generalizations implicit in the literature. The basic instrument was a pretested interview schedule administered by trained black upperclassmen. In addition to items which allowed placement of subjects in the social structure, the study attempted to secure information about the quantity and frequency of alcohol use; definitions of and preoccupation with alcohol, complications associated with drinking, and self-esteem. The interview included cards from the Murray Thematic Apperception Test. The generalizations were supported. In comparison with youth described in other studies, the subjects were less likely to be abstainers (10%), and more likely to be light drinkers (55%) but not more likely to have experienced complications as a result of drinking. Compared to adults of another study they were more likely to be preoccupied with alcohol (45%) and to drink for personal effect (59%). Low self-esteem was found to be a general correlate of both preoccupation and drinking for effect. A negative image of alcohol was reflected in the projective material: alcohol was thought of more often in terms of its capacity to modify reality. The most persistent theme was inebriety and alcoholism (32%), followed by family disruption (13%), personal trouble, accident, death or some other personal loss (12%), and physical aggression (6%). 63% had been advised by some adult, primarily their parents, to abstain, and 67% also had advised some other persons, usually a close friend, to abstain. Only 4 subjects (8%) described both parents as drinkers or social drinkers. 20 (41%) described both parents as either nondrinker or abstainer, and 25 (51%) indicated a situation in which one parent was described as an abstainer and the other not. 80% of the respondents accepted the notion that drinking is too expensive to enjoy, 55% rejected the proposition about leisure time being more enjoyable than work, and 84% rejected the proposition that achievement connects with factors outside themselves. Only 39% rejected the proposition that work is primarily a way of making a living rather than a calling. These findings were interpreted to indicate substantial internationalization of a "Protestant Ethnic" orientation in most subjects.

## 1965

9
Bailey, Margaret B.; Haberman, Paul W.; Sheinberg, Jill. Distinctive Characteristics of The Alcoholic Family. New York: National Council on Alcoholism, 1965. pp. 1-35.

This is the final report of a pioneering 3-year study (1962-1965) of marital interaction and family roles in families with alcoholism and 2 matched comparison groups of nonalcoholic families. Interviews with both spouses were conducted among community samples as opposed to clinical patients. One of the comparison groups consisted of families in which members had stomach ulcers or other chronic gastrointestinal ailments. The other was a "normal" comparison group. The alcoholic group had a higher proportion of Irish and black families, whereas the gastrointestinal disorder group included a greater number of Jews. A total of 430 interviews were conducted. Alcoholic couples reported more disagreements, in addition to conflict about the drinking itself, but they tended to deny their frequency or their seriousness. In the alcoholic group, quarrels, frequently characterized by physical or verbal abuse, had a low rate of resolution.

10
Blacker, E., Demone, H.W., Jr. and Freeman, H.E., "Drinking Behavior of Delinquent Boys," Quarterly Journal of Studies on Alcohol, 26(2), 223-237, 1965.

Examination of the drinking practices of 500 delinquent boys in the Massachusetts Youth Reception Center. Of the 500 (average age, 15 yrs.), 28% were abstainers, 9% had used alcohol once (one-timers), and 63% were considered drinkers (2 or more experiences). The type of drinker correlated significantly with race, and with previous court involvement, but was not significantly related to social class. Blacks had a lower rate of alcohol usage and lower rates of relief and pathological drinking than whites did.

11
Larkins, John R., Alcohol and The Negro: Explosive Issues. Zebulon, NC: Record Publ., 1965, 251 pgs.

Alcohol, negro, history, religion, economics, politics, social control, patterns of consumption, colonial days, slave trade,

8

whiskey, taxes, southern states, civil war, reconstruction, Progressive Era, riots, Prohibition, World War I, racial conflict, Volstead act, Eighteenth Amendment, Depression, New Deal, repeal, World War II, Korean War, civil rights, temperance, American Temperance Society, Christian Church, preacher, schism, baptist, methodist, reform, postwar problems, WCTU, antisaloon league, licenses, economic value, alcoholic beverage, constitution, the sixties, territorial expansion, disfranchisement, twentieth century.

12
Wilson, John M., "Sociological Investigation and Comparative Analysis of Patterns of Beliefs of Negro and White Male Alcoholic Offenders Regarding The Use of Alcoholic Beverages." Dissertation. Ann Arbor, MI: University Microfilms, 1965.

The author describes nine subordinate hypotheses developed to substantiate a central hypothesis which contains the statement that negro alcoholic offenders of Washington D.C. Differ from white alcoholic offenders in patterns of belief concerning the use of alcoholic beverages. Positive results of a study indicate a need for future research to be aimed at providing treatment practitioners with realistic frames of reference for helping specific categories of offenders.

## 1966

13
Globetti, G. and McReynolds, M., "A Comparative Study of White and Negro Students' Use of Alcohol in Two Mississippi Communities," *Social Science Research Center Preliminary Report*, No. 4, 1966. Also publ., 1964, Mississippi State University.

A comparative analysis of the social factors involved in the use of alcohol by a sample of white and black high school students in two Mississippi communities. Explanations of a teenager's drinking behavior are explained in terms of the cultural prescriptions for alcohol use included in his or her social system.

14
Halverson, Darrell R. *Tuberculous Alcoholic and His Ethnic Group: An Exploratory Study.* Seattle: University of Washington, Medical Student Research Meeting (Psychiatry): 12 Sept., 1966.

White, Indian, Negro, and Oriental tubercular alcoholic and nonalcoholic discharged patients (117) from the Firland Tuberculosis Sanatorium were compared. Differences were found in age, education, religion, marital status, disease level, hospital treatment, and duration of illness.

15
Kuller, L., Lilienfeld, A., and Fisher, R. "Sudden and Unexpected Deaths in Young Adults: An Epidemiological Study," *Journal of the American Medical Association*, 198(3): 248-252, 1966.

A study of sudden unexpected deaths in the 20- to 39-year age group indicated that cirrhosis and fatty liver caused more deaths among black males (24.5%) and females (39.1%) than among white males (19%) and females (37.5%).

16
Sherman, M.J. "Abstention: An Exploratory Analysis of Reference Group Behavior and Non-Use of Alcohol among Negro Male Collegiates." Master's Thesis. Durham, North Carolina: Duke University, 1966.

## 1967

17
Globetti, G., Attitudes Toward Alcohol Education: A Comparative Study of Negro and White Community Members. State College, Miss.: Mississippi State University, State College, Report, 1967.

Results showed that (1) attitudes toward alcohol education varied according to ethnic affiliation; (2) neither black or white groups had committed any effort to a systematic study of alcohol and alcoholism; and (3) black respondents had a negative image of the alcoholic and were confused as to the cause of alcoholism.

18
Globetti, G., "Comparative Study of White and Negro Teenage Drinking In Two Mississippi Communities." Phylon - The Atlanta University Review of Race & Culture. 28(2): 131-138, 1967.

A comparative analysis is made of the social factors related to the use of alcohol among young people of different racial and ethnic backgrounds. The author suggests that the use of alcohol in American society is a culturally defined pattern which varies according to subgroup affiliation and membership. The analysis was based on a sample including 314 white and 214 black high school students living in two Mississippi communities. Contrary to the belief held by many that the use of alcohol is unrestrained in black society, this study demonstrated that black students were governed more by adults than were white students.

19
Liebow, E., Tally's Corner: A Study of Negro Streetcorner Men. Boston: Little-Brown & Co., 1967.

This study concerns a "shifting collection of anchorless adult black males who come together more or less regularly on Tally's Corner in a blighted section of Washington D.C.'s inner city during the early 1960's." The stress here is on "the acting, as well as the classic acting-out behavior, and the varying levels of responses of these poor and marginally poor urban Negro males." Adaptive patterns of habits and habitats, the "up-tight" buddy system as a resource and buffer protecting dignity and rationalizing and concealing failure when necessary are studied here. Means of adaptation and alleviation considered here are drug and alcohol use, as well as gambling.

20
Stern, M.W., "Drinking Patterns and Alcoholism Among American Negroes," In Pittman, D.J., ed., Alcoholism, New York: Harper and Row, 1967, pp. 69-98.

Explored here are the following dimensions of black alcoholism: 1) normative orientations toward alcohol use (ritualistic, rites de passage, conviviality, abstience, utilitarian); 2) tolerance for intoxication and intoxication-related behaviors; and 3) culturally consistent, stable drinking customs for which there is consensus. The alcoholism rates for blacks, as suggested by most studies, are generally higher than for whites, with the same being true for problem drinking rates. Black alcoholism rates are 2 to 4 times higher than white rates. When one controls for socioeconomic status, migration status, and for urbanization, black alcohol rates are still higher than those for whites. Alcoholism rates for black females are uniformly higher than those of white females. Controlling for education, urban female rates are higher at each educational level for blacks than for whites, from 3 to 6 times higher; with increased education, the gap is greater. Employed black females have alcohol rates over 3 times higher than those of employed white females. Black female homemakers have an alcoholism rate that is 5.5 times higher than white female homemakers. The sex ratio of alcoholic males to females differs by race. The ratio for blacks is much lower than for whites: black females run a greater risk of alcoholism, relative to black males, than do white females, relative to white males. Unlike white females as compared to white males, black females appear to be at more disadvantage than black males, having a slower decline in alcoholism of alcoholism mortality rates than do males. There are few generalizations that can apply to the drinking behavior of the American black as a whole because of the differences in lifestyle between lower status blacks and the black middle class. Systematic and quantified data about alcohol use are not available and therefore no generalizations are possible regarding the prevalence of drinking and abstaining or the distribution of types of drinkers by age, gender, social status, urban-rural and regional differences.

## 1968

21
Aronson, S.M. and Aronson, B.E., "Clinical Neuropathological Conference." Diseases of the Nervous System, 29(5): 336-343, 1968.

The case of a 41-year-old black male with complaints of muscle stiffness, weakness, and alcoholism was diagnosed as primary myopathy, implicating alcohol as a primary cause.

22
Maddox, G.L., "Drinking Among Negroes; Inferences From the Drinking Patterns of Selected Negro Male Collegians," Journal of Health and Social Behavior, 9(2): 114-120, 1968.

The material presented in the Quarterly Journal of Studies on Alcohol, 29: 117-129, 1968 is considered, with the additional conclusion that the heavy escape drinking and self-derogation characteristic of older black collegians provides inferential evidence of the drinking patterns of adult black males.

23
Nathan, Peter E.; Lipson, Alberta G.; Vettraino, Anthony P.; Solomon, Philip., "Social Ecology of an Urban Clinic for Alcoholism: Racial Differences in Treatment Entry and Outcome," International Journal of The Addictions, 3(1): 55-63, 1968.

The alcoholism clinic at Boston City Hospital undertook to examine for racial differences the utilization rates of their clinic. Twenty demographic, personal history, treatment frequency and treatment outcome variables were elicited from 129 patients. The percentage of negroes attending the clinic was 16. The data showed that when negroes came to the clinic, they sustain continued treatment less often and drop out prematurely more often than do white patients. Age and treatment outcome are positively related and age predicts outcome of treatment more consistently than any other demographic variable, including race. This clinic does not attract the older negro patient who would probably do well in treatment and thus does not perform the function of treating the general population as it was set up to do.

24
Robins, Lee N., "Project Follow-up Summary: Childhood Predictors of Mobility and Criminality." St. Louis, Missouri: Washington University Medical School, Psychiatry Dept., 1968.

This is a follow-up of negro boys who attended St. Louis elementary schools between 1930 and 1934. The negro male population offers a sample in which is concentrated a high proportion of the urban problems of poverty, crime, delinquency, and disrupted homes, which provides cases to test hypotheses concerning the variables of deviance and class. Findings indicate that: drug use and heavy drinking had serious effects on adult adjustment as measured by employment, marital stability, and arrests for non-drug and non-alcohol offenses; the effects of drug use and heavy drinking were independent of the effects of high school graduation and the home environment; and that potentially serious school problems can be identified in first and second grade.

25
Robins, L.N., Murphy, G.E. and Breckenridge, M.B., "Drinking Behavior of Young Urban Negro Men," _Quarterly Journal of Studies on Alcohol_, 29(3): 657-684, 1968.

Drinking behavior was studied in 235 black males aged 30-36, born and reared in St. Louis, Mo., whose names had been selected from elementary-school records. Information about drinking was obtained by interview with 95% of the sample (and by searching agency records). Of the 223 subjects, 61% were at some time heavy drinkers (7 or more drinks per week and 7 or more per occasion or 4 daily), 30% currently; 18% once distributive drinkers (7 or more drinks per week but less than 7 per occasion), 23% currently, 17% once light drinkers (less than 7 drinks per week), 37% currently; 4% once nondrinkers, 10% currently. The subjects began drinking at an early age, and early drinking was associated with becoming a heavy drinker: 13% before age 11 (of whom 79% became heavy drinkers), 38% before age 15 (73% heavy drinkers), 66% before age 17 (69% heavy drinkers), 84% before age 19 (67% heavy drinkers). Heavy drinking was twice as common in these males as in a previously studied sample of white males similarly identified in the St Louis school records (abstract in _Quarterly Journal of Studies on Alcohol_, 24: 567-568, 1963), and problems from drinking were found to be more than 3 times as common. 20% had a public record of some drinking problem; 46% reported problems due to drinking and 53% reported personal concern about drinking excessively: 27% had a history of medical problems (6% alcoholic psychosis, 3% liver damage, 9% hospitalization for alcohol-related problems, 20% tremulousness, 2% gastritis): 44% had a history of social problems (20% arrests for alcohol-related offenses, 35% family complaints, 6% job difficulties)... Failure to graduate from school together with late delinquency predicted that heavy drinkers (89%) would become problem drinkers (94% of heavy drinkers); 49% of high-school graduates without elementary-school problems became heavy drinkers, and of these 49% became problem drinkers.

26
Vitols, N. M., "Cultural Patterns of Drinking in Negro and White Alcoholics," Diseases of The Nervous System, 29(6): 391-394, 1968.

Discusses negro drinking patterns from data based on the admission of negro alcoholics to North Carolina Mental Health facilities. The data indicated a lower incidence of negro alcoholics than white, but was not considered to be a true reflection of the incidence or rate of alcoholism in both races. Negro drinking patterns were believed to reflect the inseparability of historical, social and cultural factors. The drinking problem in the negro is believed to be one of adaptation where it is predicted that the negro will share the patterns of white alcoholics if he comes to share the white man's culture and society more fully.

## 1969

27
Brunswick, A.F., "Health Needs of Adolescents: How the Adolescent Sees Them," _American Journal of Public Health_, 59(9): 1730-1745, 1969.

This article presents the findings of a study designed to understand how adolescents view their health and problems and to determine whether ethnic groups show differences on these matters. The Washington Heights Study of Adolescent health was a pilot study, involving a personal interview and a physical examination. This report is based solely on findings from personal interviews with 122 males and females aged 12-17 years. The research instrument was a largely precoded, structured interview schedule, administered by interviewers who were matched to the respondents by sex and ethnicity. The interviews were with individual males and females in their homes during May and June of 1967...The ethnic composition of the sample was 20% black (32--17 boys and 15 girls, 32% Hispanic (51--25 boys and 26 girls), and 48% white (39--25 boys and 14 girls)...Black girls and Hispanic boys were most often critical of their general state of health...Four-fifths of Hispanic and black youth said being healthy mattered a lot. Hispanic boys were fatalistic about being able to avoid illness. Of the representative sample of 122 adolescents aged 12 to 17, 32% considered drinking a major health problem among their peers. Of the 25 Hispanic males, 25 white males, 17 black males and 15 black females, 32, 24, 30, and 26% drank at least one can of beer weekly; 12, 16, 18, and 13% respectively, drank 3 or more cans. At least one drink of distilled spirits weekly was reported by 33% of the black girls and 18% of the black males, 16 and 8% of the Hispanic males and females, and 8 and 7% of the white males and females. Three or more drinks weekly were reported by 13 and 6% of the black females and males, 8 and 4% of the Hispanic boys and girls.

28
Cahalan, D., Cisin, I.H., and Crossley, H.M., _American Drinking Practices_, New Brunswick, NJ: Rutgers Center of Alcohol Studies, Monograph No. 6, 1969.

This study identified 2511 white, 200 Negro and 35 other race respondents, and contains a table and a brief description of drinking practices by ethnicity and sex. There is considerably more discussion (including numerous tables) of ethnic differences in drinking where respondent-specified "national identity" is employed as the ethnic identification variable...There was little difference in the drinking rates of black and white males; however, black females had higher proportions than white females of abstainers (51 vs. 39%) and heavy drinkers (11 vs. 4%)...The proportion of U.S. born non-white drinkers (which included black respondents) who were heavy drinkers was one of the highest (30% among Latin-American, Caribbean; 23% among U.S. non-white, 22% among Italians). Among the heavy drinkers, the percentage of U.S. born non-whites who were identified as heavy escape drinkers was also high. Non-white respondents were not more likely to say having a drink is helpful when depressed or nervous. They were more likely to say that tranquilizers, other pills and going to church were helpful. These respondents were considerably higher than average on 4 of the 5 "escape" reasons for drinking.

29
Carson, J.E., Gorwitz, K., "Is There a Revolving Door?", Maryland State Medical Journal, 18(3): 123, 1969.

In this survey of 904 non-white and 2279 white men in Maryland State mental hospitals, 24 and 15% were admitted in acute alcoholic states; 65 and 77% were admitted with a primary diagnosis of alcoholism.

30
Dohrenwend, B.P., "Social Status, Stress and Psychological Symptoms," Milbank Memorial Fund Quarterly, 47(1, pt. 2) (January), 137-150, 1969.

Studied the incidence of psychiatric disorder among black and Puerto Rican groups relative to their social class counterparts in more advantaged ethnic groups in the Washington Heights area of New York City. Results suggest that there are strong ethnic and class differences in ways of expressing stress.

31
Journal of the National Medical Association, "Negro-White Differences in Alcoholic Psychoses," 61(2): 197, 1969.

Blacks tend to suffer from alcoholic psychosis in adolescence, but among whites, alcoholic psychosis is a disease mainly of middle age.

32
King, Lucy Jane; Murphy, George E.; Robins, Lee N., "Alcohol Abuse: A Crucial Factor in The Social Problems of Negro Men." _American Journal of Psychiatry_, 125(12): 1682-1690, 1969.

Increasing degrees of alcohol use were found to be associated with increasing evidence of social deviance in an interview study of 223 urban black males. Alcohol abuse is described as an important variable in the cycle of broken home, delinquency, and underemployment, rather than simply a symptom of social deviance.

33
McCord, William, Howard, John, Friedberg, Bernard, Harwood, Edwin, _Life Styles in the Black Ghetto_, New York, NY: W.W. Norton, 1969.

This study of the urban Black featured interviews with 1,185 urban Blacks in three American cities. Another 620 people were interviewed who represented different responses to ghetto life. The authors "attempted to unify the sociological and psychological approaches to the problem by examining the collective responses of urban Negroes to their condition and the reaction of the white establishment to these movements." William McCord, in Chapter 7, "The Defeated" discusses alcohol and drug use and abuse in the ghetto environment.

## 1970

34
Cahalan, D., Problem Drinkers: A National Survey. San Francisco, CA: Jossey-Bass, Inc., 1970.

Only a small portion of this book focuses on ethnic differences. The major conclusion regarding blacks was that they (and those of Latin-American and Caribbean backgrounds) had higher than average scores on an alcohol problems scale which involved social consequences, on an Alienation and Maladjustment measure, and on an Unfavorable Expectations measure. The relationship between these two measures (and four other social-psychological variables) and demographic variables was discussed.

35
Globetti, G., "The Drinking Patterns of Negro and White High School Students in Two Mississippi communities," Journal of Negro Education, 39(1): 60-69, 1970.

It is stated here that the use of alcohol in the U.S. represents culturally defined patterns which vary according to sub-group affiliation and membership.

36
Globetti, G. and Pomeroy, G., "Characteristics of Community Residents Who Are Favorable Toward Alcohol Education," Mental Hygiene, 54(3): 411-415, 1970.

Two communities were surveyed to ascertain their attitudes toward alcohol education. Factors of race, sex, social class and age were important. White parents in both communities were equally favorable while black parents in one community were less favorable... Regardless of class the white community appeared to be more favorable. The relation between communities and alcohol education program acceptance was discussed.

37
Harrison, D.E., "Emerging Drinking Patterns of Pre-Adolescents: A Study of the Influence of Significant Others." Dissertation. Ann Arbor, MI: University Microfilms International, 1970.

This study examined the nature and extent of alcohol use among pre-adolescent sixth graders in a Mississippi community, and the influence of significant others on the use and non-use of alcholic beverages... When the data were examined with racial status controlled, it was found that males of both racial sub-groups were more likely to be users than females. With sexual status controlled, there appeared to be no significant differents in the proportion of white and Black males classified as users. A significantly higher proportion of white females are users as compared with Black females...

38
Maddox, G.L., "Drinking and Abstinence: Emergent Patterns Among Selected Negro Freshmen," In: G. Maddox, Ed., _The Domesticated Drug: Drinking Among Collegians_, New Haven: College and University Press, 1970, pp. 146-175.

Research on 262 young black males (median age of 18.7), was conducted (1963). A direct relationship between quantity/frequency and socioeconomic status was found. The lowest socioeconomic group contained the highest number of abstainers: Heavier drinkers were located in the highest socioeconomic status group. Social role aspirations influenced whether they chose to drink while in college, and peer influence encouraged abstainers to drink.

39
Robins, L.N,. and Guze, S.B. "Drinking Practices and Problems in Urban Ghetto Populations," In N.K. Mello and J.H. Mendelson, _Recent Advances in Studies of Alcoholism: An Interdisciplinary Symposium_. Washington, DC: June 1970, pp. 825-842.

Two follow-up studies of the consequences of drinking problems in the ghetto are considered. The first, a study by interview and record search of urban born and reared black males in their early 30s, found that half had some history of medical or social problems attributable to drinking excessively. Those with problem drinking subsequently suffered for the first time drug use, divorce, arrests, and incarceration with a frequency one-and-a-half to three-and-a-half times that of males from similar backgrounds without drinking problems with an equivalent numbr of years at risk...Like White males previously studied, Black males develop problems with alcohol when they have been raised by inadequate parents, and when they themselves have had a history of juvenile behavior problems.

40
Siegal, H.A., "The Drinking Man: Lower-Class Negro Drinking Patterns and Alcoholism in an Urban Setting." Criminology, 8(3): 263-278, 1970.

The drinking patterns and life style of 16 black males living in the basement of an apartment building in the South Bronx area of New York City are discussed. Their lives are structured around alcohol. The men work only for subsistence, and everything is shared among all the group members. Wine is the most frequently consumed beverage (Because it is cheapest), and a constant level of intoxication is usually maintained. Several roles are distinguished: the "main man" provides living facilities for the group, the "hustler" has contacts with the outside world, especially the job market, and the "advocate" obtains goods and services from the social agencies in the area. This group is a much more cohesive one than Skid Row drinking groups, probably because the South Bronx ghetto is a primarily family-oriented area where "sticking together" is the norm. It lacks caretaker institutions which characterize the Skid Row environment, and makes reliance on the drinking group a necessity for survival.

## 1971

41
Davis, Fred T., Jr. "The Para-Professional; An Essential Component in a Multi-Discipline Team Approach to the Treatment of Ghetto Alcoholism," In R. Brock, Ed., Selected Papers Presented at the General Sessions, 21st Annual Meeting, San Antonio, Texas, 1970. Washington, DC: North American Association of Alcoholism Programs, 1971, pp.27-29.

The alcoholism unit at the Harlem Hospital Center began in 1967 as a 3-year research project, and has since become a permanent outpatient unit at the hospital. A multidisciplinary team approach to the treatment of the urban ghetto alcoholic is employed. Several paraprofessionals who are recovered alcoholics are employed, with a day room for the unemployed patients being staffed mainly by the para-professionals. Various treatment approaches are used at the unit, including group therapy, individual counseling, occupational therapy and follow-up home visits and crisis intervention are provided. The paraprofessionals work in conjunction with the rest of the staff in most of these areas. Case histories of three patients are presented here.

42
Garrett, G.R., "Drinking Behavior of Homeless Women." Ph.D. Dissertation, Ann Arbor, MI: University Microfilms International, 1971.

The life histories and drinking patterns of homeless women were examined and compared with those of homeless men. Interviews with 52 women were conducted at the Women's Emergency Shelter in New York City in the summer of 1969...The Shelter women were younger, more often black, and more financially deprived than the men...A general self-perception test and a quantity-frequency index were used as measures of current drinking...Over half of the Shelter women had been heavy drinkers at some time; their mean age at onset of heavy drinking was 32 years (men, 28 years). The women were more likely to drink alone...Significantly more women heavy drinkers came from large families. All the women, irrespective of their drinking status, had experienced a major crisis event which, in most, occurred in their late 20s or early 30s. The "skid careers" of heavy drinkers, as measured by life-time patterns of affiliations (employment, organizational membership, living with other persons) were similar to the careers of other homeless women.

43
Lipscomb, W.R., "Drug Use in a Black Ghetto," California Mental Health Research Digest, 9(1): 28-29, 1971.

Data are presented here on drug use in urban, black ghettos. Information was gathered from a group of black males considered representative of the ghetto residents, because they possessed three or more of the characteristics employed to define hard core poverty. Subjects were interviewed when they were admitted to a work training program and again 6 to 12 months afterward. 87% had at some time used alcohol, 54% marijuana, 20% amphetamines, 5% hallucinogens, 4% barbituates, and 3% heroin. Poorly accounted for discrepancies in data garnered at the second inverview are apparent, however, with only 37% admitting to marijuana use. The figures are considered as comparable to non ghetto drug use and it is concluded here that drug use and experimentation are fully acceptable phenomena of the ghetto community.

44
Robins, L.M., et al., "Adult Psychiatric Status of Black Schoolboys," Archives of General Psychiatry, 24(4): 338-344, 1971.

The adult psychiatric status was studied of 235 black males of average or better intelligence who were urban born or urban educated between 1930-1934. Despite discrimination, young urban black males apparently differ little from whites in rates of psychiatric disorders. Three childhood variables were studied, and it was found that the child's own antisocial behavior was a more powerful predictor of adult psychiatric status than was either his family's social status or his father's history of antisocial behavior (this same result was also noted for whites). All three childhood predictors were positively associated with the diagnosis of antisocial personality in adult life.

45
Rubington, E., "The Changing Skid-Row Scene," Quarterly Journal of Studies on Alcohol, 32(1): 123-135, 1971.

Skid row is a vanishing social system with a declining population of deviants, now predominantly of older whites and young blacks and a rising rate of both violent internal crime and alcoholism. Only one third were alcoholics and one third were abstainers; but in the newer population alcoholics predominate. These changes will affect the caretakers who deal with homeless alcoholics both on and off skid row.

46
Rutgers University Center of Alcohol Studies, Drinking Behavior of Young Urban Negro Men. New Brunswick, N.J., 1971, 29 pages.

A study of drinking behavior of negro men born and reared in St. Louis, MO., is described. Drinking patterns and elements in the life histories leading to heavy drinking are discussed. It is pointed out that inadequate parents and a history of juvenile behavior problems contribute greatly to the development of heavy drinking and accompanying medical and social problems.

47
Siegel, H.A., "The Drinking Man: Notes on the Lifestyle of the Ghetto Alcoholic," Yale Sociology Journal, Spring 1971.

A 13-month study was conducted in the southeast Bronx, New York City, on the lifestyle of the middle-aged black alcoholic living in a ghetto area. The patterns of consumption and the types of beverages are discussed, along with the subculture of the drinking man - who does not consider himself an alcoholic. The exploitation of this subculture by the non-drinkers in the area is seem by living arrangements, and the normative elements of the culture are discussed. Sharing is the most pervasive of the mores, and "mutual protection" is in effect. The daily round is spent socializing with friends, which includes extensive discussion of current events and the telling of dirty tales and jokes. The liquor store owner is another exploiter of this group. Patterns of consumption are considered therapeutic, symbolic, and instrumental, providing mutually reinforcing elements. Other cultural traditions in ghetto life demand that persons stick together in the face of adversity, combining with the drinking patterns to give this subculture a unique stability and strength over the individual.

48
Zimberg, S., Lipscomb, H. and Davis, E.B., "Sociopsychiatric Treatment of Alcoholism in an Urban Ghetto," American Journal of Psychiatry, 127(12): 1670-1674, 1971.

The treatment program for socioeconomically deprived Negro alcoholics at the Harlem Hospital Center is discussed. Previously unpublished research found that 60% of the males and 34% of the female inpatients at the hospital had "diagnosable levels of alcohol abuse;" approximately 18% of admissions to the medical service were for alcoholism-related conditions... Of the 79 male alcoholics, aged 25 to 44, randomly assigned to the day care program, 55% achieved stage 4 and 33% achieved stage 5. Despite the severe state of social and economic deprivation experienced by these alcoholics, more patients could have achieved a higher level of functioning if more vocational rehabilitation had been available.

## 1972

49
Bluestone, H. and Connell, S., "Treatment Goals for the Alcoholic in an Urban Ghetto." Conference paper presented at the 23rd Annual Meeting of the Alcohol and Drug Problems Association, September 23-26, 1972, Atlanta, GA.

Treatment goals for a poor urban ghetto black and Puerto Rican population are discussed. An alcoholic treatment program in the East Bronx is described. The area is poor, has few services, is high in crime and disease, and is generally rundown. The average alcoholic client is a black male between 31 and 40 yers of age, separated from his spouse but living with relatives, usually unemployed and physically ill. Physical treatment is provided immediately and drug therapy is limited as a guarantee of this return to the program. Antiabuse is employed for selected patients, assistance with pressing environmental problems is provided, and regulations (primarily, no alcohol) are enforced. The usual motivations to stop drinking (good job, family) are lacking, and history taking and specific psychiatric goals serve no useful purpose. Patients are instead placed in problem-oriented groups concerned with their specific needs. Abstinence is not stressed in ghetto areas.

50
Chaucer, N.G., "The Brotherhood Approach to Alcoholism," _Connecticut Medicine_, 36(8), 435-436, 1972.

A new approach (about two years old at the time of this writing) to treatment of alcoholics through interaction with ex-alcoholics working through a club is discussed. After a history of failures in the medical approach to treating homeless male alcoholics, especially blacks and Puerto Ricans, an ex-alcoholic, Willie Cousin, convinced the Hartford City Director of Health to try a direct, personal approach through interaction with ex-alcoholics. With the aid of the local council on alcoholism he established a black branch of Alcoholics Anonymous and developed the Brotherhood Club as an interim facility. There were four or five evening meetings a week, including one Alcoholics Anonymous meeting, one educational and social meeting and one purely social meeting, with group participation in cooking and eating. 259 men and 132 women have been helped in some substantial way by the program (at that time). Clients are brought to a major care center and are picked up by a Brotherhood member when they are ready for discharge. During a 9-month period, 1758 people made contact with the program. About half, 814, left after the first contact. 20% (362) have remained in the program and attend at least three meetings every month. 7% (134) have remained sober and have returned to gainful work.

51
Davis, Fred T., Effective Delivery of Services To Black Alcoholics. Washington, D.C., Roy Littlejohn Associates, 1972. 85pp.

A study of alcoholism programs in the black community reveals a lack of cohesion between multiple program elements resulting in inadequate service delivery. Suggested elements of a comprehensive program for successful treatment and rehabilitation of the black alcohol abuser include: (1) acute medical care and nonmedical emergency services, (2) inpatient and outpatient treatment, (3) intermediate care, (4) rehabilitation services, (5) custodial care, (6) societal and welfare services, (7) consultation and education, and (8) research and evaluation. It is further felt that all programs must be responsive to changing community needs and resources.

52
Edmundson, W.F., Davies, J.E. and Acker, J.D., "Patterns of Drug Abuse Epidemiology in Prisoners," Industrial Medicine and Surgery, 41(1): 15-19, 1972.

A health survey of two-thirds (470) of the population (92 percent male) of a county jail disclosed that a larger proportion of the whites (58 percent) than the blacks (43 percent) were regular users of illicit drugs. Regular alcohol use was equally distributed, however, among all age groups of both races.

53
Gross, Milton M.; Rosenblatt, Sidney M.; Lewis, Eastlyn. "Acute Alcoholic Psychosis and Related Syndromes: Psychosocial and Clinical Characteristics and Their Implications", British Journal Of Addiction, 67(1):15-31, 1972.

The authors examined 63 variables in 567 males admitted to Downstate Medical Center suffering from acute alcohol withdrawal syndromes, and found that demographic variables and clinical factors affect the etiology of the disease. Black patients tended to be younger and had a higher incidence of hallucinations. Older, less educated patients had a greater clouding of the sensorium. Previous admissions had a higher incidence of disrupted marriages, and aggressive behavior upon admission. Deaths occurred largely among middle-aged white first admissions, while seizures occurred among white, middle-aged multiple admissions. Hallucinations occurred in those with more clouding of the sensorium and were not present in those with suicidal/homicidal behavior. Clouding of the sensorium was related to the severity of the disease, duration of hospital stay, and fevers. Convulsions did not worsen the prognosis as fevers did.

54
Hyman, M.M., Helrich, A.R. and Bessen, G., "Ascertaining Police Bias in Arrests for Drunken Driving," Quarterly Journal of Studies on Alcohol, 33(1-Part A): 148-159, 1972.

It is concluded here that the high ADWI rate among minority and disadvantaged groups probably reflects accurately a greater frequency of drunken driving among them rather than a police bias in arrests.

55
Littlejohn, R. and Assocs., An Exploratory Study of Distinctive Problems in Alcohol Abuse Among Black Americans in Four Communities. Washington, DC: Report prepared for NIAAA, DHEW, NIMH, 1972. See United States. National Institute on Alcohol Abuse and Alcoholism.

56
Lowe, George D., Hodges, Eugene H., "Race and the Treatment of Alcoholism in a Southern State", 1972. Social Problems , 20(2): 240-252, 1972.

A study is made of the relationship between race and the delivery of services to patients in a southern state facility for alcoholic rehabilitation. In this study, questions to be answered were: (1) How were black alcoholic persons treated within the state alcoholism program, (2) Where were they treated, and (3) Why were they not found in treatment programs. Findings indicate that local communities exercise alternatives with deviant drinkers and disproportionately channel white alcoholic individuals toward treatment, and black alcoholic individuals to prison. These findings were supported by a comparison of commitment and incarceration rates. Possible outcomes of such a practice are discussed. Statistical tables are given.

57
Marshall, Harvey, and Purdy, Ross., "Hidden Deviance and The Labelling Approach: The Case For Drinking and Driving," _Social Problems_, 19(4): 541-553, 1972.

Two alternative theories to explain the overrepresentation of certain social classes - such as blacks and lower-class males - in official conviction statistics for drinking and driving were examined. According to the first, or "impartial" model, the probability of conviction is determined primarily by the degree and frequency of deviance. The second, or "labeling" model, holds that the probability is at least partially independent of degree or frequency. The findings in general are consistent with the "labeling" model, although some support is given to the "impartial" model as well.

58
National Institute For Community Development Inc., _Final Report On Alcohol Abuse and Alcoholism, Workshop On Alcoholism and Blacks_. Washington, D.C., 1972.

Alcohol-related problems among black Americans are discussed. Recommendations are offered on how to use the resources of NIAAA to meet the needs of the black community.

59
National Institute For Community Development, Inc., _Final Report On National Institute Of Alcohol Abuse and Alcoholism Workshop On Alcoholism and Blacks_. Washington, D.C., 1972, 153 pages.

The 1972 New York Conference on Alcoholism and Blacks sponsored by NIAAA and The Center for Minority Group Mental Health Programs (CMGMHP) is summarized. The report includes an excerpt of an 1882 essay by Frederick Douglass on efforts to perpetuate black slavery through alcoholism. It covers reasons for the workshop, its background, organization and design, activities, and findings and recommendations. An "exhibits" section contains materials intended for use by workshop participants.

60
Robins, L.N., "An Actuarial Evaluation of the Causes and Consequences of Deviant Behavior in Young Black Men." In: Life History Research in Psychopathology. Volume 2. Eds. M. Roff, L.N. Robins and M. Pollack. Minneapolis, Minnesota: University of Minnesota Press, 1972, pages 137-154.

61
Stern, Muriel W., Pittman, David J., Drinking Patterns In The Ghetto. St. Louis, Mo.: Washington University Social Science Institute, 1972, 713 pgs.

The drinking behavior and orientations manifested in an urban American Negro slum population are examined in depth. Most of the data were collected from residents of the Pruitt-Igoe Housing Project in St. Louis, Mo. The authors describe the social organization of drinking behavior in this urban ghetto, and relate the pattern of alcohol use to the larger system of social roles and values within which it is manifested; and explore some of the parameters of alcohol-related deviance in this population. Major emphasis is placed on alcohol use patterns, attitudes, and motives, and the social contexts within which they are learned and displayed, with less attention to the problematic aspects of drinking.

62
Stroup, A.L. and Robins, L.N., "Elementary School Predictors of High School Dropout Among Black Males," Sociology of Education, 45(2): 212-222, 1972.

Elementary school predictors of high school dropouts were analyzed in a sample of 223 black urban males. School retardation, truancy, early drinking activity, parental social status and number of elementary schools attended were most clearly associated with high school dropout. It is suggested here that elementary schools could offer greater incentives for regular attendance, individualized instruction to prevent failure, and could allow children to stay on in a familiar school when families move across school district boundaries.

63
United States. National Institute on Alcohol Abuse and Alcoholism. _Executive Report of The NIAAA Workshop On Alcoholism and Blacks._ Rockville, Md., 1972.

NIAAA and the National Institute For Community Development, contracted with each other to conduct a workshop on alcoholism and the black community. The purpose of the workshop was to assist NIAAA in planning, establishing priorities and implementing strategies designed to initiate programs concerned with alcohol abuse in the black community. Of paramount importance were the areas of physical health, mental health, sociocultural subsystems, economics, and law. The major finding to emerge from the workshop was that reliable data concerning blacks and alcoholism are unavailable or nonexistent, making the effort to plan activities and programs for blacks nearly impossible.

64
United States. National Institute on Alcohol Abuse and Alcoholism. _Exploratory Study Of Distinctive Problems Of Alcohol Abuse Among Black Americans In Four Communities_. Rockville, MD., 1972, 116 pages.

A study was made of the distinct problems of alcohol abuse among black Americans in four diverse communities: Gary, IN; Atlanta, GA; Rural and small/town Mississippi; and the borough of Manhattan, New York City. At issue were the problems of linking blacks with effective rehabilitation services and of uncovering ways of improving services to meet the needs of blacks. Findings are stated in terms of: (1) The views of blacks (versus whites) on problem drinking; (2) demographic characteristics of black alcohol abusers; (3) the variation in "systems" of agency services; (4) the distinct drinking habits of the four communities; (5) major problems associated with drinking; (6) major causes of drinking; (7) priorities in perceived needs, both for those in treatment and for those not in treatment; (8) experience with helping agencies, including the number and types of agencies used; and (9) suggestions on improving local services.

## 1973

65
Bourne, Peter G., "Alcoholism in The Urban Negro Population." In: P. Bourne & R. Fox, Eds., Alcoholism: Progress in Research and Treatment. New York: Academic Press, 1973. 439 p.

The author reviews the history of alcohol use and alcoholism within the black population of America. Drinking patterns and psychological factors are illustrated in case histories that show how social forces and family disorganization lead to, and compound, individual drinking problems. The author describes current innovative treatment approaches, and predicts that long overdue attention will be given to the black problem drinker in urban America.

66
Brunswick, A.F. and Tarica, C., "Drinking and Health: The Relationship Among Urban Black Adolescents," Paper presented at the 23rd Annual Meeting of the Society for the Study of Social Problems, 1973.

Personal home interviews were conducted with a representative sample of 668 black youth, 12-17 years old from one inner city health district. Physical, social and emotional aspects as well as psychosocial attitudes were studied.

67
Clark, W.A., "Black Pride, Drug Attitude, and Drug Use as They Relate to Black College Students." Dissertation. Ann Arbor, MI: University Microfilms International, 1973.

The purpose of this study was to investigate the relationships between (1) black pride and drug attitude, (2) black pride and drug use by categories, and (3) drug attitude and drug use by categories. 150 black students were polled at 14 sites. A random sampling was done, which included every fourth black subject who passed a predetermined site. Results indicated a positive correlation between the subjects' degree of black pride and their drug attitude, with males having a higher correlation than females (although females used less drugs)... It was concluded here that the best way to minimize drug abuse among black college students is to increase optimally their feelings of black pride.

68
Davis, Fred T. "Alcoholism Among American Blacks." Conference Paper. 24th Annual Meeting of Alcohol and Drug Problems Association, 1973.

The author believes that special programs need to be provided for minority group alcoholic persons and continued while efforts are made to teach these persons to use the system as it now stands. This paper focuses particular attention on alcoholism among black Americans, examining the cultural, economic, psychological, and social elements contributing to the development of alcoholism in the black population. The goals of NIAAA poverty alcoholism programs are cited. The need for continuity of care coupled with comprehensive care is stressed.

69
Davis, W.E. and Jones, M.H., "Race-Related Variations in Psychiatric Diagnosis," _Newsletter for Research in Mental Health and Behavioral Sciences_, 15(4): 31-32, 1973.

A race related survey was conducted to compare the type of psychiatric diagnosis given to blacks and Caucasians in a VA hospital at Downey, Illinois. A larger portion of blacks were diagnosed as being schizophrenic. A larger number of Caucasians were seen as alcoholic and depressed. The race of the psychiatric patient is a seminal subject variable in practice and in research.

70
Gillis, L.S.; Lewis, J.; Slabbert, M., "Alcoholism Among The Cape Coloureds." _South African Medical Journal._ 47(30):1374-1382, 4 Aug. 1973.

A random sample of cape peninsula blacks was interviewed in a community survey to determine alcoholism rates and drinking patterns. The prevalence of alcoholism in blacks, as indicated by the survey, was significantly higher than estimates of alcoholism elsewhere. The study revealed correlations, possibly causal, between alcoholism and the availability of wine, poverty and adverse social circumstances, and the role and status of individuals in the family.

71
Goodwin, D.W., "Alcohol in Suicide and Homicide," _Quarterly Journal of Studies on Alcohol_, 34(1): 144-156, 1973.

Suicide rates are lower among blacks than among white alcoholics. The low suicide rate among black alcoholics is possibly due to the early onset of problem drinking which may produce enough brain damage by middle age to dull the sufferings, and to the fact that few black alcoholics have had much wealth or status to lose.

72
Goodwin, Frances H., _Summary of Conference Lectures._ Dallas, TX.: El Centro College, Ethnic Alcohol Problems Conference, 1973.

Conference papers focusing on alcohol problems among the poor, American Indians, Chicanos, and blacks are summarized. Prevention and treatment approaches for these populations are discussed.

73
_Human Behavior._ "Black and White Drunks," 2(7):40-41, 1973.

Discriminatory rehabilitation practices in Georgia toward black alcoholics as compared to white alcoholics are briefly discussed.

74
Lowe, George D.; Alston, Jon P., "Analysis of Racial Differences in Services to Alcoholics in A Southern Clinic." _Hospital and Community Psychiatry_, 24(8):547-551, 1973.

An investigation was made to determine if delivery of services in the Georgian Clinic was influenced by racial differences. Data gathered through the use of seven indexes of service indicated no pattern of discrimination against black patients, neither did racial comparisons of patients with similar social characteristics show evidence of discrimination. The clinic's treatment philosophy and organizational structure encourage staff to relate to patients as individuals and discourage bureaucratic procedures, thus eliminating racial bias.

75
<u>Nation.</u> "Moistly Sober," 217:614, 1973.

Theorizing that heavy drinking is the result of an inability to conserve "precious" bodily fluids, the owner of Schick-Shadel Hospital has established a chain of clinics to eliminate alcoholism by retaining fluid levels in patients.

76
Phelps, Donald G., "Do Ethnic Minorities Need Special Alcoholism Programs?" <u>Addictions.</u> 2(3): 7-8, 1973.

The question of special treatment programs for minorities is discussed. Alcohol has been a part of black history since the establishment of slavery in the mid-1600s and today is a major source of recreation and relief in the black community. A study conducted among black Americans indicated that they are less likely to view excessive drinking as a problem requiring professional help. Spanish-speaking people often find no available services because Spanish-speaking people are not involved in the various agencies. It is necessary for those in the health care field to recognize the differences among people and see that these differences are accommodated in the mainstream of treatment centers.

77
Phelps, Donald, "Do Ethnic Minorities Need Special Alcoholism Programs?" Conference Paper. 1973 Annual Meeting of The National Council on Alcoholism, Inc. Washington, DC: 1-6 Apr 1973.

The author advocates greater sensitivity and responsiveness to the needs of different ethnic groups in the provision of alcoholism treatment services. Alcoholism problems applicable to different groups are reviewed, with emphasis on the history and extent of the problem among black Americans. The findings of a study by Roy Littlejohn Associates, Inc. on the distinctive problems in four black American communities are cited. The practicality of specialized treatment programs for ethnic minorities is questioned; in lieu of such programs, complete access by all minorities to a comprehensive treatment and health delivery system is urged. A renewed effort to train large numbers of people to meet the demands on such a system is recommended.

## 1974

78
Berberian, R.M., "Differential Rates of Drug Use Among Black and White, Affluent and Non-Affluent Adolescents." New Orleans: Paper presented to the Epidemiology Section of the Annual Meeting of the American Public Health Association, October 24, 1974.

79
Brunswick, Ann F., and Tarica, Carol. "Drinking and Health: A Study of Urban Black Adolescents", Addictive Diseases, 1(1):21-42, 1974.

Findings are presented of an investigation of relationships between drinking and health in 659 black adolescents aged 12-17 as self-reported in personal interviews. In general, the subjects recognized alcohol drinking and alcoholism as a major health threat. Drinking increased among the sample with age and did so considerably more sharply among boys than girls. Subsequent multivariate analysis showed that age alone was not a highly predictive drinking determinant. Drinkers, especially older girls, were more likely to have 16 out of the 51 health problems studied. On a composite measure of overall health status, younger boys and older girls evidenced the strongest relationship between drinking and poor health. Drinkers tended to worry more than nondrinkers. Older drinkers reported more sleep disturbance, although they demonstrated more self-regard than nondrinkers. Adolescent drinking is recognized as symptomatic of other health problems.

80
Chafetz, Morris E. Book Review of Alcoholism: Progress in Research and Treatment, Contemporary Psychology, 19(10): 724-725, 1974.

Alcohol serves many complex social functions, good cross section of contemporary alcoholism studies, interesting to students of far-flung disciplines, material for readers with limited knowledge and for experts. Peter Bourne on urban black alcoholism. Number of chapters regrettably quite technical. Barry Leach on Alcoholics Anonymous, Jared Tinklenberg on alcohol and violence, alcoholic withdrawal by Victor and Wolfe. Role that laws play in drinking behavior.

81
Davis, Fred T. "Alcoholism Among American Blacks." Addictions, 3(2):8-9, 12-16, 1974.

The problem of alcoholism among black americans is explored, with special emphasis on the cultural, economic, psychological, and social elements contributing to the development of alcoholism in the black population. Historical factors and the influence of black migrations are discussed, as are the nature and extent of alcoholism among blacks today. Special attention is accorded the question of the unique needs of black people and the appropriateness of services to meet such needs. The author advocates a dual approach consisting of special programs for minority-group alcoholic people and instruction of these people in the use of the prevailing treatment system.

82
Davis, William E., and Jones, Mark H. "Negro Versus Caucasian Psychological Test Performance Revisited." Journal of Consulting and Clinical Psychology, 42(5):675-679, 1974.

Differences in proportion of Negroes versus Caucasians receiving schizophrenic, alcoholic, and depressive psychiatric diagnoses are discussed. Greater number of Caucasians diagnosed as alcoholic individuals as compared to negroes.

83
Engler, Richard. Exploratory Study of Distinctive Problems of Alcohol Abuse Among Black Americans In Four Communities: Modified Report, (Report to NIAAA, 30 Sep 1972). Washington, DC, Ray Littlejohn Associates, Inc., 30 Sep 1974. 121 p.

Survey data from 4 different US communities (Gary, Indiana; Atlanta, Georgia; Rural-Smalltown, Mississippi; and New York City) indicate that agency alcoholism services vary greatly from one location to the other. Mississippi does not provide any services, Gary is typified by loss of services and institutional support, and Atlanta facilities are growing toward satellite center approaches in rehabilitation under OEO funding. New York City has a wide range of agencies and programs plagued by problems due to the control aspect of treatment referral. Forty-six agencies and 1085 black alcohol abusers or abusers" relatives were canvassed; the study was limited to accessibles, largely skid-row types. Areas of concern were linking alcohol abusers to rehabilitation and discovering service improvement methods. Drinking patterns, knowledge and use of agencies, and sex and age variables are covered. The authors suggest a new agency configuration to reach black abusers.

84
Feagins, Jack L. "Descriptive Study of Variance In Sources of Referral Pathways to Treatment For Black and Nonblack Alcoholics." Dissertation. Ann Arbor, MI: University Microfilms, 1974, 216 p.

Results of a questionnaire study examining the referral system and pathways to treatment for both black and nonblack alcoholic persons are reported. The study includes an evaluation of hypotheses on race, age, and sex in terms of data obtained from individual respondents, and an assessment of criteria used by certain social agencies in referring alcoholic persons to treatment. It also looks at black and nonblack groups at 2 specific treatment facilities, namely, Mercy Hospital Outreach Clinic in Pittsburgh and Chit Chat Residential Treatment Center in Wernersville, PA. Limitations of the study that lend themselves to follow-up research are noted, and implications for social work policy are discusses.

85
Harper, Frederick D., "Alcohol and Blacks: State of The Periodical Literature." Conference Paper. Rosslyn, VA: National Center for Alcohol Education: Seminar 1, 22 Oct., 1974. 25 pages.

The classified abstract archive of alcohol literature in conjunction with the Quarterly Journal of Studies on Alcohol were used as primary sources to access the status of literature on alcohol and blacks. Only abstracted articles were included in the survey. Each abstract was reviewed to ascertain focus in terms of topic and sample description, was categorized according to focus as indicated by title, purpose, and findings, and was placed in 1 of 6 topic areas such as treatment or alcohol education and prevention. Only 77 articles with discussion or findings pertinent to blacks were located of which only 11 dealt solely with black Americans out of some 16,000 studies reported over the last 30 years. Analysis by topic indicated drinking patterns and behavior articles to be most frequent. General findings from the literature are presented along with recommendations toward balancing the deficit of research on alcohol and blacks.

86
Herrera, C., "Substance Abuse Program at The New York Veterans Administration Hospital." Conference paper. New York: Proceedings of Puerto Rican Conference on Human Services, 14 Nov 1974. 263 p. (pp. 91-95).

The substance abuse program at the New York Veterans Administration Hospital is described. The combined drug and alcohol treatment program provides inpatient care, detoxification, and ambulatory methadone maintenance. The program has a strong outreach component that goes out to find patients, on the streets, in jail, and in the community. Alcohol and drug rehabilitation counselors in the program reflect the ethnic characteristics of the population being served, about 35 percent black and 20 percent Spanish-speaking.

87
Kuller, Lewis H., Perper, Joshua A., Cooper, Malcolm, "Epidemic of Deaths Attributed to Fatty Liver in Baltimore." Preventive Medicine, 3(1): 61-79, 1974.

Liver Cirrhosis, now the leading cause of death in the 25-44 year-old age group in Baltimore, is examined in an epidemiological study which revealed that (1) the increase in cirrhosis death rate is especially prominent among blacks, (2) the increase is primarily due to fatty liver sudden deaths rather than classical cirrhosis, (3) most fatty liver sudden deaths were unwitnessed, and (4) cirrhosis and fatty liver death rates were much higher in men than in women. Most of the classical cirrhosis, and probably nearly all the fatty liver deaths, were associated with alcohol consumption. The alcohol fatty liver sudden death rates were much higher in the lower as compared with the upper social class.

88
Maclachlan, Sharon D., Black Alcoholic: A Prospective Study. Berkeley. University of California, School of Public Health, 1974.

Thirty-one alcoholic patients at San Francisco General Hospital were interviewed in order to assess their reasons for drinking, the psychosocial stress and environmental factors in their behavior, and the availability of community resources for rehabilitation and prevention measures. The survey population was predominantly black (23 subjects), admitted to the hospital for causes other than alcoholism (26). Survey responses defined 4 alcohol abuse discord areas: loneliness, communication difficulties, lack of family ties, harmony, and support, and economic deprivation. Many subjects experienced stress from underemployment and inaccessibility of and unpreparedness for jobs. Although the community has been aware of an increasing alcoholism problem among ghetto residents, few treatment efforts have been directed to this area. Various therapy modalities are reviewed including family counseling and drug treatment.

89
McGrath, William; Owen, Uriel; Bigge, Robin. "Comprehensive Approach For The Treatment of Black Families or Individuals With Drinking Problems In Wyandotte County, Kansas." Conference Paper. San Francisco, CA: Alcohol and Drug Problems Association Conference, 12-18 Dec. 1974. 5 p.

A black alcoholism demonstration project is described as a four-pronged treatment approach for individuals or families who experience alcohol-related problems. The 4 program components include a "drop-in" facility, a transitional living group, a social skills development section, and a community development component. After outlining the program philosophy and assumptions, past and current community involvement in the program is discussed.

90
Novick, L.F., Hudson, H. and German, E., "In-Hospital Detoxification and Rehabilitation of Alcoholics in an Inner City Area," American Journal of Public Health, 64(11): 1089-1094, 1974.

A program of comprehensive care of 81 inner-city male alcoholics (aged 21 to 72, mean age 40.3, 66 blacks, 11 Puerto Ricans, 4 whites) is discussed. Representing 95 admissions over 10 months at a new 6-bed detoxication unit at the Hospital for Joint Diseases, Harlem, New York City, the patients were admitted for detoxication with the understanding that aftercare outpatient facility of the hospital would be required. Discharged patients were escorted to the first outpatient visit. The detoxication service is unique in that it provides care for urban black and Puerto Rican male alcoholics of low socio-economic class "without regard to future salvageability." The low abstinence rates achieved indicate the special problems presented in counteracting alcohol misuse in urban ghettos. The mean hospital stay was longer than anticipated, 15.7 (range 1 to 93 days) rather than 5 days. Dual addiction and coexisting social and health problems complicated treatment efforts: 23 patients were dually addicted, 75 had medical problems (usually liver complications) in addition to alcoholism and 67 were unemployed. After the first escorted visit, only 35 patients returned to the aftercare facility. Only 12 patients were still abstinent 5 to 15 months after discharge from the hospital. The program did not have residence, vocational training and placement services. Adequate aftercare in the inner city may require consideration of education, employment, housing, and multiple addiction problems.

91
Swift, Carolyn, "Utilization of Ministers As Alcohol Counselors: Increasing Treatment Alternatives in The Black Community." Conference Paper. San Francisco, CA: North American Congress on Alcohol and Drug Problems, 12-18 Dec. 1974. 20 p.

Two pilot projects designed to test the practicality and effectiveness of using black ministers as counselors for black alcoholic offenders in a municipal court or jail setting are evaluated. An alcoholism counseling workshop for black ministers was conducted in 1970 by the Wyandotte Mental Health Center in Kansas City, Kansas. As an outgrowth of this workshop, 2 separate but related programs were established in the following year: A program of court counselor aides involving ministers who attended the workshop, and a court class in alcoholism utilizing the ministers in teacher/therapist roles. These two programs proved highly effective in reducing recidivism among alcoholic offenders; providing education and therapy for offenders as an alternative to incarceration; providing a small core of dedicated community leaders in the field of alcoholism; and increasing treatment options for black alcoholic persons in the community.

92
United States. National Institute on Alcohol Abuse and Alcoholism. Revised Guidelines For The Black Alcoholism Projects. Rockville, Md., 1974.

Although a categorical grant program for alcoholism treatment projects directed toward the black population has not been established, applications for such projects are received and accepted according to certain guidelines which are presented in this report in draft form. It is hoped that treatment/rehabilitation/referral projects will be developed for all segments of the black community with the control focus in black communities. In order to help promote and deliver services that will be relevant to the special needs of black groups, it is suggested that grant applicants provide services which are consistent with the lifestyles of the people and the community to be served, i.e., culture, language, and values. These guidelines cover considerations of black self-determination and the preparation of a narrative program description for grant applicants.

93
University of New Mexico, Institute for Social Research and Development. Prevention/Rehabilitation Programs and The Black Community. Albuquerque, 1974.

A report on the prevention and rehabilitation services rendered to the black community of Albuquerque, New Mexico recommends the strengthening of existing programs over the initiation of additional or alternative programs. The basis of the report is a survey reflecting the attitudes of 90 black community residents to services and a survey describing 18 agencies' perceptions of their own programs. Results of a form questionnaire and a personal interview showed that 64 percent of the agencies and 94 percent of the black residents felt that prevention and rehabilitation services were not meeting the needs of the black community. The need for better relations and communication between the agencies and the community is emphasized.

94
Viamontes, Jorge A.; Powell, Barbara J., "Demographic Charcteristics of Black and White Male Alcoholics," International Journal of The Addictions, 9(3):489-494, 1974.

The authors surveyed charts of 100 black and 100 white alcoholic males hospitalized in Malcolm Bliss Mental Health Center to explore possible demographic differences in alcoholism between black and white males and possible differences of incidence of alcohol-related symptomatology. It was found that black members of the sample began drinking at an earlier age than the white sample, blacks were younger at hospital admission, and reported significantly more hallucinatory behavior and convulsions than whites. The reasons for these differences are discussed.

95
Wolcott, Harry F., _The African Beer Gardens of Bulawayo: Integrated Drinking In A Segregated Society._ New Brunswick, NJ: Rutgers University Center of Alcohol Studies, 1974. 261 p.

A cross-cultural study of the African Beer Gardens of Bulawayo, Rhodesia (now Zimbabwe) was conducted. Integrated drinking in a segregated society is made the focal point of this research. The author examines various environmental, social, and cultural factors related to urban beer drinking. Among these are black/white relationships and substitution by the public of beer garden problems for more serious social and political problems. The author seeks to identify the nature and extent of individual variation in behavior and attitudes toward drinking. Professional opinions on urban African beer drinking are given by churchmen, municipal welfare workers, police, and physicians. This study concludes with an analysis of the functional and dysfunctional aspects of municipal beer gardens in Rhodesian society.

96
Zimberg, S., "Evaluation of Alcoholism Treatment in Harlem," _Quarterly Journal of Studies on Alcohol_, 35(2): 550-557, 1974.

Two methods of treating socioeconomically deprived, mostly black alcoholics were evaluated at the Harlem Hospital (N.Y.) Center Alcoholism Unit. The 58 men in group 1 received comprehensive outpatient treatment, including a day care program, individual and group psychotherapy, social casework home visits, drug therapy, disulfiram, and help in finding housing, public assistance and jobs. They were seen 5 times a week for an average total of 50 visits. The 49 men in group II were seen weekly or biweekly (for an average total of 24 visits) by an internist for brief supportive therapy and antianxiety and antidepressant medication and disulfiram.... Number of clinic visits, usage of tranquilizers, antidepressants and disulfiram, and group therapy and Alcoholics Anonymous attendance were not related to outcome. The abstinent group had more intensive psychotherapy and family therapy. Because these patients were so economically deprived, they had little incentive to become abstinent. An alcoholism treatment program designed for the disadvantaged should include training and opportunities to improve their socioeconomic status.

## 1975

97
Atlanta University, School of Social Work. Alcoholism and Blacks. Atlanta, Georgia, 1975.

This monograph was written to "serve as a resource for those persons who are responsible for planning, managing and direct service delivery to the Black and minority alcoholic."

98
Beverly, Creigs C., "Toward A Model For Counseling Black Alcoholics." Journal of Non-White Concerns, 3(4): 169-176, 1975.

Factors relevant to the development of treatment methods for black alcoholic individuals are included in a discussion concerning the controversy over whether there should be specific treatment and rehabilitation programs for alcoholic individuals among the minority population. The author notes a dearth of information relative to alcoholism among blacks, along with the nontransferability of treatment modalities standardized on white populations. Three primary considerations for the establishment of workable treatment and intervention modalities for blacks are discussed: (1) a clear perspective of the meaning of the black experience; (2) isolation of the behavioral components among black people that have fostered their survival; and (3) the implications of counseling in a racist society. The treatment modality of bicultural counseling is offered as an alternative to existing therapies for black alcoholic individuals.

99
Brown, Robert W., "Some Implications of Alcohol, Drug Abuse, and Mental Health For The Black Family," Conference Paper. "Seminar on A Comparative Analysis of Black Families in The Caribbean." Nassau, Bahamas: 21 Aug 1975, 30 p.

Alcohol and drug abuse in black families in the US and Caribbean are explored, and research, training, and service projects having direct or inferential implications for black families are described. It is suggested that comparative surveys provide only an inference of cause and effect. The need to undertake scientific inquiries from a position of ethnic neutrality, formulate objective questions, and seek accurate answers is cited. Further inquiries into nonconventional medicine in the behavioral and medical scientific fields are suggested. It is felt that the dynamics of self-concept when blacks are in a majority in contrast to when they are in a minority, is one of the most important cross-cultural areas in need of further exploration.

100
Cahalan, D., and Cisin, I., _Final Report on a Service-Wide Survey of Attitudes and Behavior of Naval Personnel Concerning Alcohol and Problem Drinking_. Washington, D.C.: Bureau of Social Science Research, Inc., 1975.

Only one table in this report presents findings by ethnicity, reporting some differences. Among officers, black men had slightly higher problem scores than white men; with the reverse being true for enlisted men and women. According to the authors, additional tabulations by ethnicity will be included at a later date in a separate memorandum report.

101
Camey, Francis J., "Sociocultural Study of Alcoholism and Heroin Addiction," Dissertation. Ann Arbor, MI: University Microfilms International, 1975.

Differential rates of alcoholism and heroin addiction among Irish Americans and black Americans were studied in a cultural context with an aim toward formulation of a theoretical framework that would encompass both alcoholism and heroin addiction. Methodology included in-depth interviews of patients at an addiction center. A general review of the anthropological and sociological literature on alcoholism and heroin addiction indicated that a relationship exists between cultural or subcultural orientations toward alcoholism and/or heroin addiction. Empirical support was found for a theoretical perspective which draws heavily upon Albert Ullman's theory concerning value conflict, ambivalence, and alcoholism.

102
Clance, Robert L., _Alcoholism in The Inner City Black Community: Preliminary Observations, Definitions, and Research Implications._ Atlanta, GA: EOA Alcohol Treatment Program, 1975, 5 p.

Information, gathered in a phenomenological method, regarding attitudes toward alcoholism in the black community and factors involved in alcohol treatment programs are discussed. A need to recognize the different drinking histories of inner city low income black and whites is cited. The author feels that the strengths of the community should be explored as aids in treating alcohol abusers. It is suggested that considerable research is necessary to successfully attract and maintain black alcohol abusers in treatment programs.

103
Coney, John Charles, "Precipitating Factors in The Use of Alcoholic Treatment Services: A Comparative Study of Black and White Alcoholics." Dissertation. Ann Arbor, MI: University Microfilms International, 1975.

Factors that precipitate the use of an alcoholic treatment program by black and white alcoholics were studied, focusing on socioeconomic factors that influence health service utilization. Several theoretical models are presented that attempt to explain differential health service utilization. The study group consisted of 69 blacks and 54 whites receiving outpatient alcoholism treatment. Social and demographic profiles of each group are presented, including data on family composition, marital status, age, birth order, religion, income, and occupation. In terms of precipitating treatment factor, blacks gave "can't cope" and needing detoxification as reasons; whites more often gave "family problems." Blacks reported fewer alcohol-related arrests than whites, but whites had higher incomes and a more stable employment history. Although race accounted for some of the differences found, it was compounded by religious preference and geographical background.

104
Dandoy, Suzanne, "Treating Tuberculosis in The Poor Black Alcoholic Male," (Letter to the Editor) American Review of Respiratory Disease, 112(5): 743, 1975.

In this letter to the editor, a proposal of two concepts of inpatient tuberculosis management, one for middle class individuals and another for poor, black, alcoholic males, is refuted. The author contends that length of stay should be determined by an evaluation of all pertinent factors in the individual patient.

Gaines, Jackie, "Study on The Black Woman Alcoholic." Conference Paper. Milwaukee, Wis.: National Alcoholism Forum, 27 Apr-2 May, 1975.

The unique aspects of alcohol abuse in black women are explored through a review of literature concerning: (1) Alcoholism in general, (2) Drinking patterns of women, (3) The Historical development of alcoholism in blacks, and (4) The drinking patterns of drinking women. It was found that the scarcity of hard data on the black female alcohol abuser makes it impossible to generalize. The author outlines a possible model of the black female alcohol abuse for future research.

105
Gregory, Dick, "Racial Differences in The Incidence and Prevalence of Alcohol Abuse in Oklahoma," *Alcohol Technical Reports.* 4(4): 37-41, 1975.

Data are presented on the prevalence and incidence of alcoholism among blacks, Indians, and whites in Oklahoma. American Indians, male and female, were found to have the highest rates of alcohol abuse. Blacks were found to have the lowest male and female alcohol arrest rate in the juvenile population, but the 2nd highest rate in the adult population. Sixty nine percent of alcoholic Indians were incorporated in the treatment delivery system as compared with 18 percent of black and 19 percent of white alcohol abusers.

106
Helmer, J., *Drugs and Minority Oppression*. New York: The Seabury Press - A Continuum Book, 1975.

Helmer contends that class conflicts have determined the criminal status of drugs throughout history. He cites the identification of Chinese with opium, Mexicans with marijuana and blacks with all narcotics, and states that each "crackdown" reflected a fear of economic competition by aliens to the work force and not a concern with drugs.

107
Jacobs, Roosevelt, "Study of Drinking Behavior and Personality Characteristics of Three Ethnic Groups." Dissertation. Ann Arbor, MI: University Microfilms International, 1975.

Ethnic differences in drinking behavior were examined in blacks, whites, and chicanos. Attitudes while drinking and personality characteristics in these ethnic groups of alcohol abusers were compared. Samples of approximately 60 males from each ethnic group were randomly selected from alcoholic outpatient clinic populations in 2 California hospitals. Subjects were interviewed and administered a questionnaire and the short form MMPI. Differences were observed in drinking behavior; a fair number of the minority patients were periodic drinkers, whereas the whites tended to be daily drinkers. Younger whites showed a significantly higher incidence of alcoholism than younger blacks or chicanos. In personality differences, blacks differed significantly from whites and chicanos, who were relatively similar. Blacks scored in the deep depression range of the MMPI, indicating feelings of inadequacy and hopelessness.

108
King, Lewis M., and Lopez, Roberta L., *Black Adolescent Alcoholism: Selected Annotated References - 1945 - 1974*. Los Angeles, California. Fanon Research and Development Center, UCLA, 1975.

This bibliography provides information on the physiological, psychological and sociological aspects of alcohol abuse and alcoholism in black adolescents.

109
Kolb, D., Gunderson, E.K., Bucky, S., *Prognostic Indicators For Black and White Alcoholics.* Report. San Diego, CA. Naval Health Research Center, 1975. 20 p.

Characteristics that differentiate between samples of Black and Caucasian Navy enlisted men admitted to Alcohol Rehabilitation Centers (ARC) and units are determined, and variables that predict effective performance after rehabilitation are identified for both groups. The subjects included 2686 men admitted to ARC's during the period 1973-1974. Pay grade and prognostic rating given by treatment staff were the best predictors of effectiveness for both groups. Ethnicity was not a factor in overall effectiveness. Lower effectiveness rates were noted for young alcoholics. Implications for program planning and future research are considered.

110
Milgram, G.G., Alcohol Education Materials: An Annotated Bibliography. New Brunswick, N.J.: Rutgers Center of Alcohol Studies, 1975.

111
Pan, L., Alcohol in Colonial Africa. Helsinki: The Finnish Foundation for Alcohol Studies, Monograph, Vol. 22, 1975.

This study includes a historical review of the liquor trade in Africa, an account of the international conference convened to devise its control, the work of the League of Nations (which came to supervise its control), and a portrait of the local circumstances and consequences of alcohol control in three of the African territories themselves. South Africa is not included here, nor the German and Portuguese colonies, and West Africa is stressed.

112
Rappaport, M., Labaw, P. and Williams, J., The Public Evaluates the NIAAA Public Education Program. Vols. I and II. Princeton, N.J.: Opinion Research Corporation, 1975.

These two volumes constitute a report of a study conducted in January 1975 and June 1975, to ascertain how the public reacted to public messages about drinking, and the public's attitudes toward and knowledge of alcoholism as a problem in the U.S. The research also obtained data about drinking practices. 11% of the 2,157 respondents were blacks in Wave I, Volume I. About two-thirds (64%) of the general public stated that they personally know someone who drinks too much. When those who responded in the affirmative were asked if that person was an acquaintance, friend, or relative, blacks were more likely than whites to state that it was a relative (38% as compared to 28%). 25% of the general public say they have tried to help someone with a drinking problem during the six months prior to interview. Half of the blacks report trying to help someone as contrasted with almost one-fourth of the whites (49% compared with 23%). The higher rate of black efforts to help someone could be because: (1) they prefer personal help in such matters or (2) they are less aware of places in the community to go to for help. Seven out of 10 (71%) blacks report not knowing of places in the community where people with drinking problems could get help or counseling as compared with 43% of whites. Blacks are more likely than whites to indicate that ministers would be "most successful in handling people with drinking problems" (26% compared with 14%), and more likely to classify themselves as abstainers (47% compared with 33%). Both are equally likely to classify themselves as semi-abstainers (10%). Among those who do drink, half (49%) of the blacks are classified as infrequent drinkers, contrasted with 40% of the whites. 23% of the blacks are classified as heavy drinkers compared with 28% of the whites... Blacks are more likely than whites to report feeling that alcoholism "is not a real illness," that "people bring it on themselves" (40% as compared with 26%). There is no presentation of findings by race in the analysis summarized in Volume I. Volume II consists of tables by the various demographic variables: sex, race, education, age, region, income and marital status.

113
Siegal, H.A., Petersen, D.M., and Chambers, C.D., "The Emerging Skid Row: Ethnographic and Social Notes on a Changing Scene," *Journal of Drug Issues*, 5(2): 160-166, 1975.

Changes in Skid Row life in 10 American cities were assessed during 1972-73 by participant observation and by interviews with 560 Skid Row residents. The history of Skid Rows and their design as viable, integrated social worlds are discussed. Not all Skid Row residents are alcoholics. The distinctive Skid Row Life is disappearing... Urban renewal has reduced the number of missions serving Skid Row residents, reducing access to free food and sociability... Minority groups (Hispanics, Native Americans, blacks) tend to be overrepresented, and the members of these groups are 10 years younger (average) than their white counterparts. Unlike the whites, many have had no previous experience with Skid Row living. Long-time residents of Skid Row themselves observed increases in the number of blacks, in the use of drugs other than alcohol, and in the increase in violence, the victims of which are usually Skid Row residents. Patterns of single-room occupany appears to be replacing much of Skid Row life. The process is beginning in New York City and is accelerating or nearing completion in Minneapolis, St. Paul and Salt Lake City.

114
Treiman, Beatrice, *Progress Report: Prevalence Data On Drinking Practices of Five Population Groups In California.* Report. Berkeley: University of California, School of Public Health, 1975.

This summary report presents findings that supplement the 1974 California drinking survey, which summarized California data on three groups: women, Chicanos, and Blacks. Progress report summarizing findings, minority groups, Blacks, Spanish-speaking individuals, women, Native Americans, youth, treatment modalities, evaluation of programs, statistics, relation of alcoholism or drinking to socioeconomic, health, and legal phenomena.

115
Viamontes, J.A., and Powell, B.J., "Unequal Trials of Boozing," Human Behavior, 4(3): 44, 1975.

Epidemiological comparisons between black and white alcoholic individuals highlight significant differences in drinking patterns, problems, and treatment. Epidemiological information on black and white alcoholic individuals, blacks forced into treatment at an earlier age, skid row, low socioeconomic background, earlier loss of drinking control by blacks.

## 1976

116
Allen, Chaney. I'm Black and I'm Drunk. See 1978 listing (same author).

117
Argeriou, Milton, and Zinkowski, John, "Black Alcoholism: A Comment On NIAAA'S Plan To Combat The Problem," Journal of Studies on Alcohol, 37(7):1003-1007, 1976.

The NIAAA'S interim guidelines for establishment of black alcoholism projects are criticized for their possible latent function of redirecting treatment energies away from the primary problem of alcoholism. The authors decry what they regard as an NIAAA effort to establish separate and unequal treatment facilities for black alcoholic persons, and its alleged emphasis on resolution of irrelevant societal conditions. They see the black alcoholic person's problem as alcoholism, not social justice, and failure to recognize the medical-moral distinction as deleterious to the program and to the people it is intended to serve.

118
Benjamin, Rommel, "Rural Black Folk and Alcohol." In: Frederick D. Harper, Ed., Alcohol Abuse and Black America, Alexandria, VA: Douglass Publishers, 1976. 229 P. (pp. 50-60).

Drinking behavior and drinking patterns of rural blacks in Mississippi indicate that drinking is a functional and pervasive activity for persons in the lowest economic category. The author notes that American society has fostered black male dependency on the black female, respect for the white female, and fear of the white male. In such an environment drinking among black males becomes an expression of manhood, a method for coping with boredom, monotony, loneliness, and low self-esteem. Attitudes toward drinking are tolerant within the black community, and there is often positive evaluation of men who can "hold" their liquor. Among upper income blacks, drinking takes place on weekends and week-nights, often in semiprivate places. Implications for treatment and prevention are discussed.

119
Beverly, Creigs, "Toward A Model For Training Black Alcoholic Counselors." In: Frederick D. Harper, Ed., Alcohol Abuse and Black America. Alexandria, VA.: Douglass Publishers, 1976. 229 p. (pp. 86-98).

It is stated that black alcoholism counselors must be aware of the systematically induced socioeconomic differences between blacks and whites and of the black experience as it relates to counseling and training models. This being the case, some core content areas are suggested for the special training of counselors to black alcoholics. Firstly, counselors must learn to live with the organizational constraints that inhibit and prevent their effectiveness. Secondly, counselors should be knowledgeable about existing counseling modalities. Several briefly described courses are recommended, and observations are offered that deal with the specifics of counseling black alcoholics.

120
Bourne, Peter, "Alcoholism in The Urban Black Population," IN: Frederick D. Harper, Ed., Alcohol Abuse and Black America. Alexandria, VA: Douglass Publishers, 1976. 229 p. (pp. 39-47).

Incidence of alcoholism among blacks, patterns of drinking, psychological factors, and various treatment approaches are discussed. Existing data indicate that ingestion of alcohol by urban blacks, particularly men, is several times higher than for an average cross section of urban society. The influence of historical patterns of alcohol consumption is detailed, and the use of alcohol as a prestige symbol is noted. Until recently, most treatment and rehabilitation programs were unavailable to blacks; Alcoholics Anonymous was clearly oriented toward white, middle-class Americans. This has changed in recent years and a variety of such programs are now directed toward the poor. The detoxification center is called the critical element in breaking the drinking cycle. Halfway houses are considered the next step as the individual gains a measure of sobriety.

121
Brisbane, Frances, "Causes and Consequences of Alcohol Use Among Black Youth," Journal of Afro-American Issues. 4(2):241-254, 1976.

Interviews with black preteens and adolescents in poor socioeconomic communities revealed that there are massive societal pressures approving the use of alcohol, and the black adult who drinks is frequently perceived as a hero. Many of the youth had relatives who drink heavily but are not perceived as alcoholic persons. Moral issues appear to confuse certain attitudes. A large number of teenagers reported drinking regularly themselves. The survey confirms findings that, for the disadvantaged, alcohol provides a way to cope with the intolerable conditions of living and the added miseries of ethnic rejection and poverty. However, it would be an oversimplification to say that poverty is the cause of alcoholism among blacks. Drugs, including alcohol, are seen as a part of the transition from childhood to adulthood.

122
Cahalan, D, _Ethnoreligious Group Differences, 1974 California Drinking Survey_. Supplement to D. Cahalan, et al., _Alcohol Problems and Their Prevention: Public Attitudes in California_, Berkeley, Ca.: Social Research Group, revised, 1976.

Data for this study were taken from personal interviews with 1,024 people, forming a probability sample of adults 18 years and over in California. Interviews were conducted August 1974, and contained questions regarding the respondents' drinking, and their attitudes related to the drinking practices of California adults, the extent of alcohol problems in the state, and strategies for the control of alcoholism problems. The findings were reported here for the following groups: White Protestant, White Catholic, Jewish, All Other White, Black, Asian, Chicano and Not Ascertained. Tables are included indicating the responses of the black respondents (N=83) to all the above topics. Rates of problems with social life, health, home life, job, or financies were higher than usual among blacks, particularly among black females. When asked about means of prevention and treatment of alcohol problems, a higher proportion of blacks (and Chicanos) mentioned teaching abstention. It was suggested that this attitude, coupled with the relatively high rate of heavy drinking and drinking problems among blacks, reflected some ambiguity among blacks and supported previous research that people of below average socio-economic status tend to be more fearful of the consequences of drinking. "Ethnoreligious groups were not found to differ materially or consistently in their perception of alcoholism as a serious problem, nor in their support of various measures to prevent or minimize drinking problems--although it was noted that a slight majority of blacks felt that 'alcohol taxes are high enough as it is,' whereas a majority of White Protestants, Jews, and Asiatics said they would favor increasing alcohol taxes for the purpose of providing for more treatment and prevention."

123
Cahalan, D. and Treiman, B., Drinking Behavior, Attitudes, and Problems in San Francisco. Berkeley, CA.: Social Research Group, School of Public Health, University of California, 1976.

Data for this study were collected in a 1975 general population survey that discussed measures of drinking behaviors and drinking problems and related issues concerning drinking, alcoholism and treatment for alcoholism, such as levels of information, felt needs and attitudes. This study presents detailed findings by sex and age groups and by socioeconomic level and by ethnocultural subgroupings (including white, black, Asian and Hispanic). This survey was designed particularly to provide data for the youth, blacks, Hispanics, women and the elderly, as well as for San Franciscans in general. Blacks (as well as those of Latino or Asian ancestry) were not as likely as others to drink at all and to report having been high or tight during the previous year. Blacks were less likely (than were whites or Latinos) to report difficulties due to their drinking. Blacks reported lower rates (than whites) of concealed drinking and of being in drinking conducive environments... Fewer black respondents (26%) than those in other ethnic groups rated their own health as excellent; and more of them (86%) reported having seen a doctor in the past 12 months; and more of them (69%) said they really attempted to look out for their own health.

124
Davis, Fred T., "Counseling The Black Alcoholic," In: Frederick D. Harper, Ed., Alcohol Abuse and Black America. Alexandria, VA: Douglass Publishers, 1976. 229 p. (pp. 79-98).

After discussing characteristics of black alcoholic men on several socioeconomic levels, a few specific problems encountered by the black counselor are described. Because both the black alcoholism counselor and his client are victims of an unresponsive social system, there are certain difficulties with confrontation. For instance, the client may say that he cannot get a job because of his color. It is difficult for the counselor to convince him to work on the drinking problem first, fully knowing that he may find that color is the real reason his patient is not employed at his trade or profession. The lack of treatment facilities in the black community is noted. Blacks, as well as other ethnic groups, suffer from pressures not experienced by members of the larger society. Having determined that the inability to cope with certain degrees of stress is one of the major causes of alcoholism, the black counselor must examine some of these stresses among blacks in America.

125
Dawkins, Marvin P., "Alcohol Use Among Black and White Adolescents," In: Frederick D. Harper, Ed., Alcohol Abuse and Black America. Alexandria, VA: Douglass Publishers, 1976. 229 p. (pp. 163-175).

Differences between black and white adolescents in a rural community are examined in terms of several sociocultural aspects of drinking, and the relative effect of race and other social factors on the use of alcoholic beverages. Findings based on data collected from a sample of 111 high school seniors revealed that: (1) the majority of respondents were alcohol abusers; (2) whites were more likely to have received their first drink from friends, whereas blacks usually received their first drink from parents; (3) the parents of all respondents tended to disapprove of adolescent drinking, but white parents were more likely to disapprove; and (4) having a closest friend who considers himself a drinker proved to be the most reliable predictor of alcohol use.

126
Dawkins, Marvin P., "Research Issues on Alcohol Abuse and Blacks." In: Frederick D. Harper, Ed., Alcohol Abuse and Black America. Alexandria, VA: Douglass Publishers, 1976. 229 p. (pp. 141-152).

A critique is offered of descriptive and explanatory research concerning alcohol and blacks, and suggestions are made for enhancing the theoretical and practical value of both kinds of research. Many explanatory studies have taken a social deviance perspective based on white, middle-class norms. Despite the existence of some descriptive studies, conditions of alcoholism among blacks have not been given adequate treatment. In the view of the author, the most crucial needs for descriptive studies are analyses of basic data regarding alcohol abuse and its relation to demographic factors, such as sex, age, income, region, and education. However, the author considers it important to move beyond the descriptive level to avoid encouraging possible biases in the interpretation of the differences.

127
Gaines, Jackie Jenkins, "Alcohol and The Black Woman," In: Frederick D. Harper, Ed., Alcohol Abuse and Black America. Alexandria, VA: Douglass Publishers, 1976. 229 p. (pp. 153-162).

Myths detrimental to the black woman are challenged with empirical evidence, and drinking patterns of black women are described, although insufficient data works against making generalizations about the black female alcohol abuser. Available data are mainly demographic in nature, and only one study attempts to deal with personality and motivational characteristics of the black female alcohol abuser; there are no studies which attempt to assess effective treatment modalities for black women. However, the author feels that the same factors that induce excessive drinking can also serve as a motivating force in the search for sobriety. A hypothesis is offered for use in a prevention model.

128
Genovese, E.D., Roll, Jordan, Roll: The World the Slaves Made. New York: Random House, Vintage Books, 1976.

The slaves "neither drank to excess nor acted on their knowledge of the narcotic effects of hemp..." However, the slaves were featured as being drunkards with "drunkenness (running) rampant in the quarters." Slaves were thought to be easily corrupted innocents who were preyed upon by opportunitistic declassé whites. Liquor was viewed as a threat to the institution of slavery because grogshops were places where slaves met with poor whites and freed blacks and it was felt that through this contact uprisings against the plantations would occur. Heavy drinking was permitted at holiday parties on the plantation by slaves. Slaves "preferred a safer vice than heavy drinking--chewing, sniffing, and smoking tobacco." "The availability of liquor and the general sobriety of the slaves speaks well for their community strength and resistance to demoralization.... and the depth of the religious commitment and the moral influence of the preachers."

129
Harper, Frederick D., Ed., Alcohol Abuse and Black America. Alexandria, VA: Douglass Publishers, 1976. 229 p.

The author, in this overview of the use and abuse of alcohol among Black people, notes that alcohol has been linked to over 50 percent of homicides among Blacks. The abuse of alcohol by Blacks has resulted in pedestrian and automobile fatalities, occupational and home injuries and fatalities, family hardship, chronic and extreme illnesses, house fires, and physical assaults that include wife and child beating. Economic considerations, role of religion, political influences, why do blacks drink, theories of black drinking behavior, the black woman, alcoholism in the urban black population, rural black folk and alcohol, case studies of black alcoholics, counseling the black alcoholic, training of black alcoholism counselors, the helping relationship, minority input and relation to NIAAA, black vs white physiological differences, alcohol and crime in black America, research issues in alcohol abuse by blacks, alcohol use among black adolescents, alcohol abuse and the black family, summary and recommendations.

130
Harper, Frederick D., Alcohol and Blacks: An Overview. Monograph. Washington, DC: Howard University, School of Education, 1976.

A brief review of research findings on the topic of alcohol and blacks is presented, with particular emphasis on the causes and consequences of heavy drinking among blacks and the distinctions between blacks and whites in terms of drinking behavior and drinking problems. Specific areas of inquiry include: The nature of alcohol; the need for research data on alcohol and blacks; black drinking behavior and practices; the etiology of heavy drinking by blacks; alcohol-related language peculiar to the black American culture; the association of alcohol with crime in urban and rural black communities; and counseling and treatment strategies for black alcoholic people. Conclusions based on the research findings are provided, and suggestions for alcohol professionals and loved ones of black alcoholic people are offered. Sources of further information on alcohol and blacks and of volunteer and funding support for alcohol-related programs are also listed.

131
Harper, Frederick D., "Overview: Alcohol and Blacks." In: Frederick D. Harper, Ed., Alcohol Abuse and Black America. Alexandria, VA: Douglass Publishers, 1976. 229 p. (pp. 1-12.)

Alcohol abuse, the number 1 health and social problem in Black America, has been so ingrained in black American culture that its impact and role have been overlooked. Alcohol has many ambivalent meanings to Black people of different socioeconomic groups. Over the last 30 years only 11 research articles on alcoholism have been written which involved Blacks only as the main concern. Many studies include a small number of Blacks, which perpetuates the tendency to look at white drinking patterns and behavior as the norm, while interpreting Black differences as variation or deviance. Another trend in the literature is toward studies which deal with captive Black audiences in hospitals, prisons, and welfare centers, which limits generalizing from findings. Due to the paucity of research and to the bias in existing literature, there are many unresolved questions on the topic of alcohol and Blacks. Some of these questions and issues are stated here.

132
Harper, Frederick D., "Alcohol and Crime in Black America." In: Frederick D. Harper, Ed., Alcohol Abuse and Black America. Alexandria, VA: Douglass Publishers, 1976. 229 p. (pp. 129-140.)

Data on alcohol-related homicides in Atlanta, Cleveland, Miami, and Washington, DC are examined. The conditions that influence alcohol-related crimes are discussed, as are the consequences and prevention of such crimes. Alcohol is said to be associated with over 50 percent of homicidal deaths. A much larger proportion of blacks, as compared with whites, are victims of homicide. The statistics also suggest that black females are much more likely than white females (although less likely than black males and white males) to be victims of alcohol-related homicide. The high incidence of criminal acts in black America is influenced by a number of socioeconomic and psychological conditions, such as stress, which interact with alcohol abuse. Some concrete recommendations for community action in minimizing and preventing alcohol abuse and alcohol-related crime are offered.

133
Harper, Frederick D., "Case Studies of Black Alcoholics," In: Frederick D. Harper, Ed., Alcohol Abuse and Black America. Alexandria, VA: Douglass Publishers, 1976. 229 p. (pp. 61-78).

Case studies of black alcoholics who were in various treatment programs throughout the country are reported by counselors or program directors familiar with the alcoholic client. Black male and female alcoholics of different age groups are presented. Personalized information, insight, and practical solutions are provided. Information is also provided on the progression of alcoholism for people of different drinking patterns and developmental backgrounds.

134
Harper, Frederick D, "Etiology: Why Do Blacks Drink?" In Frederick D. Harper, Ed., Alcohol Abuse and Black America. Alexandria, VA: Douglass Publishers, 1976. 229 p. (pp. 27-37).

Etiological theories of why Americans drink are primarily based on the drinking patterns of white Americans, but drinking patterns among black Americans differ in that there is a tendency either to drink heavily or not at all. Theories of black drinking behavior are briefly reviewed, and the author offers several hypotheses in an attempt to develop an etiological theoretical framework which would explain a variety of black drinking patterns based on sociological, economic, historical, and psychological considerations. Motivations for nondrinking are also considered, including several possible reasons why a large proportion (51 percent) of black women are nondrinkers.

135
Harper, Frederick D., "Helping Relationship," In: Frederick D. Harper, Ed., Alcohol Abuse and Black America. Alexandria, VA: Douglass Publishers, 1976. 229 p. (pp. 99-107).

Techniques of the helping relationship and various counseling theories are described. Helping persons are told they must understand the current forces that influence and shape black drinking behavior - the alcohol industry, advertisements, alcohol-related government policies, and the role of church and family. Economically, helping persons should understand the impact of unemployment, underemployment, and misemployment on the behavior and destinies of black families. In addition to this generalized knowledge concerning Black America, understanding the local community in which they serve is seen as essential to successful treatment.

136
Harper, Frederick D., "Summary, Issues, and Recommendations." In: Frederick D. Harper, Ed., Alcohol Abuse and Black America. Alexandria, Va.: Douglass Publishers, 1976. 229 p. (pp. 187-200).

Approaches toward providing helping services to Black alcoholics and their families are summarized. Summarization of ideas concerning alcohol abuse among black Americans, counseling the black alcoholic, recommendations for better serving black alcoholics, recommendations to family, government, and black community.

137
Harper, Frederick D., and Dawkins, Marvin P., "Alcohol and Blacks: Survey of The Periodical Literature," British Journal of Addictions, 71(4): 327-334, 1976.

The state of the periodical literature on alcohol and blacks is assessed, and although 16,000 alcohol-related studies have been reported in scientific journals over the last 30 years, only 77 have dealt with blacks. Nonscientific studies have also been scarce; only 11 of these focused solely on blacks, while the remainder included blacks in samples with whites, or various other ethnic groups. Articles with the greatest frequency of occurrence dealt with drinking patterns and behavior. The next largest number of articles covered treatment modes. Surprisingly, none were found under the headings of alcohol education and prevention. The drinking problems of blacks tend to be viewed from an intrapsychic causation, a point of view that faults blacks as the cause of their own drinking problems as opposed to causation by external societal factors. Some recommendations are offered.

138
Iiyama, P., Nishi, S.M., Johnson, B.D., Drug Use and Abuse Among U.S. Minorities: An Annotated Bibliography. New York: Praeger Publ., 1976.

139
Inge, Rosalind, "Alcoholism and Blacks: A Synthesis of Findings," Urban League Review, 2(1):19-24, 1976.

A brief review of the scientific literature on alcoholism and blacks covers the following areas: drinking patterns, sociopsychological correlates, health and physiological effects, nature of treatment, and relationship to criminal offenses. The overwhelming majority of the 127 identified studies dealing with blacks tend to focus almost exclusively on adult males. Most contemporary social scientists usually equate excessive drinking in public with the black lower class, and not with the middle class. However, drinking is not unique to the poor. Overall, 79 percent of black men drink alcoholic beverages, compared to 77 percent among white men. Black women tend to be overrepresented at the polar extremes; either they do not drink at all or drink intensively. Black alcoholics are much less likely than white alcoholics to be reached by either private or public treatment programs.

140
Journal of Studies on Alcohol, "Black Alcoholism: A Response From NIAAA," 37(7):1007-1009, 1976.

An NIAAA rebuttal of criticism by Milton Argerioux and John Zinkowski of the Institute's interim guidelines for black alcoholism projects is presented. The basic premise of the detractors, that the program represents NIAAA'S sole mechanism of project grant support for black alcoholic persons, is rejected. Also disputed are claims that the program provides for separate and unequal services to black and white alcoholic persons and that it is not sufficiently patient-oriented.

141
King, Lewis M., and Lopez, Roberta L., Black Adolescent Alcoholism: Useful and Related Annotated References, 1945-1975. Los Angeles, CA. UCLA Adolescent Drug Abuse Etiologies Project, 1976.

This bibliography contains literature summaries and abstracts on the topic of alcoholism among black youth. Literature summaries, abstracts, black alcoholic persons, black adolescents, black youth, young black people, teenage alcoholism, hereditary/genetic studies, physiological studies, psychological studies, familial studies, sociocultural studies, multivariate studies, related studies, survey studies, experimental studies, correlational studies, comparative studies, review papers, chronological listing.

142
Larkins, John, "Historical Background," In: Frederick D. Harper, Ed., Alcohol Abuse and Black America. Alexandria, VA: Douglass Publishers, 1976. 229 p. (pp. 13-25).

The early history of blacks in America is traced, as well as the history of alcohol use, and economic considerations which influenced both are outlined. Colonial statutes created a climate conducive to the sale and use of alcoholic beverages and the enslaving of black Americans. The period from 1825 to 1860 was one of considerable religious activity against slavery and the use and abuse of alcohol. Theories concerning the excessive use of alcohol by blacks are briefly reviewed, but complex factors make any single theory inadequate. Black Americans have played an influential role in the growth of the alcohol industry as consumers without enjoying the economic benefits from the manufacture and sale of alcoholic beverages.

143
Martinez, Julio, "Minorities and Alcohol/Drug Abuse." American Journal of Drug and Alcohol Abuse. 3(1):185-187, 1976.

As far as the overall population of New York is concerned, Puerto Ricans are a minority, yet they, with blacks, comprise the majority of the people who are most affected by drug use and abuse. They do not have a voice in policy and planning of treatment services, a function which is carried out by middle class professionals who have little real knowledge about the Hispanic culture. The author pointed out some important considerations in the treatment of Spanish-speaking addicts, including the need for bilingual therapists and reading materials. He stressed that social prejudices had to be confronted if any changes were to be made. He criticizes the therapeutic community for trying to impose middle-class values upon clients who are still defined and contained in a lower-class reality.

144
Morgan, John P., and Tulloss, Thomas C., "Jake Walk Blues: A Toxicologic Tragedy Mirrored In American Popular Music," Annals of Internal Medicine, 85(6):804-808, 1976.

Consumption of an adulterated Jamaica Ginger extract ("Jake"), an illicit beverage popular in the Southern and Midwestern United States in 1930, caused an epidemic of thousands of cases of muscle pain, weakness of the upper and lower extremities, and spinal cord damage. Although an alcoholic extract of ginger had been available as a drug store remedy since 1863, a different additive, tri-ortho-cresyl phosphate, appeared in the beverage in 1930. Research showed that this adulterant was capable of producing a similar paralytic illness in animals. Before this association was made, 4,837 cases of paralysis were reported. One author estimates the actual total at 60,000. Victims with resultant gait impairment were said to have the "Jake Leg" or "Jake Walk." Twelve commercial phonographic recordings made between 1928 and 1934 by southern rural artists, black and white, which refer to this infirmity are discussed in detail.

145
Patterson, Bentley, "Alcohol and The Body," In: Frederick D. Harper, Ed., Alcohol Abuse and Black America. Alexandria, VA: Douglass Publishers, 1976. 229 p. (pp. 117-126).

The effects of excessive alcohol on the liver, the digestive system, the cardiovascular system, the nervous system, and the development of cancer are discussed. Questions are raised concerning black vs white physiological differences and how they relate to the differential effects of alcohol. In the black community, alcohol-related physical effects are associated with other health factors which makes it difficult to tell which are truly the effects of alcohol abuse. The fact that whites and blacks differ in proneness to certain diseases might affect differential reactions to alcohol abuse. Since alcohol affects all human bodies similarly, the question would mainly concern differentials with regard to quality, incidence, and magnitude of physiological effects.

146
Sampson, Calvin C., and Braxton, Edwyn L., "Esophageal Carcinoma in Blacks: Analysis of 88 Necropsied Cases," Journal of The National Medical Association, 68(4):278-280, 311, 1976.

Results of an etiological study of esophageal carcinoma in all black patients dying of this disease at Freedman's Hospital, Howard University, during the period 1957-1975 are presented. A significant number of the patients were tobacco users and alcohol drinkers, either singly or in combination. A clearly defined etiological agent could not be identified, and the cause for the rate increases in esophageal carcinoma in black persons remains unknown.

147
Samuels, Frank G., _Negro Tavern: A Microcosm of Slum Life._ San Francisco: R and E Research Associates, 1976. 121 p.

Frances and the negro community, churches, school, recreational facilities, police and community, business community, tavern society, lower-class and working-class taverns, local environment, tavern sociability, ritualization of the pickup, adversary relationships: men and women, men and wives, girlfriends, children, drinking rituals, tavern interaction among regular customers, games, contests, social clubs, bartenders and clients, owners, behavioral aspects. Aspects of social organization in slum areas are examined, focusing on tavern-based groups and local cultural settings in a Negro inner-city neighborhood in Milwaukee, Wisconsin. 121p.

148
Smith, William R., Varvel, Walter A., Leunes, Arnold D., "Rural Alcohol Abuse," _Annals of The New York Academy of Sciences,_ 273(May 18): 659-664, 1976.

A representative sample of 148 rural Texas males aged 18 to 20 were compared with regard to psychologic and background information items selected to predict alcohol abuse or nonabuse. Subjects were classfied as white abusers, white nonabusers, black abusers, and black nonabusers. Determinations of abuse and nonabuse were based on information on quantity consumed, circumstances of drinking, drink-related problems, and estimates from the subjects' acquaintances. The format of the study included measures of achievement need, alienation, tolerance of deviance, leisure time, religious fundamentalism, general deviation, mobility, age, family size, and education. Analysis of variance revealed significant differences between abusers and nonabusers in tolerance of deviance, religious fundamentalism, general deviation, mobility, age, and education. The findings were used to develop recommendations for education, information, and treatment in strictly rural American areas.

149
Sterne, Muriel W., and Pittman, David J., "Alcohol Abuse and The Black Family," In: Frederick D. Harper, Ed., _Alcohol Abuse and Black America._ Alexandria, VA: Douglass Publishers, 1976. 229 P. (pp. 177-185).

Alcohol use patterns, attitudes and motives and the social contexts within which they are learned and displayed are examined in an urban, black ghetto population. There are complex and subtle interactions between drinking behavior and life in an urban, low-status black family, in which the family influences whether and how its members drink, and in which the family is in turn affected if this drinking becomes abusive. The seductions of street life are such that adolescents experience an early and pronounced ease of entry into adult drinking patterns. Abstainers constitute a significant minority. Adults in this environment tend to have chronic problems in maintaining a secure sense of self-esteem. Observations in this report are based mainly on data collected in a 1966 study of residents in a St. Louis housing project.

150
Treiman, Beatrice R., Street, Pamela B., Shanks, Patricia, _Blacks and Alcohol: A Selective Annotated Bibliography._ Berkeley: University of California, School of Public Health, 1976. 87 p. Available from the Department of General Services Publications, P.O. Box 1015, North Highlands, California, 95660.

This annotated bibliography provides a compilation of reference material dealing with the drinking patterns and alcohol-related problems of the black population.

151
United States. National Clearinghouse for Alcohol Information. _Report on the Workshop on Black Materials_. Gaithersburg, Md., 1976.

A report is given of a workshop sponsored by NCALI during which a multidisciplinary group of black Americans from various sections of the country met to review and evaluate a selection of current NIAAA alcohol publications to determine appropriateness for various strata of the black populace, to identify target audiences within the black community, to develop guidelines for communications efforts, and to determine the appropriate methods of field testing and ultimate dissemination of materials produced from this effort. Many of the publications reviewed contained both misleading and false information. Suggestions and comments are offered concerning materials. General guidelines for communication efforts are given, and it was felt that dissemination should be carried out by local groups rather than from Washington.

152
Washington, Veneita, "Alcohol Information: A Potential Source," In: Frederick D. Harper, Ed., Alcohol Abuse and Black America. Alexandria, VA: Douglass Publishers, 1976. 229 p. (pp. 109-115).

The capabilities and components of the National Clearinghouse for Alcohol Information are described, and a proposal for minority programs is offered that would provide information services to the black community. The operations division of the Clearinghouse has seven major components: Acquisitions, analysis and reference, current awareness, technical publications, computer liason, communications and media, and warehouse and distribution. The development of information dissemination programs for minority groups is described. However, it is pointed out that any program must be based on the idea that before viable alcohol information can be disseminated to, for, and about black people, it must first be gathered, conceptualized, and documented from a cultural frame of reference. Several areas of concern are listed, and the possibilities for minority input are outlined.

## 1977

153
Andrews, T., _A Bibliography of Drug Abuse, Including Alcohol and Tobacco_. Littleton, Colorado: Libraries Unlimited, Inc., 1977.

This bibliography includes 725 references. It might be helpful to check Chapter 1 "Bibliographies, Indexes, and Abstracts" (pp. 11-29) and Chapter 2 "Dictionaries, Glossaries, and Directories" (pp. 30-34) and other sections.

154
Brunswick, Ann F., "Health and Drug Behavior: A Study of Urban Black Adolescents." _Addictive Diseases._ 3(2):197-214, 1977.

Results of a survey to determine the relationships between health and drug use in a sample of adolescents from a large inner-city and largely black ghetto area of the eastern United States are presented. Areas of analysis include demographic and social structure variables, general health status, emotional health, smoking and drinking, and psychosocial factors. The known drug users are compared with the total sample and, when appropriate, qualified for possible differences between the younger (14 to 15 years old) and older (16 to 17 years old) age segments. The fit between these findings and those of previous studies is assessed, and implications for future research are noted.

155
Cahalan, Don. _Ethnoreligious Group Differences, 1974 California Drinking Survey: Supplementary Report._ Report. Berkeley: University of California, School of Public Health, 1977.

Ethnoreligious group differences in drinking behavior and problems in California are reported as a supplement to an earlier (Oct. 1974) report entitled "Findings of a Statewide California Survey on Attitudes Related to Control of Drinking Problems." The present report gives additional details on certain key items of drinking behavior and attitudes, subdivided by a combination of ethnic and religious classifications which were separated in the earlier report. Where justified by sizes of samples, findings are stated for eight groups, subdivided by sex: white ("Anglo") Protestants, white Catholics, Jews, all other whites, blacks, persons of asian ancestry, chicanos, and those whose race was not ascertained. The report follows the same general guidelines as the initial detailed report, taking up first drinking behavior and problems, then alcohol abuse and alcoholism as a problem, and, finally, prevention and treatment measures.

156
Carter, James H., "General Perspective of The Alcohol Abuse Problem in North Carolina," Conference Paper. "Conference: Alcohol & Alcohol Abuse in The North Carolina Black Community," Reidsville, NC: 31 May - 3 June 1977, 11 p.

The author presents a general perspective of the alcohol abuse problem in the North Carolina black community. The issue of racism is suggested as a key factor for alcoholism among blacks. Racism is cited as the nation's number one mental health hazard, with a parallel being drawn between alcoholism and mental health. Arguments are presented to dispel myths about the black family and alcoholism. It is contended that although treatment is important, emphasis should be on prevention, especially among teenagers and young adults.

157
Carter, James H., "Mental Health Service In A Black Community," _Urban Health_, 6(6):36-37, 1977.

The Mental Health Unit of the Lincoln Community Health Center, Durham, North Carolina, is described. Lincoln Community Health Center, Mental Health Unit, Durham, North Carolina, End the Old Habit Program, ETOH Program, minority alcoholism services, black alcoholics, black female alcoholics, evaluation.

158
Coney, John C., _Precipitating Factors in The Use of Alcoholic Treatment Services: A Comparative Study of Black and White Alcoholics._ San Francisco: R & E Research Associates, 1977. 142p.

This study was designed to explore circumstances under which black and white alcoholics utilize the same treatment program, and within the study, the author sought to develop social and demographic profiles of black and white program participants who are currently receiving care at the Dimock Community Health Center Alcoholism Program in Roxbury, Massachusetts. An underlying assumption for the Dimock program model was that the 2 groups would vary with respect to family composition and personal characteristics. Study findings are discussed in terms of the underutilization of treatment services by black alcoholics, and differences in in family composition and alcoholic symptoms between the 2 groups. The author offers an assessment of the conceptual model, a projection of study conclusions, and a review of implications for future research.

159
Dupree, Dick, and Charay, Art, "Development of Alcoholism Programs in a Mixed Ethnic Community," Conference Paper. 1st International Action Conference on Substance Abuse. Phoenix, AZ: 9-13 Nov 1977. 208 p. (pp. 200-206).

Guidelines are offered for developing an alcoholism program in an intercultural setting. Vol. 2: Education and Health, published by Do It Now Foundation, structure and development of programs in intercultural setting, methods of inducing community involvement, Mexican and Black youth.

160
Fialkov, M.J., "Alcoholics and The Emergency Ward. Part II: A One-Year Follow-Up Study," South African Medical Journal, 52(16):653-656, 1977.

The outcome of specialized alcoholism treatment for an unselected group of South African black and white males was unsatisfactory at follow-up 1 year after their initial contact with a hospital emergency psychiatric unit in Cape Town. Only 7 to 10 percent of the patients referred to specialized treatment units attained sobriety, a figure which is less than the 15 percent abstinence reported for other patients who received no treatment at all. The results point to the unsuitability of the patients for treatment at these units, and suggest the need for more effective management at the first point of contact.

161
Fine, Eric W., and Steer, Robert A, "Relationship Between Alcoholism and Depression in Black Men." In: F.A. Seixas, Ed., Currents In Alcoholism. Vol. 2. New York: Grune & Stratton, 1977. 565 p. (pp. 35-43).

Depression was found to be an extremely common phenomenon among 103 black male alcoholic outpatients being treated at a Philadelphia Community Mental Health Center. Answers to alcohol usage and impairment indices, developed by the Stanford Research Institute for the NIAAA treatment center monitoring system, were gathered during an interview at the time the subjects were admitted to the alcoholism program. Findings showed evidence of depression in 65 percent of the sample. On the Beck Depression Inventory, administered after the interview, 28.2 percent of the subjects scored 24 or above - a level indicating severe depression. The relationship between depression and the average daily consumption of alcohol was linear and highly significant, supporting the contention that increasing levels of depression lead to attempts at self-medication with alcohol.

162
Galchus, D.S. and Galchus, K.E., "Drug Use: Some Comparisons of Black and White College Students," Drug Forum, 6(1): 65-76, 1977.

A questionnaire was administered to 342 Black undergraduates (from a largely Black private college) and to 374 White undergraduates from a largely White state-supported college. Results indicated that a significant racial difference was found in the use of cocaine, heroin, amphetamines and barbiturates, and no significant difference was found between male and female use of marihuana. Tobacco was associated with marihuana use for both Blacks and Whites. The correlation between marihuana use and that of heroin and cocaine was low for both samples, and religious beliefs were negatively correlated with the decision to use marihuana. Approximately 50% of both Blacks and Whites were occasional or frequent users of marihuana.

163
Gillis, L.S., and Stone, G.L., "Fate of Drinkers: A Six-Year Follow-Up Study of A Community Survey," South African Medical Journal, 51(22):789-791, 1977.

The drinking patterns of black persons over the age of 18 in the Cape Peninsula (South Africa) remained remarkably stable over a 6-year survey period. Excessive drinkers tended to retain their drinking pattern. Very few persons ceased drinking on their own account, and a negligible proportion came forward for treatment. Social drinkers and abstainers also tended to maintain their drinking habits, with only a few becoming excessive drinkers. The mean age of excessive drinkers was lower than that of the social drinkers and abstainers. There was much less excessive drinking among women.

164
Globetti, Gerald, Alsikafi, Majeed, Morse, Richard J., "Alcohol Use Among Black Youth In A Rural Community," _Drugs And Alcohol Dependence,_ 2(4):255-260, 1977.

An alcohol use survey among young black students in a rural community (i.e., An abstinence setting) pointed up circumstances of youthful drinking that clearly differ from those recorded elsewhere. Although fewer students drink, the drinking styles show several dimensions frequently associated with alcohol abuse. As a rule, users do not have parental permission to drink and for the most part they identify with churches that condemn alcohol on moral grounds. Because many of the youth procure alcoholic beverages illegally, they tend to drink in a surreptitious manner under conditions devoid of restraint. Consequently, a significant number of youths drink without normal propriety and exhibit various alcohol-related social problems. These findings suggest that less youthful drinking can be expected in abstinence settings, but that problems may be more frequent among those young people who do drink.

165
Harper, Frederick D., _Background Review, Analysis, and Guidelines Toward Three Workshops On Alcoholism Treatment And Blacks._ Report. Washington, DC, Howard University, 1977.

A brief review is presented of the quality and quantity of literature on alcohol use and alcoholism among Black Americans. Major research findings and theories are summarized and followed by an extensive discussion about treatment and rehabilitation of the Black alcoholic.

166
Harper, Frederick D., and Dawkins, Marvin P., "Alcohol Abuse in The Black Community," _Black Scholar,_ 8(6):23-31, 1977.

The health and social consequences of alcohol abuse among black people are examined, with special emphasis on the role alcohol plays in impeding progress by the black community toward a better way of life. A brief review of the nature of alcohol and alcoholism is provided, and survey data on the incidence of heavy drinking and problem drinking among blacks are summarized. The epidemiologic and sociologic impact of alcohol on blacks is discussed, and the lack of awareness of this source of victimization is decried. Prevention programs aimed at a revision of attitudes and values contributing to alcohol abuse among blacks are advocated. In line with this objective, suggestions on alcoholism problem prevention for individual black drinkers and their loved ones are provided.

167
Heilbrun, Alfred B., and Heilbrun, Kirk S., "Black Minority Criminal and Violent Crime: The Role of Self-Control," British Journal of Criminology, 17(4):370-377, 1977.

Behavioral studies of 126 male felons referred for parole evaluation at the Georgia diagnostic and evaluation center in Jackson confirmed the importance of deficient self-control in violent crimes committed by black criminals. Assessment was by: (1) previously used scales of impulsivity of prisoners' crimes; (2) the MMPI psychopathic deviate and hypomania scales; and (3) direct behavioral measures of impulse control, namely, a mirror-tracing task and the stroup color-naming test. Results of these investigations disclosed a tendency toward poorer impulse control among black violent criminals than among their white counterparts. By contrast, no racial differences in self-control by nonviolent criminals were found on those measures for which complete data were available. The potential value of this and related studies to eventual understanding of both violent criminal behavior and parole outcome among minority groups is acknowledged.

168
Higgins, Paul, Albrecht, Gary L., Albrecht, Maryann H., "Black-White Adolescent Drinking: The Myth and The Reality," Social Problems, 25(2):215-224, 1977.

Results of a 1970 study of drinking behavior among black and white adolescents in Atlanta, Georgia are analyzed and discussed. The authors find that contrary to inferences developed from research on adult drinking in the U.S. as a social problem, black teenagers in this study drank less frequently than white teenagers and were more likely to drink at home with the family. Results imply that problem drinking among black adults may not be as strongly related to adolescent drinking as previously supposed. It is suggested also that disorganization of the black family as a causative factor in the development of alcoholism has been overemphasized.

169
Hodges, H.E., and Lowe, George D., "Race and Change In Rates of Treatment and Deaths Due To Alcoholism In A Southern State: 1970-1974," Phylon, 38(2):152-159, 1977.

Both availability and utilization of alcoholism services in the State of Georgia increased over the period 1970-1974, but rates of death associated with alcoholism and the racial disparity in these rates - higher for blacks than for whites - remained stable over the same period. The only dramatic decrease in death rates occurred among black males over 65 years of age. These findings suggest that the health care system in Georgia has not had any great success in intervening in the process of alcoholism, at least insofar as falling death rates are concerned. Differing interpretations of the Georgia experience in terms of the relationship between alcoholism services delivery and alcoholism death rates are discussed.

170
Klatsky, Arthur L., Friedman, Gary D., Siegelaub, Abraham B., "Alcohol Consumption Among White, Black, or Oriental Men and Women: Kaiser-Permanente Multiphasic Health Examination Data," American Journal of Epidemiology, 105(4):311-323, 1977.

Patterns of alcohol consumption were investigated among persons who took automated multiphasic health checkup examinations in a California program between 1964 and 1968 (N=91,659). Substantial age, sex, and race differences in alcohol consumption were reported. Generally, men drank more than women, and drinking was most prevalent among whites and least prevalent among orientals. The proportion of drinkers declined steadily in both sexes with advancing age, but even in the eighth decade of life almost two-thirds of men (64.2 percent of all races) reported alcohol consumption. Alcohol use showed a strong positive association with cigarette smoking, a weaker positive association with coffee use, and no relation to blood group within race. A complex relation was observed between alcohol use and adiposity, which differed for the various sex-race subgroups.

171
McCreary, Charles, and Padilla, Eligio, "MMPI Differences Among Black, Mexican-American, and White Male Offenders," Journal of Clinical Psychology, 33(1):171-177, 1977.

Racial/ethnic variations on the MMPI were examined by contrasting separate groups of male black and Mexican-American misdemeanor offenders with white offenders matched and unmatched on social class. Cultural factors seemed to be related to black-white differences in 'MA,' 'K,' and 'HY' scales. Black-White differences on the 'MF' and 'Alcoholism' scales are tentatively attributed to socioeconomic factors.

172
Minnesota Institute on Black Chemical Abuse, Annual Report: October 1, 1976 - June 30, 1977. Minneapolis, 1977, 13 pages.

The history, financial status, and activities of the Minnesota Institute on Black Chemical Abuse (MIBCA) are highlighted in this annual report. Message from Director, program history, program outline, history, service components, alcoholism services for black people, financial report and update summary, numerical program goals and rates of attainment, attachments, staff monitoring system, qualitative program assessment process, training outline, support group evaluation form, pre/post training form, goal attainment form.

173
Multicultural Drug Abuse Prevention Resource Center, Can Drug Abuse Be Prevented in The Black Community?, Inglewood, CA., 1977.

This booklet deals with the problem of drug abuse, including alcohol abuse within the Black community. Areas addressed include past failures at prevention, classifications of users, different drugs used at each stage of use, reasons for using drugs, who the users are and prevention strategy.

174
Myers, Vincent, "Drug-Related Cognitions Among Minority Youth," Journal of Drug Education, 7(1):53-62, 1977.

Lengthy interviews with a nationwide sample of young, low-income Black, Chicano, and Caribbean men and women, and with their nonminority counterparts, revealed that most were uniformed about the effects of licit and illicit drugs. Only 9 percent responded accurately to more than two-thirds of the 42 questions developed to gauge the accuracy of their knowledge of the dangers and effects of drugs. Respondents were 1357 Job Corps enrollees, drawn from a population of about 20,000 at 19 Job Corps Centers in 17 states. Of the ethnic groups queried, Caribbean men, and white men and women were the best informed. These data, combined with other findings drawn from a more lengthy report, lead to the conclusion that new sources of accurate information, attuned to the culture and language of youthful minorities, are needed to inform the one-half who use illicit drugs.

175
Myers, Vincent, "Drug Use Among Minority Youth," _Addictive Diseases,_ 3(2):187-196, 1977.

Results of a nationwide sample survey of young and low-income Black, Chicano, and Caribbean men and women, as well as their nonminority counterparts, indicate that a majority disapprove of illicit drug use. While one-half of the sample report having had experience with illicit drugs, most have renounced their involvement and no longer use them. Of the racial and ethnic groups queried, white youth are the most likely to have been drug-involved. These data, together with other findings drawn from a more lengthy report, suggest that dysfunctional drug use patterns among many low-income minorities are not pronounced.

176
National Center for Alcohol Education, _Decisions and Drinking: An Ounce of Prevention._ Arlington, Va., 1977. DHEW Publication (ADM) 77-454.

Instructional materials are offered for a course intended to support responsible decision-making about drinking. The course is focused on Blacks. Drinking decisions, drinking problems, attitudes, facilitator's handbook, flip chart, facilitator's presentation outline cards, 8 take-home summaries, myths and realities, influences of American History and popular history on decisions about drinking, reasons for drinking, effects of alcohol on body functions, mixing drinks with other drugs, social drinking and antisocial driving, influence of family and peers, environmental factors, self-image related to decision-making.

177
Oldroyd, Richard J., and Howell, Robert J., "Personality, Intellectual, and Behavioral Differences Between Black, Chicano, and White Inmates in The Utah State Prison," Psychological Reports, 41(1): 187-191, 1977.

A correlational study compared 668 Caucasian, 103 Chicano, and 73 Black inmates on 47 variables considered relevant to the prison setting. Religious differences were prominent as were differences in scores on standard intelligence tests. Chicanos tended to be more assaultive. Blacks posed less escape risk, and fewer Blacks used alcohol. Blacks scored as better adjusted on bipolar psychological inventory scales relating to feelings of personal inadequacy. Other differences are also discussed.

178
Primm, B.J., "Poverty, Folk Remedies and Drug Misuse Among the Black Elderly," In: W.H. Watson, I. Lewis, et al., Eds., Health and The Black Aged. Washington, D.C.: National Center on Black Aged, 1977. 151 p. (pp. 63-70).

The author discusses how poverty among elderly Blacks has led them to rely on folk remedies and the misuse of drugs (including alcohol) to cure their ailments. Methods of prevention and major issues concerning drug misuse are described, including some determinants of dosage requirements for the elderly.

179
Robey, Floyd, "Kentucky's Task Force On Minority Alcohol Concerns - A Report." Conference Paper. NCA National Alcoholism Forum. San Diego, CA: 29 Apr - 4 May 1977. 14 P.

This brief address comprises an elaboration of the development, growth, and some of the accomplishments of the Kentucky Task Force on Minority Alcohol Concerns. Information on the incidence of problem drinking among Black people in Kentucky and on the goals, plans, and activities of the Task Force in response to the needs of the Black community is presented. Special mention is made of Task Force contributions to: (1) A Black workshop at the 6th Kentucky School of Alcohol Studies, 12-15 Jul 1976: (2) A public awareness exhibit booth at the 39th Annual Louisville Defender's Black Exposition, Oct 1976; and (3) "Project Awareness 77," involving the training of task force members in Cottage Program Techniques for Application in the Black Communities of Louisville and Lexington. Conclusions based on the Task Force experience and proposals for meeting future treatment and prevention needs of Black alcoholics are noted.

180
Schuckit, Marc A., "Geriatric Alcoholism and Drug Abuse," Gerontologist, 17(2): 168-174, 1977.

Substance abuse among the elderly is described, including use of opiate drugs, nonopiate drugs, and alcohol abuse. As is the case with other older addicts, the elderly opiate addict has great need for medical care and housing. Nonopiate abusers are those who inadvertently abuse prescribed drugs. The elderly, due to their decreased physical reserve, are twice as likely to react adversely to medications in even normal doses. New data indicate that the elderly have a higher percentage of Blacks, are more likely to receive treatment at a hospital and are more likely to be treated with Methadone maintenance. Elderly alcoholics may not be a homogeneous group, but there are few studies of large groups of older alcoholics. Compared to a younger group of alcohol abusers, the elderly alcoholic group has a higher proportion of men, Caucasians, and individuals with a lower educational level.

181
Seftel, H.C., "Diseases In Urban and Rural Black Populations," South African Medical Journal, 51(5): 121-123, 1977.

In a review of diseases encountered by urban and rural Black populations in South Africa, two groups of new disorders are described as having serious impact on urban residents: (1) A large range of alcohol-related illnesses having deleterious effects at the social, economic, psychological and physical levels; and (2) A large variety of diseases similar to those found in western populations. In rural areas, the major problems are centered around infection and malnutrition. Other significant disorders include cancer of the esophagus, liver and cervix, rheumatic heart disease, and cardiomyopathy.

Urban Blacks in South Africa comprise a population in a state of transition with all gradations of development. This population exhibits a correspondingly wide and varied range of diseases including both the ancient afflictions of the tribe and the new diseases of the city. It is felt that more epidemiological research is needed to obtain reliable knowledge about disease prevalence among these populations and to determine the most effective methods of applying present knowledge to existing and future treatment resources.

182
Southern Area Alcohol Education and Training Program, Inc., _Alcohol Abuse Training Relevant To Minority Populations. Handbook: Blacks._ Report. Atlanta, GA., 1977.

The intent of this manual is to provide trainers with essential background information about alcohol abuse among Black populations and to present a practical, workable model for organizing and structuring a training program. Training manual, alcohol abuse professionals, training of paraprofessionals, concerned caregivers, interested citizens, helping professions, alcoholism among minority groups, black people, background information, black self-image, black alcoholism, black vocabulary test, model training program outlines.

183
Steer, Robert A., Shaw, Brian F., Beck, Aaron T., "Structure of Depression In Black Alcoholic Men," _Psychological Reports,_ 41(3): 1235-1241, 1977.

Factor analyses of the scores of Black alcoholic men (N=103) on the Beck Depression Inventory revealed dimensions of depression similar to those previously reported for racially heterogeneous alcoholic patients and primarily depressed patients. Meaningful dimensions of depression identified were cognitive-affective impairment, retarded depression, and escapism. The most replicable dimension in this Black sample appeared to be cognitive-affective in nature. Only 1 factor was composed of more than 5 salient variables, however, casting some doubt on the generalizability of the structure to other Black alcoholic samples.

184
Texas Commission on Alcoholism, Alcoholism Among Blacks. Communications Aid. Austin, Texas, 1977.

This information packet contains material titled: (1) Resource guide to Black alcoholism in Texas; (2) Alcoholism and the Black community; and (3) Perspective on Black alcoholism in Texas.

185
Thomas, G.E., Wicks, A.C.B., Clain, D.J., Loon, N., Seggie, J., Bramstom, B., "Hepatocellular Carcinoma In The Rhodesian African," Digestive Diseases, 22(7): 573-581, 1977.

The authors carried out a prospective survey of 28 primary liver carcinomas in Rhodesian Blacks during the period from July 1973 to June 1974. Hepatocellular Carcinoma is the most common malignancy seen in Rhodesian Blacks. Results indicate that the age distribution was evenly spread through adult life with no definite peak incidence. Some of the patients were young and without evidence of chronic liver disease. However, many had the stigmata of established hepatic disease. This contrasts with the common assertion that in areas of high incidence for primary liver cancer, those affected are mainly young and lack signs of chronic liver disease. The most common presenting symptoms were abdominal pain and swelling and weight loss. Hepatomegaly, often tender and nodular, was present in all but one of the patients. The incidence of alpha-feto protein, 46.5 percent, is low compared to other countries where primary liver cancer is common. Hepatitis B antigen was absent in all 28, suggesting that there is no association between the persistence of the antigen and hepatocellular carcinoma in Rhodesia (now Zimbabwe). Liver function tests, although abnormal, were never diagnostic of primary liver cancer. The authors have confirmed a high association between alcohol consumption and cirrhosis and hepatocellular carcinoma.

186
United States. National Institute on Alcohol Abuse and Alcoholism. An Ounce of Prevention - A Course for Blacks. (ADM-77-454). Rockville, Maryland: 1977.

It is assumed here that an exploration of black drinking decisions must take place within the context of the fundamental importance of black identity and self-image in making any kind of life decision. There is consideration here of a responsible model for decision-making about drinking. This model includes "an opportunity for examining some myths and realities about being a black person in this country; where the myths came from and why; how the myths affect black life; and how the realities can be dealt with positively in today's society. By starting with the here-and-now world in which they live, in combination with a clear look at the past, blacks will be better able to rid themselves of the myths and misinformation which can breed problems associated with drinking."

187
United States. National Institute on Alcohol and Alcoholism. *The Unseen Crisis: Blacks and Alcohol*. Washington, D.C.: U.S. Government Printing Office, 1977. (DHEW Publication No. ADM 77-478).

This 14 page booklet begins with a Foreword by the Rev. Jesse L. Jackson, and includes helpful information on the nature of black alcoholism, and some action steps that could be taken to help to rectify the problem.

188
United States. National Institute on Drug Abuse. *Drugs and Minorities*, Ed. by G.A. Austin, B.D. Johnson, and E.E. Carrcll and D.J. Lettieri. Rockville, Maryland, 1977.

This volume contains summaries of research focusing on the extent of drug use and abuse among racial and ethnic minorities, and the factors influencing it.

189
Wicks, A.C., Thomas, G.E., and Clain, D.J., "Cirrhosis of The Liver In Rhodesian Blacks." *South African Medical Journal.* 41(25): 911-914, 1977.

Clinical features of both alcoholic and cryptogenic cirrhosis of the liver were observed in a prospective study of 35 black patients (predominantly men) admitted to the medical wards of The University of Rhodesia over a 1-year period. Alcohol consumption in the form of African beer was significantly higher in the cirrhotic patients than in a control population, but the clinical picture was predominantly that of neither alcoholic nor cryptogenic cirrhosis. Hepatomegaly, porphyria cutanea tarda, ascites, splenomegaly, and esophageal varices were common. There was a complete absence of gynecomastia, spider nevi, and liver palms. Histologically, the majority of patients had macronodular cirrhosis, and only 1 patient had micronodular cirrhosis and minimal fatty change. Hepatitis B surface antigen (HBSAG) was not detected in any patient, despite a positive HBAG rate of 4 percent in Black African blood donors, determined by means of the same laboratory technique.

## 1978

190
Aguirre, Marilyn, and Zambrana-Shojaei, Ruth E., "Evaluation of An Alcohol Prevention Program For Urban Poor Minority Youths: Lessons Learned." Conference Paper. NCA Meeting. St. Louis, MO: 1978. 23 P.

The difficulties encountered in evaluating primary alcoholism prevention programs in poor inner-city areas are discussed. The authors identify those factors which serve to hinder implementation of an effective evaluation design. They also analyze the implications of these factors for policy with regard to the evaluation of primary prevention in poor inner-city communities. The experiences of a particular program for Hispanic adolescents in East Harlem are used as an illustration of how specific evaluation problems are manifested.

191
Allen, Chaney, *I'm Black and I'm Drunk*. Minneapolis, Minnesota: CompCare Publications, 1978.

This book is an autobiography of a daughter of a minister who was an alcoholic. She relates her experiences in fighting alcoholism, before she finally won the battle over alcoholism and became an alcoholism lecturer and counsellor in San Deigo. She gives credit here to AA, and includes practical aids she developed while working with alcoholics (this same story was published in 1976 under the title: *I'm Black and I'm Drunk*).

192
Blumberg, Leonard U., Shipley, Thomas F., Barsky, Stephen F., *Liquor and Poverty: Skid Row As A Human Condition.* New Brunswick, N.J.: Rutgers Center of Alcohol Studies, 1978. 298 P.

The view that skid row is the intersection of alcohol and poverty is explored. The authors define skid row as a lifestyle and alcohol and poverty as central to the lifestyle whether it is found in the skid row area or elsewhere. The development of skid row areas in Philadelphia and Detroit is examined as well as the problem of predicting the development of other skid rows. Skid row-like people and where they might be found are discussed. The authors suggest that the relevant question is not so much, "Where will skid row move next?" As it is, "What kind of social policies and programs are necessary and desirable to inhibit the development of a skid row lifestyle?"

193
Christmas, June J., "Alcoholism Services For Minorities: Training Issues and Concerns," _Alcohol Health and Research World,_ 2(3): 20-27, 1978.

This article comprises a status report, with recommendations, on current outreach programs for minority alcoholics. Separate consideration is given to: (1) reasons for the concern for minorities; (2) the minority alcoholic as an individual in society; (3) considerations in addressing the needs of minorities; (4) caretakers who should be trained in alcoholism treatment; and (5) specific training issues and concerns. The author stresses the need for a cultural perspective in treatment and for an appropriate balance between alcoholism efforts and efforts in related human service areas.

194
Clark, Lemuel B., _Alcohol, Drug Abuse, and Mental Health Manpower Issues Involving Racial and Ethnic Minorities._ Report of the ADAMHA Manpower Policy Analysis Task Force. Rockville, MD: National Institute of Mental Health, 2: 218-260, 1978.

The alcohol, drug abuse, and mental health manpower issues and problems facing different racial and ethnic minorities, and the poor are addressed. The four major racial and ethnic minorities are referred to as Blacks, Hispanics, Native Americans, and Asian Americans. Charts are presented representing various socioeconomic parameters taken by the U.S. Bureau of the Census. Recommendations are presented for the various issues and problems addressed.

195
Coney, J.C., _Exploring the Known and Unknown Factors in the Rates of Alcoholism among Black and White Families._ San Francisco, CA: R and E. Research Associates, 1978. 94 p.

Available literature is consolidated to answer specific research questions on alcoholism among white and black females. The problem is formulated and a framework for considering the problem is outlined. The journals and books researched to provide a methodology for studying this problem are cited and abstracts of key articles are included. A critical review of empirical findings and a summary of critical reviews of known facts about the problem are presented. The unknown facts are discussed in relation to unsettled questions and needed research. Implications of the research for social work are also discussed.

196
Eversmeyer, W.H., Rosenstock, David, Biundo, Joseph J., "Aortic Insufficiency with Mild Ankylosing Spondylitis in Black Men," Journal of the American Medical Association. 240(24): 2652-2653, 1978.

Two black male patients with aortic insufficiency were found to have mild, asymptomatic ankylosing spondylitis, evident from roentgenograms and from the presence of HLA-B27 antigen. One patient, admitted because of an alcohol withdrawal syndrome, was found to have a grade 3/6 blowing, diastolic murmur along the left sternal border. He had a history of heavy ethanol abuse of several years' duration, but had no prior record of a heart murmur. The two cases emphasize that even "subclinical" ankylosing spondylitis may have aortic insufficiency, and that the uncommon occurrence of ankylosing spondylitis in black patients may also be associated with this extra-articular manifestation.

197
Expand Associates, Inc., Overview of Comments, Issues, Findings, and Recommendations for Three Series of Workshops On Alcoholism Treatment and Black Americans. Report. Silver Springs, MD., 1978.

Three series of workshops held in Washington, DC, during the period 6-21 April 1978 were held concerning alcoholism treatment and rehabilitation for Black Americans. Each of the workshops had a different focus: (1) Black programs, (2) Blacks in predominately White programs, and (3) Role of institutions, organizations, and agencies in meeting the needs of the Black alcoholic. The first series discussed topics such as perspectives on clinical technique, funding, and the future of Black programs. The second series examined the effective rehabilitation of the Black alcoholic through staff awareness and orientation and outreach in the Black community.

The third series focused on strategies for responsive treatment of the Black alcoholic and subgroups within the Black population.

198
Famutimi, E.O., "Training of Ministers As Alcohol Service Agents For The Black Community." Dissertation. Ann Arbor, MI.: University Microfilms International, 1978.

Ministers serving Black communities, recruited from Washington, D.C., churches, participated in a 3-phase training program involving lectures and presentations on the psychological, cultural, social and economic causes and effects of alcohol misuse and alcoholism. They attended workshops on alcoholism therapies and received practical experience at alcohol resource centers; they were also trained in the planning and initiation of neighborhood alcoholism service programs. A post-program test for changes in attitudes toward and knowledge about alcohol problems are given; scores were compared with those of a control group. The trained ministers' test scores showed that their knowledge about alcoholism had increased significantly and their attitudes had shifted in the desired direction. Compared with no alcoholism counseling in the year prior to training, after their training the ministers counseled and referred hundreds of clients. The program is seen as a model for preventing and combatting alcoholism and other diseases in ethnic populations.

199
Freeman, Don, "The Black Community and Marijuana Legalization." In: _Drug Abuse: Modern Trends, Issues and Perspectives_. Proceedings of the Second National Drug Abuse Conference, Inc., New Orleans, Louisiana, 1975. Comp.: A Schecter, H. Alksne and E. Kaufman. New York: Marcel Dekker, Inc., 1978, pp. 803-817.

This chapter is divided into subsections on drug abuse policy and the Black community, the national debate on the legalization of marijuana, recent research, marijuana, tobacco and alcohol, tobacco and marijuana, marijuana and alcohol, availability, use and the impoverished, the extent of current use in the Black community, achievement and emotional development of Black youth, and Black social-political activism and marijuana.

200
Gearing, F.R., D'Amico, D.A., Toussie, S., "Does Methadone Maintenance Lead to Increased Alcohol and Polydrug Use?," In: Critical Concerns in the Field of Drug Abuse New York. NY: Marcel Dekker, 1978. (pp. 280-286).

Methods and results from cohort experiences in determining the alcohol and polydrug involvement of patients in methadone maintenance treatment are described and discussed. It is concluded that: (1) alcohol problems are more prevalent among both black men and women and tend to increase with age at onset of treatment, whereas polydrug problems are more prevalent among white men and women, and among the younger patients; (2) among the patients who have remained under observation and treatment with methadone for four years or longer, previously reported alcohol and drug abuse problems tend to disappear, supporting the hypothesis that in this group these problems are transient and remediable if necessary ancillary services are put into operation, and patients are not discharged too soon; (3) unrecognized problems with alcohol and polydrug use in the earlier cohort (1964-1969) appear to have been somewhat more prevalent than expected; and (4) results for comparative figures for the communities from which these patients came with reference to multiple drug use were inconclusive. It is noted that only one study (1972), which reviewed admissions to several municipal and voluntary hospitals in New York City, could be cited, and that if the results from this study are used as a crude index of the size of the alcohol problem in New York City, the proportion of patients in methadone maintenance treatment who present a major alcohol problem is no greater than might be expected.

201
Gibson, D.P., $70 Billion in the Black: America's Black Consumers. New York: Macmillan, 1978.

This book, like its earlier version, The $30 Billion Negro, examines how minorities (with a focus here on blacks) react in the marketplace. Blacks as consumers of alcoholic beverages are discussed on pp. 130-132, 147-151 and 160.

202
Gordon, A.J., "Hispanic Drinking After Migration: The Case of Dominicans," Medical Anthropology 2 (No. 4): 61-84, 1978.

The drinking behavior of migrants from the Dominican Republic who currently live in Newton, MA., is examined; 7700 Dominicans live in an "inner city" neighborhood shared with other Hispanics (primarily Puerto Ricans), blacks and the remnants of a once much larger white population. Previous studies suggested that recent minority group migrants generally experience alienation, increased reliance on alcohol and consequently problem drinking, but the current study found a decrease in drinking among Newton Dominicans. The style of drinking is noticeably different: drinking is done on weekends rather than during the week, rarely leads to fights and is far less associated with the "macho" image. Reasons for this shift in drinking patterns, including the need to economize, to progress and to sacrifice, are examined. Home-owning is very important. Some Dominicans have 2 full-time jobs and the transition from the "macho" male ideal to the "hombre serio" has been accelerated by the heightened roles and expectations of wives. The fewer opportunities for socializing in Newton, as opposed to the Dominican Republic, also cuts down on drinking. When socialization does occur, people strictly observe codes of moderation in drinking. Another very potent factor is the charismatic Catholic movement, which holds to a conception of the good life as a life without vice, in which one's commitments, time and energy ought to be dedicated to the church, the home and the workplace; excessive drinking and drunkenness are especially disparaged.

203
Harper, Frederick D., "Alcohol Use Among North American Blacks." In: Israel, Y., et al., Eds., _Research Advances in Alcohol and Drug Problems._ New York, NY: Plenum Press, 1978. 497 P. (pp. 349-366).

A review of 77 studies involving drinking practices among North American Blacks is presented. Drinking patterns of Black Americans appear to differ from those of whites; the group tends toward weekend drinking, and lower-class blacks tend toward status drinking of high priced liquors. The health and physiological effects of alcohol abuse among blacks are more severe than among whites, probably due to living conditions and limited health care services. Alcohol and heavy drinking was found to be a causative factor of criminal behavior in blacks. Comprehensive treatment programs are suggested as most effective in providing for both individual and family needs of the black alcoholic. Further study is recommended for testing etiological theories on why blacks drink as opposed to why whites drink.

204
Isaacson, C., "Changing Pattern of Liver Disease in South African Blacks," South African Medical Journal, 53(10): 365-368, 1978.

Results of a comparative study of liver biopsies of South African blacks for the periods 1959-1960 and 1975-1976 show significant differences in the histological picture of micronodular cirrhosis. The data point to the recent appearance in this population of fatty change, alcoholic hepatitis, alcoholic hyaline, and alcoholic cirrhosis, conditions which were never observed when alcohol consumption was confined to heavily iron-laden home brew. The changed disease pattern is attributable to 1962 liquor law revisions permitting blacks access to all varieties of alcohol. No corresponding change in the histology or incidence of macronodular cirrhosis and hepatocellular carcinoma is indicated.

205
Jackson, Reid E. (Ed.), Health Policy, Planning, and Financing the Future of Health Care for Blacks in America: A National Conference Held in Washington, D.C., 28-29 Oct 1977. National Center For Health Services Research Proceedings Series. Silver Spring, MD: Expand Associates, Inc., 1978.

This conference, entitled "Health Policy, Planning, and Financing the Future of Health Care for Blacks in America," was convened in response to a need to focus on problems that must be addressed in anticipation of a national health insurance program and equitable access to care for blacks and other medically underserved populations.

206
Jarvis, Edna, "Alcoholism: A New Perspective for Black Americans," Crisis,85(7): Aug-Sept: 237-239, 1978.

The alcohol problem among the black community is discussed. Blacks, probably due to strong fundamentalist traditions, have both a high abstaining rate and high rate of alcohol abusers. The author feels that alcohol abuse has been accepted without much question in black communities. Many religious people think alcoholism is a sin and assess the disease as a moral issue. Various alcohol-related disorders have been recognized and facts about them as well as myths concerning alcohol are presented.

207
Keenan, T.P., "Study of Alcohol Knowledge and Information Sources Among Rural High School Students." Dissertation. Ann Arbor, MI: University Microfilms International, 1978.

An alcohol information test (AIT) was developed to determine the level of information on alcohol in 8th-, 10th- and 12th-graders and the extent to which that level differs by grade, gender and race and to examine the information sources and students' perception of the credibility of the sources; 692 students completed the questionnaire. It was found that information increased from the 8th to the 10th grade and then remained stable. Mean scores for boys and girls did not vary significantly among whites, but black girls outscored black boys by a substantial margin. Concerning white respondents, (a) a relative increase in using peers as a source of alcohol information occurred between the 8th and 10th grade; (b) 12th-graders demonstrated more confidence in the relative accuracy of information received from medical personnel than did 10th graders; and (c) as a group, whites had more confidence in the relative accuracy of people than did blacks. The following trends were identified within the black group: (a) a relative increase in the use of television as a source of information between the 10th and 12th grades. Boys indicated more relative use of television as a source of information than girls; (b) girls demonstrated more confidence in the relative accuracy of information from medical personnel; and (c) blacks viewed medical personnel as more accurate concerning alcohol information than did whites.

208
Ludmar, J.M., "Selected Personality Characteristics of Black and White Male Alcoholics in a State Treatment Facility." Dissertation. Ann Arbor, MI.: University Microfilms International, 1978.

The dependence of MMPI on age, race and formal education was studied in 50 white and 30 black men (aged 25 to 62; mean age 38) who entered the Manhattan Alcoholism Rehabilitation Unit between April 1976 and June 1977. The patients had the classic MMPI profile for alcoholics, that is, an elevated D and PD scale combination. The blacks scored significantly higher than the whites on the MA and lower on the SI scale. Alcoholics who had not graduated from high school had significantly higher scores on the HS, D, PT and SI, and significantly higher scores on the HS, D and HY scales and lower scores on ES that those aged 25-35.

209
Meade, T.W., Brozovic, M., Chakrabarti, R., et al., "Ethnic Group Comparisons of Variables Associated with Ischaemic Heart Disease," British Heart Journal, 40: 789-795, 1978.

Alcohol consumption was measured in 412 white (61 women) and 141 black (55 women) British workers (mean ages ranged from 34 to 40 years) in a prospective study of ischemic heart disease. Cigarette and alcohol consumption were greater in the white than the black men. Race, blood platelet counts, fibrinolytic activity and other hemostatic variables are apparently more closely associated with the onset of ischemic heart disease than is the level of alcohol consumption.

210
Miller, R.M., Hunt, J.A., "Radiological Features of Alcoholic Ulcero-Osteolytic Neuropathy in Blacks," South African Medical Journal, 54: 159-161, 1978.

All patients admitted with a neurotrophic ulcero-osteolytic process to a surgical ward in Johannesburg, South Africa, between June 1976 and July 1977 were black men (mean age 43; N = 15) with a history of excessive drinking; all of them had dark complexion due to excess iron intake from home-brewed alcoholic beverages. These patients had trophic ulcers and infections of the feet, with varying degrees of bone resorption and clawing and deformation of the toes; some changes in the distal vessels were present in all, and typical angiographic features were present in the distal arteries of the feet. It is concluded that the etiology of the disease is related to alcoholism and that the term alcoholic ulcero-osteolytic neuropathy accurately describes the findings in this condition.

211
Morehouse, E.R., "Treating the Alcoholic on Public Assistance," Social Casework 59(1): 36-41, 1978.

This article discusses specific approaches for treating the Department of Social Services (DSS) or Supplementary Security Income (SSI) mandated alcoholic, and on issues that arise with this particular population.

212
Paton, Stephanie M., and Kandel, Denise B., "Psychological Factors and Adolescent Illicit Drug Use: Ethnicity and Sex Differences," Adolescence, 13(50): 187-200, 1978.

An attempt is made to clarify the relationship between four psychological factors (depressive mood, normlessness, sense of isolation from the world, and self-esteem) and drug use in a random sample of New York State Public High School students. Of the four psychological factors examined, only two, depressive mood and normlessness, show a positive relationship with the use of illicit drugs, especially drugs other than marijuana. The association of depressive mood and normlessness with illegal multiple drug use varies by ethnicity and sex, being consistently stronger among girls and among whites. In addition, depressive mood is negatively related to multiple drug use for black and Puerto Rican boys. The authors believe these findings suggest that psychological factors play a different role in adolescent drug involvement within various social and cultural groups.

213
Schneider, B.A., Schneider, E.L., Hardesty, A.S., et al., "Interrelations of Psychiatric Diagnosis, Psychological Profile and Ethnic Background," Psychological Reports, 43(1): 55-61, 1978.

The relationship between psychopathology and ethnic background was studied via the structured clinical interview in a random sample of 200 psychiatric patients (134 whites, 48 blacks, 18 Hispanics; 87 women) divided among 4 major diagnostic categories (114 had functional psychosis, 16 organic brain syndrome, 33 neurosis and personality disorder, and 30 alcohol and drug dependence). Chi-square analyses comparing ethnicity and diagnosis yielded no significant differences. Analysis of variance of the structured clinical interview scores showed no significant ethnic differences on overall severity of illness, but 3 of the 10 subareas showed such differences ($p < .02$ or $< .04$): incongruous behavior (dirty clothes, scratching, tremor, etc.) occurred most frequently in whites and least frequently in blacks, while physical complaints and behavioral and verbal indices of perceptual dysfunction (hallucinatory experiences) were more frequent among Hispanics and blacks than among whites.

214
Steele, R.E., "Steele's Reply to Bedrosian and Beck," Journal of Consulting and Clinical Psychology, 46(6): 1500-1501, 1978.

This article replies to the criticism by R.C. Bedrosian and A.T. Beck (Journal of Consulting and Clinical Psychology, 46: 1498-1500, 1978) of the authors' article "Clinical Comparison on Black and White Suicide Attempters" (Journal of Consulting and Clinical Psychology, 45:982-986, 1977). The criticism revolves around two issues: (a) the appropriateness of the variables chosen to examine black-white differences in suicide attempt behavior, and (b) the prematurity of the authors' claim that one empirical "box score" study is sufficient to question the viability of black psychology. On the point of the omission of alcohol consumption, a key variable known to be related to suicide attempt behavior, the author concedes that the study would have been improved had this variable been included. Although not reported in the original study, information from the medical workups on alcohol and drug abuse revealed no statistically significant differences between the black and white suicide attempters which the author contends is consistent with his interpretation that there are no meaningful "clinical" differences between the two groups. In answer to the second issue, the author stresses that his original intention was not to suggest that this one study be sufficient to invalidate the claim that a black psychology is needed. He reinterates that his interpretation of the study results does not provide supportive evidence for a black psychology notion and that his call for a reexamination of the need for a black psychology in light of empirical evidence is a valid one.

215
United States. National Institute on Alcohol Abuse and Alcoholism. National Conference on Minority Group Alcohol, Drug Abuse and Mental Health Issues Conference Proceedings. Denver, CO: 22-24 May 1978. 102 p.

Alcohol, drug abuse, and mental health concerns among the various racial minority groups which were addressed at this conference are summarized. Asian American minority network,

Black American minority network, Hispanic American minority network, American Indian minority network, accreditation workshop, institutionalization workshop, nonmetropolitan communities.

216
Wanberg, K., Lewis, R., Foster, F.M., "Alcoholism and Ethnicity: A Comparative Study of Alcohol Use Patterns Across Ethnic Groups," International Journal of the Addictions, 13(8): 1245-1262, 1978.

Ethnic and sociodemographic or sociocultural differences in alcohol use and alcohol-induced problems were studied in 70 American Indian, 48 Black, 75 Hispano and 78 White Anglo inpatient alcoholics. Personal income did not, but family income did, differ across the 4 groups. All groups experienced significant disruption in social and vocational areas, but American Indians showed the greatest social disruption. Almost 86 percent of American Indians had never been married or were divorced or separated (vs. 70 percent of Blacks and 75 percent of Hispanos and 65 percent of White Anglos whose marital or family relationships were disrupted). The groups did not differ in sustained vs periodic drinking, but American Indians and Hispanos were more likely to drink in gregarious, convivial settings and drank more and showed greater deterioration in social roles (i.e., joblessness, problems with the law) due to alcohol use. The groups did not differ in use of alcohol to enhance self or manage anxiety and depression. A need is seen for specialized staff to work with American Indian and Hispano alcoholics.

217
Webb, L.F., "Is Crisis in the Alcoholic Black Family Different from the Crisis in the Average Alcoholic White Family?" In: Critical Concerns in the Field of Drug Abuse. New York, NY: Marcel Dekker, 1978. 142 p. (pp. 857-861).

The author contends that both black and white families, particularly those in crisis, share what is called "participational identification," but the similarity of the two families ends with the existing caste system in America. Black families are discussed in relation to white families, and to the lack of black family service agencies to help them with their specific problems. A program for the black alcoholic family in crisis, which relates to the strengths of the black family, and builds on "peoplehood," is introduced.

The program spans 13 weeks, exposing family members to immediate resources available to them with emphasis on their rights as first-class citizens. The spouse is shown that the family structure foreign to the white world has been the determining factor for black survival. Effort is spent to help the spouse see herself or himself as capable of dealing with alcoholism as he or she is capable of dealing with many other stresses that occur within the black family. Within the program, the role of the family members is identified and stressed, and family members are urged to communicate with each other, with great emphasis placed on seeing themselves as black. It is hoped that scholars will begin to conduct studies that include the "peoplehood" of the black and focus on the effect that this has on the black alcoholic family.

218
Zeiner, Arthur, and Paredes, Alfonso, "Differential Biological Sensitivity to Ethanol As A Predictor of Alcohol Abuse," In: Smith, David E. Ed., Multicultural View of Drug Abuse. Cambridge, MA: Schenkman Publishing. 1978. 615 P. (pp. 591-599).

The epidemiological evidence for racial and ethnic differences in ethanol use and abuse is reviewed. A strong relationship between alcohol abuse and mortality from liver cirrhosis is drawn in an international study. The rate of alcoholism in Oklahoma is lowest among Caucasians, higher among Blacks and highest among Indians. Other studies indicate as large a degree of variation exists within Indian groups as it does between racial groups. Genetic determinants of ethanol metabolism have been investigated using identical and fraternal twin studies. Racial differences in ethanol clearance rates and in response to an acute dose of ethanol have been noted. Possible neurochemical bases for ethanol addiction are hypothesized.

219
Zimberg, S., "Treatment of Socioeconomically Deprived Alcoholics." In: Zimberg, S., Wallace, J., and Blume, S.B., Eds., Practical Approaches to Alcoholism Psychotherapy. New York: Plenum, 1978. 288 p. (pp. 205-218).

Treatment approaches and incidence and characteristics of alcoholism in the urban poor, specifically among Blacks and Ruerto Ricans in New York (skid row population excluded), are described along with the approaches and outcome of a pilot treatment program at Harlem Hospital (ABST. No. 412, *Journal of Studies on Alcohol*, Vol. 35). Day-care was established as the core treatment approach, providing a structured 9-5 treatment program in an alcohol-free environment. When patients had achieved at least 90 days of sobriety, they were provided with vocational counseling and over 160 patients became involved in training. Compared with Blacks, Puerto Ricans are less likely to use Alcoholics Anonymous, but are more often accompanied by their families during the initial visit to the treatment program. Bilingualism and cultural knowledge are essential for treating Puerto Rican alcoholics. Puerto Rican women alcoholics had poorer treatment outcomes than do Black women alcoholics. Contrary to middle-class alcoholics, most deprived individuals do not experience treatment as enough of an incentive to give up alcohol. The advantages of an outpatient day-care program for the socioeconomically deprived are noted. For outcome evaluation, variables other than drinking status should be utilized (e.g., changes in vocational status, health and hospital usage, public assistance costs, etc.).

## 1979

220
Arnold, S.D., "Tuberculous Peritonitis Associated with Alcoholic Liver Disease," _New York State Journal of Medicine,_ 79(6): 922-924, 1979.

Case reports of three black patients (one male and two females), initially diagnosed as having ascites secondary to alcoholic liver disease, are presented. The presence of high fever and inanition, the indolence of presentation, the paucity of peritonitis signs, and the exudative nature of the ascitic fluid suggested tuberculous peritonitis. It is concluded that the presence of fever and ascites in the patient with alcoholic liver disease requires an aggressive diagnostic approach, including pericentesis with culture for mycobacteria and peritoneal biopsy with a repeat procedure, if necessary.

221
Bell, P., "Some Considerations in Counseling Black DWI Offenders," Conference Paper. 2nd National DWI Conference. Rochester, MN: 30 May-1 Jun 1979. 188 p. (pp. 150-151).

Guidelines for discussion of cultural and ethnic issues related to the delivery of alcohol abuse services in the black community are outlined. Population-specific programming, Community approval of substance use, Access to health care, Cultural defenses, Survival skills, Role models, Black community as homogeneous, Trust in alcoholism service system, Alcohol awareness, Cultural forces.

222
Best, Josefina E., "Comparative Analysis of Alcohol Abuse Among Two Ethnic Minority Groups." Dissertation, Thesis. May 1979. 129 P.

The socio-cultural aspects of alcohol abuse among Native and Black americans are compared. A review of literature is presented concerning alcohol abuse among teenagers and its implications for nursing practice. Teenage abuse was found to be widespread among both sexes, with parents, peers and television making a tremendous impact on the learning process. The author proposes a preventive alcohol educational program for youth. Master's dissertation seminar paper, adolescent drinking, psychotherapy, halfway houses, vocational rehabilitation, Alcoholics Anonymous, Al-Anon, Alateen.

223
Bobo, S.E., and Wright, D.F., "State of the Art of Black Women in the Prevention of Substance Abuse." Conference paper. Bicultural Women's Forum, Center for Multicultural Awareness Conference. Washington, DC: 23-25 Aug 1979. 17 p.

The authors contend that in viewing prevention from the perspective of ethnic minorities, the person-oriented view must be expanded to include a system-oriented view, to ensure that prevention activities address the root causes of substance (including alcohol) abuse in the community. Social, economic, and cultural conditions within the black community are described. Black women's functions and influence in community activist roles are examined, and areas of possible change are identified. Prevention strategies that utilize these key roles, and that will impact on individual, small group, institutional, and community levels are suggested.

224
Bourne, P.G., and Light, E., "Alcohol Problems in Blacks and Women." In: J.H. Mendelson & N.K. Mello, Eds., Diagnosis & Treatment of Alcoholism. New York, NY: McGraw-Hill, 1979. 405 p. (pp. 83-123).

The first part of this chapter discusses alcoholism and Blacks: the history of alcohol use; drinking patterns; and drinking problems. The second part discusses alcoholism and women: etiology of alcoholism; differences between male and female alcoholics; subgroups of women alcoholics; biomedical consequences; and alcohol use during pregnancy. It is concluded that alcoholism treatment for Blacks and women must be based on the unique nature of the alcohol problem in each of these groups, with the therapeutic strategy tailored to the needs of each specific group if it is to be effective.

225
Brunswick, A.F., "Black Youths and Drug Use Behavior." In: G.M. Beschner & A.S. Friedman, Eds., Youth Drug Abuse. Lexington, MA.: D.C. Heath, 1979. 681 p. (pp. 443-493).

A study of youthful drug abuse in the black community in New York City's Harlem found what was called the highest prevalence of heroin use and addiction of any recent representative household community survey or high school survey yet reported. Alcohol was the drug used earliest in the life of the user. One in five male users reported first use of alcohol by the age of 10. By the age of 14, half of male drinkers and almost the same proportion of females had experienced some involvement with alcohol. The model frequency of alcohol use was daily and/or several times a week for males and slightly less often for females. At the time of interview, three-quarters of the alcohol users had been drinking for at least five years, and a similar proportion had taken at least one drink within the past month. Data from this study are shown in tabular form.

226
Buckalew, L.W., "Alcohol: A Description and Comparison of Recent Scientific vs. Public Knowledge," Journal of Clinical Psychology, 35(2): 459-463, 1979.

A 23-item true-false alcohol knowledge questionnaire was completed by 190 respondents including 69 high-school students, and 67 undergraduate and 52 graduate college students (mean ages 17, 20 and 31, respectively); each group was fairly well balanced in terms of race and sex. Despite a relatively high awareness of the general and gross effects of alcohol, the composite mean of 59 percent correct answers suggested significant misinformation. Overall, 52 percent responded that alcohol is a chemical poison; 19 percent were unaware that alcohol kills brain cells; 66 percent thought alcohol bad for the heart; 55 percent considered alcohol a stimulant; 40 percent did not feel that children's drinking would affect development; 21 percent did not consider alcohol a drug; 77 percent regarded alcoholism as a mental problem; 40 percent believed that people drink only from personal desire; 56 percent did not believe a desire for alcohol can be inherited; 32 percent classified light drinking during pregnancy as harmless; 28 percent were unaware of relationships between alcohol and metabolism; 45 percent felt that there is no way to drink a lot without getting drunk. There was a positive, though minimal, relationship between knowledge of alcohol and education; whites showed more alcohol knowledge than did blacks.

227
Costello, R.M., Baillargeon, J.G., Biever, P., et al., "Second-Year Alcoholism Treatment Outcome Evaluation With A

Focus on Mexican-American Patients," American Journal of Drug and Alcohol Abuse, 6: 97-108, 1979.

The first 75 patients treated at the alcohol treatment unit of the Audie Murphy Memorial Veterans Hospital in San Antonio, Tx, were evaluated with a focus on ethnic differences. The group included 44 Anglo-American men (current mean age 49), 26 Mexican-American men (current mean age 40), 2 Black men and 3 Anglo-American women. A 6-component social adjustment inventory (SAI) measuring residential stability, interpersonal relationships, recreational and social activities, general health status, employment status and drinking status, was used to index poshospital adjustment 2 years after discharge. The overall success of the program was 39 percent; the validity of the treatment difficulty scale as a predictor of success was demonstrated. Anglo and Mexican-Americans had success rates (based on drinking status) of 34 and 58 percent, respectively, in the 1st year and 42 and 39 percent in the 2nd. The average stability of 1st-year findings of SAI components compared with 2nd-year results was 79 percent. Use of standardized index of pretreatment patient characteristics is recommended to facilitate comparative program evaluation research.

228
Darity, W.A., "Alcohol and Other Drugs as Cripplers: A Crucial Problem in the Black Community," Urban League Review, 4(1): 36-46, 1979.

Alcohol and other drugs, as cripplers, can be considered from various points of view, particularly as having a crippling effect on the individual, on the family, and on society and the community. In interpreting crippling and the crippling effect, the cultural context, psychological context, the social context, and the physiological context are all crucial. This article addresses in a microscopic form a macroscopic problem from the point of view of (1) attitudes toward drugs and altered states of consciousness, (2) alcohol, (3) black Americans and alcohol, (4) narcotics, psychedelics, and other drugs, (5) government drug programs, and (6) a challenge for the black community and the National Urban League, and other black civil rights organizaitons.

229
Del-Villano, B.C., Tischfield, J.A., Schacter, L.P., et al., "Cupro-Zinc Superoxide Dismutase: A Possible Biologic Marker

For Alcoholism (Studies in Black Patients)," Alcoholism-Clinical and Experimental Research. 3: 291-296, 1979.

Cupro-Zinc Superoxide Dismutase (SOD-1) was measured by competition radioimmunoassay of erythrocyte lysates of 62 alcoholics (Median age 44; 19 blacks) and 27 controls (Median age 35; 9 blacks). Normal amounts of SOD-1 were found in the extract from controls and from white alcoholics (815 and 874 NG per MG of Hemoglobin). However, the level of SOD-1 in lysates from black alcoholics (1033 NG/MG) was significantly increased ($p < .0001$, rank-sum test) compared with black and white controls. This increase was not related to any other observed hematologic disorder or to any historical, demographic or laboratory value examined.

230
DeLuca, J.R., "Address to the National Black Alcoholism Council," Rockville, MD. DHEW, NIAAA. 19 Oct. 1979. 11 p.

Issues related to alcohol abuse and alcoholism problems among Black Americans are reviewed. Treatment goals, NIAAA initiatives, Cultural factors, Program development, Policy and planning, Program funding, Federal and state support for treatment, Prevention goals, Organizations.

231
Dembo, Richard, Burgos, William, Desjarlais, Don, Schmeidler, James, "Ethnicity and Drug Use Among Urban Junior High School Youths," International Journal of The Addictions, 14(4): 557-568, 1979.

Results of a survey of substance use in a junior high school in New York City are examined. Three factors influencing drug involvement were studied: (1) ethnic subculture, (2) social class, and (3) social adjustment. Alcohol was one of the seven categories of substances and 31 percent of the students reported using only alcohol; 15 percent used both marijuana and alcohol, and 12 percent were multidrug users. No significant differences in drug involvement were found between Black, Puerto Rican, and White students. Social class was also found to not be a valuable predictor of drug involvement. Results supported the social adjustment perspective and also indicated that ethnicity did interact with other variables such as home composition and machismo values to predict drug involvement.

232
Dembo, R., Schmeidler, J., Burgos, W., "Factors in the Drug Involvement of Inner City Junior High School Youths: A Discriminant Analysis," International Journal of Social Psychiatry, 25(2): 92-103, 1979.

Data from a 1976 survey of 1045 Junior High-School students (mean age 13; 43 percent Puerto Ricans and 41 percent Blacks) from an inner city were subjected to discriminant analysis to determine how the youths' demographic characteristics, sociocultural experiences (spare-time activities, own and peers' perceived status of different person types, etc.) and drug use among neighborhood peers related to their involvement with specific drugs. Of the 833 pupils studied, 35 percent denied ever using any drug, 35 percent used alcohol ("Ever," i.e., Lifetime use), 21 percent used marihuana, and usually alcohol as well, while 9 percent used other substances, and usually alcohol and marihuana. Discriminant analysis uncovered 2 factors associated with the respondents' drug taking: (1) a street-scene/recreational drug use factor, and (2) a cluster reflecting friends' use of alcohol/marihuana and other drugs. The 1st dimension separated out the nonusers and alcohol users from the other 2 user categories, and the 2D dimension separated out the users of "other drugs" from the rest. The results suggest that continued involvement in street life could increase the marihuana users' risk of moving on to the use of other substances, while the risk of becoming further involved with substances is smaller in the nonuser and alcohol groups.

233
Ellington, Jo L., Goolkasian, Paula, Rawson, Jane C., MacDonald, Donald E., Alcoholic Woman: A Descriptive and Comparative Analysis. Charlotte, NC., Randolph Clinic, 1979, 36 p.

Profiles of women alcoholics were developed and contrasted with findings from a group of nonalcoholic women to identify a discriminant function which would successfully separate women alcoholics from the comparison group. The measures used included demographic variables and psychological measures selected because of their sensitivity to behavioral and personality maladjustment rather than psychotic manifestation. For white female alcoholics, the composite profile depicts a 42 year old protestant of either high or low socioeconomic background, who has completed 11.8 years of school, is unemployed, unmarried and with two children. Her drinking has been out of control for 5 years and in comparison with an average nonalcoholic spouse she is older, has an alcohol-related arrest record, low feelings of self-worth, and more nervous symptoms. For the black female alcoholic, the composite depicts a 36 year old woman with 2.6 children who has completed 10.7 years of education, and who is unemployed. She tends to show an intermittent drinking pattern, to come from a low socioeconomic background, and her alcoholism is at a more advanced stage than the white female alcoholic. Her problems are in general similar to, but more severe than those of the white woman alcoholic. It is suggested that treatment programs take into account these individual differences in providing services to subgroups of women and minorities within the alcoholic population.

234
Harper, F.D., Alcoholism Treatment and Black Americans. Rockville, MD: National Institute on Alcohol Abuse and Alcoholism, 1979. DHEW Pub. No. ADM-79-853.

This report opens with critical reviews of the literature on alcohol use and alcoholism among Black Americans (51 items) and alcoholism treatment and Black Americans (32 items). Presentations and discussions at 3 community and counseling-oriented workshops on alcoholism treatment programs for blacks, predominantly white treatment programs, and organizations, institutions and agencies with an interest in alcoholism among blacks are summarized and analyzed. The 19 treatment methods used or favored for black alcoholics are listed in order of priority and assigned to 5 categories; counseling and therapy, vocational rehabilitation and financial aid, health care, information and support services, and personal development training. The 17 types of problems encountered by treatment agencies servicing blacks are classified under descriptions of problems related to community relations, program management, survival and growth, race relations and treatment. Among the stronger recommendations made were increased support from the National Institute on Alcohol Abuse and Alcoholism (NIAAA) and state agencies to alcoholism programs in black communities, research on drinking and alcoholism among blacks, and education and training for staff members working with black alcoholics. Opposition to NIAAA funding of alcoholism services through state contracts was voiced. Appendices include a directory of workshop participants, a questionnaire on the planning of black alcoholism workshops, and the workshop agendas.

235
Headlam, H.K., Goldsmith, R.J., Hanenson, I.B., Rauh, J.L., "Demographic Characteristics of Adolescents with Self-Poisoning," Clinical Pediatrics, 18(3): 147, 151, and 154, 1979.

Demographic characteristics of 235 adolescents observed at the emergency unit of the Cincinnati General Hospital are presented and discussed. It is noted that nearly 50 percent of the repeaters (adolescents with a previous history of self-poisoning), and 25 percent of the total study group had a history of alcohol abuse. It was found that: (1) self-poisoning occurred equally in male and female adolescents, particularly those between ages of 15 and 17 years; and (2) drug abuse and self-poisoning (including previous self-poisoning) rates were higher among whites than among blacks. It is concluded that adolescent self-poisoning appears to be a chronic disease associated with family turmoil, depression, alcoholism, drug abuse, and repeat self-poisoning. The long-term outlook for adolescent self-poisoning is not well defined, and needs further study.

236
Huba, G.J., Wingard, J.A., Bentler, P.M., "Adolescent Drug Use and Intentions to Use Drugs in the Future: A Concurrent Analysis," Journal of Drug Education, 9: 145-150, 1979.

Current drug use (113 drugs, including beer, wine and distilled spirits) were (nonsignificantly) associated with intended saline use in 1634 pupils attending grades 7, 8 or 9 in metropolitan Los Angeles schools (64 percent female, 56 percent Caucasian, 24 percent Black, 15 percent Hispanic and 5 percent Asian). Only about 20 percent of the variance in 12 intentions of future use could be explained by the current levels of use of the 13 drugs. A 2nd hypothesis-that intentions to use a particular drug would be better predicted by all current drug taking behavior than by only the level of use of that particular drug-was supported for all drugs studied. The overall pattern suggests that sources other than previous drug experience must be considered in attempting to explain intentions of future use.

237
Kurpiel, R.A., "Follow Up Study of Black Alcoholics." Dissertation. Ann Arbor, MI: University Microfilms, 1979.

The relationship of a planned treatment approach to contact rates, improvement levels and program impressions was studied in a primarily black population of alcoholics (aged 18-70; 85 percent men; 85 percent blacks) from the Rubicon Black Alcoholism Research and Demonstration Program. The subjects were divided into 3 groups based on treatment duration: (1) $< 30$ days, (2) 31-90 days and (3) $> 90$ days. Follow-up data on vocational status, drinking habits, attitudes toward various program features and services, overall rating of the program and suggestion for improvement were gathered through a questionnaire and compared with intake data from a contact sheet. The contact rate was considerably higher than the average reported in the literature (84 vs. 65 percent), with the 3 groups showing contact rates of 72-91 percent. Each of the 3 groups had higher improvement levels than the average reported in the literature (62 vs. 55 percent). Client perceptions of treatment were related to treatment duration, level of improvement and race.

238
Lopez-Lee, David, "Alcoholism Among Third World Women: Research and Treatment," In: V. Burtle, Ed., Women Who Drink: Alcoholic Experience and Psychotherapy. Springfield, ILL: Charles C. Thomas, 1979. 247 P. (pp. 98-115).

Current studies are reviewed which reflect the influence of cultural and socioeconomic factors on drinking patterns and the incidence of alcoholism. Comparative statistics are presented for males and females of various ethnic backgrounds. Data are then examined to clarify some of the special treatment needs of minority group women. Recommendations for treatment are offered. Prevalence of alcoholism among Black women, American Indians, Chicano women, Latina women, sex bias in therapy, influence of the family group.

239
Lowenthal, M.N., "Hypertensive Heart Disease and Cardiomyopathy in Blacks: Diagnostic Confusion," South African Medical Journal, 55(14): 547-549, 1979.

Case reports of four Black South African patients who were diagnosed as having cardiomyopathy are presented. All four patients were abstainers at the time of their admission to Baragwanath Hospital (Johannesburg). It is reported that one patient, however, drank 0.5 liters of beer a day until two years before admission. These cases are regarded as evidence in favor of the hypothesis that many cases of cryptogenic heart disease (cardiomyopathy, congestive cardiomyopathy, idiopathic cardiomegaly) are in fact cases of hypertension presenting normotensive cardiac failure.

240
Macphail, A.P., Simon, M.O., Torrance, J.D., et al., "Changing Patterns of Dietary Iron Overload in Black South Africans," American Journal of Clinical Nutrition, 32(6): 1272-1278, 1979.

Over the last 17 years there has been a significant reduction in the prevalence and severity of dietary iron overload in urban Blacks of Johannesburg. This is attributed to decreased consumption of traditionally brewed beer of high iron content. Hepatic iron concentrations (HIC) in autopsies from 248 men who died in 1976 was 40 percent lower than in 220 who died in 1959 and 1960 (0.31 vs. 0.49 percent of dry weight). While HIC rose with age in both groups there was no evidence of iron accumulation during the period between the 2 studies. The HIC in 345 women was much lower than in men and the 1976 group did not differ significantly from the 1959-1960 group. A paradoxical increase in the prevalence of portal fibrosis and cirrhosis between the 1959-60 and 1976 group was seen ($p < .05$ for HIC < 2 percent) and may be due to increased use of distilled spirits and fortified wine in recent years. Iron overload was significantly greater in men with carcinoma of the esophagus (62 percent had HIC > 1 percent) and in those with idiopathic heart failure (11 of 17 men and 2 of 13 women had HIC > 1 percent) than in subjects who died of other causes. This suggests excessive exposure of these subjects to traditionally brewed beverages and the adulterants present in them.

241
Marshall, E., et al., "The Black Woman in Treatment." See United States. National Institute on Alcohol Abuse and Alcoholism, 1979.

242
McMillen, M.A., and Arnold, S.D., "Tuberculous Peritonitis Associated with Alcoholic Liver Disease," New York State Journal of Medicine, 79(6): 922-924, 1979.

Case reports of three black patients (one male and two females), initially diagnosed as having ascites secondary to alcoholic liver disease, are presented. The presence of high fever and inanition, the indolence of presentation, the paucity of peritonitis signs, and the exudative nature of the ascitic fluid suggested tuberculous peritonitis. It is concluded that the presence of fever and ascites in the patient with alcoholic liver disease requires an aggressive diagnostic approach, including pericentesis with culture for mycobacteria and peritoneal biopsy with a repeat procedure, if necessary.

243
Messolonghites, Louisa, <u>Multicultural Perspectives on Drug Abuse and Its Prevention: A Resource Book.</u> Report. Rockville, MD.: U.S. Dept. of Health, Education and Welfare, National Institute on Drug Abuse, 1979, 149 pgs. (DHEW (ADM) 78-671.)

This resource guide is divided into two sections. In the first section, "Perspectives", the types of drug and alcohol abuse associated with specific ethnic and social minorities in the US, and prevention efforts in multicultural communities are reviewed. In the second section, "Information and Education Resource Guide," available materials related to drug and alcohol abuse among cultural and ethnic groups as well as sources of information about this topic are listed. Information on blacks and drug abuse can be found on pp. 12-13, and in other areas of this book.

244
Rao, V.N., Rao, V.V., Benjamin, R., "Sex, Parental Background, and Drinking Behavior of Black Collegians," <u>International Journal of Sociology of the Family,</u> 9(1): 47-66, 1979.

Results are presented from a study designed to investigate the relationships between independent and dependent variables for drinking behavior among black collegians. Data were collected during the fall of 1976 from 1,521 black college students from five predominantly black colleges and universities in Mississippi. Taking symbolic interactions as an explanation of drinking patterns, the general hypothesis tested was that males and females vary in their drinking behavior, reasons for drinking, age at first drink, and place of first drink. Hypotheses found to be tenable for both males and females were: (1) parental reasons for drinking and respondents' age and place of first drink, and reasons for drinking; (2) mother's reaction toward drinking and respondents' drinking pattern; (3) father's drinking pattern and respondents' age and place of first drink; (4) father's reaction and respondents' age at first drink and drinking pattern; and (5) extent of familial and respondents' drinking behavior. Seven subhypotheses were upheld by the data for the male sample only, while data for the female sample alone supported eight subhypotheses. It is concluded that this research supports the theory which attaches importance to family as a powerful agent of socialization in the context of drinking patterns of their children.

245
Robey, Floyd, "Current Activities of the Kentucky Task Force on Minority Alcohol Concerns." Conference Paper. Annual Conference, NCA. Washington, DC: 28 Apr 1979. 12 p.

The history, goals, past activities, and current activities of the Kentucky Task Force on Minority Alcohol Concerns are presented. The primary goal of the group is to plan for alcohol prevention, education, and rehabilitation efforts in black communities state-wide. Two current activities are: (1) project awareness, phase I; a public information project where several agencies cooperated in sponsoring a series of workshops, and (2) project awareness, phase II; a demonstration project which will utilize trained volunteers as trainers/facilitators to meet community needs related to alcohol abuse and alcoholism in West Louisville, KY. The proposal for the demonstration project is offered.

246
Roizen, J., Alcohol and Crime: The Relationship in Two Populations, Blacks and Youth. Report. Berkeley: University of California, School of Public Health, Social Research Group, 1979. (117 p.)

Research studies are reviewed concerning the relationship betwen alcohol and crime in Black and youth populations. The author contends that these studies give only limited support to the proposition that drinking is responsible for the disproportionate amount of youth crime. As was found to be true of research on adult crime and drinking, little attention has been given to perceptions of alcohol's effects on delinquent behavior, or of perceived norms regarding drinking occasions; the focus has generally been on the substance itself. Ethnographic data indicate that general surveys may be limited by having too few of the types of offenders likely to commit serious criminal acts. Data also indicate that drinking and deviant behavior among lower class and minority youth may, in part, be the consequences of too little to do, in environments where neither delinquency or drinking is negatively sanctioned. It is concluded that: (1) the strongest case for the association of drinking and crime, in the absence of better data, is that both are responses to other factors in individual and social life, i.e., poverty, family disorganization, school failure; (2) the role of drinking in criminal events is no different for Blacks than for Whites, or for youth when compared to adults; and (3) although a substantial proportion of Black and youthful offenders report drinking at the time of the crime, there is little evidence as to the role alcohol plays. An extensive bibliography is provided.

247
Scoles, P.E., and Fine, E.W., "Polydrug Use Patterns, Race, and the Problem Drinking Driver: Implications for Treatment." In: M. Galanter, Ed., Currents in Alcoholism: Volume 6. New York, NY: Grune and Stratton, 1979. 345 p. (pp. 295-301).

Data related to problem drinking, polydrug use patterns, race, and blood alcohol concentration (BAC) for a sample of 3,252 men arrested for driving under the influence of alcohol (DUI) are presented. Interviews were conducted by professional interviewers in the Diagnostic Unit of the City of Philadelphia's Alcohol Highway Safety Programs. The following results are reported: (1) for 83 percent of the problem drinkers, the BAC was above 0.15 percent; (2) BAC at 0.15 and above was significantly associated with problem drinking patterns in Black offenders (65 percent of the Blacks compared to 35 percent of Whites had problem drinking patterns); (3) BAC at 0.15 and above was significantly associated with the use of barbiturates and tranquilizing drugs among problem drinkers; (4) Whites were significantly more involved in the use of other drugs than Blacks (at the time of arrest, 63 percent of the Whites were polydrug users); (5) DUI offenders who had a diagnosis of problem drinking were significantly more likely not to possess a license at the time of their arrest (69 percent of the problem drinkers had no license, as compared with 31 percent of the social drinkers); and (6) multiple arrests related to alcohol were significantly associated with a diagnosis of problem drinking (social drinkers, in general, had prior arrest records not involving alcohol, and of the alcohol-related arrest, 88 percent involved problem drinkers). These results are further discussed.

248
Stanchfield, A.D., "Myths, Misconceptions and Misinformation about Alcohol-or, Tequila Isn't The Only Alcohol To Take With A Grain Of Salt." Dissertation. Ann Arbor, MI: University Microfilms International, 1979.

Myths related to alcohol are exemplified by attitudes, demographic groupings, reasons for use, physical effects, social effects and relationships, and individual and group disorganizaiton. Factors influencing the creation and continuation of myths include emotion (as opposed to logic), generalizations from observation, explanations of observations, social control, the influence of "authorities" including the "reformed reformer" (The ex-alcoholic). Under demographic groupings, early interest in and use of alcohol, teenage preferences, stability of drinking patterns, drinking and drug use by women, misconceptions about the poor, the Black and the American Indian, are discussed. Reasons for use range from instinct and positive ideas about pleasure and effect, to negative ideas of abnormality, suicide, rebellion, anomie and the invalidity of pleasure.

249
Steeg, C.N., Woolf, P., "Cardiovascular Malformations in The Fetal Alcohol Syndrome," _American Heart Journal,_ 98(5): 635-637, 1979.

Case reports are presented of 2 unrelated black infants (1 female) with fetal alcohol syndrome in whom cardiac catheterization revealed ventricular septal defects defects and pulmonary artery dysplasia. Following a poor response to medical management both infants underwent surgery and now, both aged 2.5 years, are doing well from a cardiovascular standpoint. Both mothers had long histories of excessive daily alcohol intake; one was also a heroin addict.

250
Stratton, R., "Sober Cherokee." _Alcohol Technical Reports._ 8:21-26, 1979.

It is stated that immigrant Americans who know nothing else about Native Americans know that "they cannot hold their liquor"; that this image of the drunken Indian was formed in Colonial times and remains today, supported with contemporary statistics: death rates for alcoholic cirrhosis, accidents, and homicides are three times higher for Indians than for the general population, and Indian arrest rates for public drunkenness vary from one area to another, but are always higher than for the general population. Statistics on one Indian tribe, the Cherokees of Oklahoma, are presented and discussed as an exception to this "firewater myth." It is reported (1974) that Oklahoma Cherokees have an alcohol cirrhosis death rate of 2.9 per 100,000 as compared to 12.1 for the total U.S. population, and also have relatively low death rates for accidents, homicide, and suicide. Statistical data tables, Blacks, Whites, Drunk driving, Cultural factors, Acculturation, Alcohol-related problems, Educational levels, Political factors, Socioeconomic factors, Presented at the Oklahoma Symposia on Drinking Behavior and Alcoholism, 5 Oct 1979, Oklahoma City.

251
Torres, Jose, "Ethical Considerations in The Treatment of Special Groups Within Substance Abuse Treatment." Conference paper. 12th Annual Eagleville Conference. Eagleville PA: 11 May 1979. 7 p.

An attempt is made to explain the inability of young Hispanics to complete drug and alcohol treatment therapy as compared to Black and White abusers. Reasons include: (1) stereotyped attitudes; (2) differences between the average American "Nuclear" family and that of the Puerto Rican family; and (3) recognition of "espiritismo" as a valid belief on the part of Hispanics.

252
United States. National Institute on Alcohol Abuse and Alcoholism. Alcoholism Prevention: Guide to Resources and References. Rockville, Maryland, 1979.

This annotated bibliography on alcoholism prevention covers a 6-year time span, 1973-1979.

253
United States. National Institute on Alcohol Abuse and Alcoholism. _Black Clients Treated in NIAAA Funded Categorical Programs of Calendar Year 1977._ Report. Rockville, MD., 1979, 15 pgs.

Data concerning black clients treated in NIAAA funded facilities in 1977 are reviewed in order to determine characteristics, referral patterns, treatments, and outcomes. Data were collected from selected programs serving some of the 54,000 black clients of the NIAAA client population. Black versus nonblack clients were compared with respect to program activity, characteristics, referral sources into and out of treatment, type of care received, and changes in drinking patterns after six months of treatment. The programs selected for study were the alcoholism treatment centers, cross-population programs, poverty programs, problem drinking driver programs, public inebriate programs, and black programs. Client characteristic data showed blacks generally averaged one to two years older, reported lower household income, and reported more lack of occupation than nonblacks. Few differences in the source of referral and type care were noted. Black clients reported positive improvements at follow-up six months after treatment intake in terms of drinking behavior, employment, behavioral impairment, and income.

254
United States. National Institute on Alcohol Abuse and Alcoholism. _Services for Alcoholic Women - Foundations for Change_: _Resource Book_. Ed. by J. Brown and N. Kamar. Rockville, Md.: National Institute on Alcohol Abuse and Alcoholism, 1979. See "The Black Woman in Treatment," by E. Marshall, J.E. Hillsman and V. Patterson, pp. 181-189. (This article first appeared in the Resource Manual of _Women in Treatment_, a course developed by the National Drug Abuse Center for the National Institute on Drug Abuse, 1976).

This article examines the problems faced by Black female addicts, and recommends approaches to treatment.

255
United States. National Institute on Drug Abuse. _Multi-cultural Perspectives on Drug Abuse and Its Prevention_: _A Resource Book_, by L. Messolonghites. Rockville, Maryland, 1979.

Information on blacks and drug abuse prevention can be found on pp. 12-13, and in other pages of this book. Also, see Messolonghites - 1979.

256
United States. National Institute on Drug Abuse. Proceedings. Biocultural Women's Forum: Administrative Report. Washington, DC: 23-25 Aug 1979. 120 p.

Proceedings of the Bicultural Women's Forum, developed by the Center for Multicultural Awareness (CMA), a resource center established by the National Institute on Drug Abuse to be a focus of prevention programming for ethnic communities across the country, are presented. Functions of the CMA, and forum goals, objectives, and outcomes are described. The following state of the art papers which relate to alcohol are appended: (1) State of the Art of Black Women in the Prevention of Substance Abuse; (2) Views of Chemical Substance Abuse by American Indian Women; and (3) Substance Abuse Prevention Issues for the Hispanic Woman.

257
Warner, R., "Racial and Sexual Bias in Psychiatric Diagnosis; Psychiatrists and Other Mental Health Professionals Compared by Race, Sex, and Discipline," Journal of Nervous and Mental Disease, 167: 303-310, 1979.

In a study designed to test for sex- and race-related bias in psychiatric diagnosis, the responses of 173 mental health professionals to 4 hypothetical patient profiles were analyzed (1 of the 4 patients was described as drinking too much, allegedly to control his/her nervousness). Minimal racial bias was observed. In some instances, therapists appeared mnore likely to make judgments biased against patients who were of the same race and sex as themselves. Women therapists showed greater tendency to label white men as having alcoholism (rather than anxiety neurosis) and black men as having antisocial personalities (in preference to simple schizophrenia). The results support the contention that hysterical and antisocial personality disorders are sex-biased diagnoses; men were more often labeled as antisocial and women as hysterical, even if they had the same profile. The race of the therapist strongly influenced diagnosis. It is argued that this finding reflects resistance of non-white therapists to a majority-group-dominated diagnostic theory. Professional discipline rarely affected diagnosis with the exception that psychiatrists were more prone to diagnose psychosis.

258
Westie, K.S., McBride, D.C., "Effects of Ethnicity, Age and Sex Upon Processing Through An Emergency Alcohol Health Care Delivery System," British Journal of Addiction. 74(1): 21-29, 1979.

Age, ethnicity and sex were found to influence the type of complaint at admission, likelihood of referral for further aid, type of psychiatric diagnosis and ultimate disposition of the case in a study of 1107 patients (231 women) admitted for alcohol problems to the emergency room of a large inner-city hospital (in the United States). Non-Spanish white men accounted for 53.6 percent, Spanish people were vastly underrepresented (5.1 percent of the patients vs. 45.3 percent of the city population) and Black men overrepresented (30.4 vs. 22.7 percent); the modal age range was 35-49, with the women being on average 6.8 years younger than the men. Intoxication or alcoholism was the presenting complaint in 60.4 percent; organic brain syndrome and alcohol- or withdrawal-related psychosis in 19.7 percent; seizures or somatic difficulties in 16.3 percent; and suicide attempts or bizarre behavior under the influence of alcohol in 3.6 percent (most of them under age 35, with a strong overrepresentation of women). Black patients were most likely to present with seizure/somatic disorders and least likely to complain of intoxication/alcoholism, while the opposite was true of whites. Spanish patients were most likely to present with bizarre behavior/suicide (all of these were women under age 25). Men presented more often with Brain syndrome/psychosis than did women. Only 187 patients (16.8 percent) received psychiatric evaluation; over one-third of these were women. The diagnosis of alcoholism was given to over half of the patients, followed by organic brain syndrome, and by psychosis (given more often to those under age 35). Black patients received disproportionately more often diagnoses of more severe disorders, while Spanish people received disproportionately often less severe diagnoses (neurosis, etc.). Only 21.8 percent of the patients were referred for further help; Spanish persons were most likely to leave the emergency room against medical advice.

259
Yawney, C., "Drinking Patterns and Alcoholism in Trinidad." In M. Marshall, Ed., Beliefs, Behaviors, & Alcoholic Beverages. Ann Arbor, MI: University of Michigan Press, 1979, pp. 94-107.

Drinking patterns and alcoholism among East Indians and Negroes in Trinidad are compared... Alcoholism among the two groups is discussed in relation to cultural variables, and it is felt that variations in child-rearing and religious beliefs lead to greater problems with alcohol among East Indians. Various alcoholism treatment modalities are also discussed, and the effectiveness of treatment for each group is compared.

## 1980

260
Arkansas Office on Alcohol and Drug Abuse Prevention. Black leader's luncheon: Report, Little Rock, AR, 1980 (No authors listed.)

The following materials obtained from a black leaders' luncheon held in Little Rock, Arkansas, on 21 March 1980 are presented: (1) recommendations from the participants on Arkansas Office on Alcohol and Drug Abuse Prevention (AOADAP) services and processes in addressing the needs of the black community in Arkansas; (2) results or findings from a survey of utilization of AOADAP services by blacks; and (3) tables ranking specific needs (treatment, primary prevention, and education) by state regions.

261
Bauman, K.E., Bryan, E.S. "Subjective Expected Utility and Children's Drinking," Journal of Studies on Alcohol, 41(9): 952-958, 1980.

The role of subjective expected utility (SEU) . . .was examined in the drinking behavior of 233 children aged 10 to 12 (31 percent blacks, 56 percent girls) in Orange County, North Carolina. Each child completed a questionnaire on the quantity and frequency of his consumption of beer and distilled spirits, possible consequences of drinking, the desirability of each consequence and the probability of experiencing each consequence after drinking beer or distilled spirits . . . .The 45 children who had ever drunk beer and the 29 children who had ever drunk distilled spirits had more positive mean SEUs of beer and distilled spirits than did those who had not ($p < .001$). Similar relationships between drinking experience and SEU were found in both boys and girls.

262
Bell, P., Belmont, H., Payton, C., et al., "Perspectives: An Interview Feature on Ethnicity and Alcohol," Alcohol Health and Research World, 4(4): 27-30, 1980.

Alcohol and drug abuse prevention among Blacks, Hispanics and American Indians needs understanding of the cultural impact on alcoholism, access points to the treatment system (family and friends; jobs and school; and courts), requirements for quality education, quality health care, reduction in alcohol or drug-related crimes, better employment opportunities and quality housing. The attitudes of the various ethnic groups towards drinking and treatment of alcoholism are also discussed.

263
Berman, R. "Research and Treatment With Black Alcoholics," Alcohol Health and Research World, 5(2): 68-79, 1980-1981.

The need to consider culture, race, genetic predisposition, environmental and sociocultural differences as factors affecting the etiology and prognosis of alcoholism is stressed. It may be more important to find similarities among all alcoholics to remedy the problem. The notion that particular treatment modalities are more effective with a particular population is questioned. Treating the patient as an individual who is frightened, ashamed, embarrassed and in need of help is preferable.

264
"Black Market and Media: Trends in 1979." (No author(s) listed). The Liquor Handbook 1980.
It is stated that the black consumer market for wines and spirits in the US today suffers from a number of misconceptions, preconceptions, and inaccurate assumptions; that the market is a strong one, is in a growth situation, and offers a great many surprises for the marketer. Statistical data on alcoholic beverage preference and consumption by blacks in 1979 are presented. The use of the black media in selling alcoholic beverages is briefly discussed, and two executives offer a profile of the black consumer, and what must be done to expand this market.

265
Bowman, P.J. "Toward a Dual Labor-Market Approach to Black-on-Black Homicide," Public Health Reports, 95(6): 555-556, 1980.

A dual labor market approach to black-on-black homicide, which focuses on the employment-related experiences of black males as the root cause of their high rate of homicide, is discussed. One of five propositions that are addressed to research and intervention needs in the black community is the proposal for intervention against the direct role of alcohol and drugs in black-on-black homicide.

266
Coakley, J., Malin, H., Hoban, C., et al., "Usual and Pre-Offense Drinking Behavior Reported by Inmates of Local Jails, Alcoholism-Clinical and Experimental Research, 4(2): 211, 1980.

A survey of more than 5000 inmates of local jails in Maryland, administered by the Bureau of the Census for the Law Enforcement Assistance Administration in early 1978, indicated that there was a distinct difference in the proportions of black and white convicts drinking prior to their offense when age was controlled. Whether convicts drank alone or with others differed markedly by sex, but not by race. Other findings presented include differences between usual and offense-related drinking behavior and the nature and severity of the offense, and differences in usual drinking behavior of inmates as contrasted with the reported drinking behavior of the general population.

267
Conrad, M.E., Perrine, G.M., Barton, J.C., et al., "Provoked Priapism in Sickle Cell Anemia," American Journal of Hematology, 9(1): 121-122, 1980.

Two young (aged 19 and 23) Black men with sickle cell anemia developed relative impotence after repeated episodes of priaprism. They learned that erection was associated with excessive ingestion of alcohol and utilized this mechanism to satisfy their sexual partners even though this was painful. Several interviews were required in order to learn about the sequence of events leading to this medical problem. This synergistic relationship between alcohol and priaprism should be sought in patients with repeated hospitalizations for this complication of sickle cell anemia because it is preventable with appropriate counseling.

268
Crawford, G.A., Washington, M.C., Senay, E.C., "Socio-familial Characteristics of Black Male Heroin Addicts and Their Nonaddicted Friends," Drug and Alcohol Dependence, 6(6): 383-390, 1980.

The family background characteristics, peer group activities and school performance of 61 Black men heroin addicts, 86 who had tried heroin, and 36 nonusers were compared. Of 19 addicts and 10 nonusers who did not perceive their fathers as good role models, 12 and 9, respectively, cited their father's alcohol or drug problems.

269
Crisp, A.D., "Making Substance Abuse Prevention Relevant to Low-Income Black Neighborhoods," _Journal of Psychedelic Drugs_, 12(2): 13-19, 1980.

The author contends that substance (including alcohol) abuse prevention efforts among Black ghetto youth have not been successful because of the use of culturally and economically biased prevention models and because prevention strategies are based on person-oriented prevention instead of systems-oriented prevention. Research literature is cited in an overview of drug abuse prevention. Promising theories and approaches to substance abuse prevention are discussed.

270
Crisp, A.D., "Making Substance Abuse Prevention Relevant to Low-Income Black Neighborhoods. II. Research Findings," _Journal of Psychedelic Drugs_, 12(2): 139-156, 1980.

The nature, perceived purpose and perceived impact of substance abuse prevention programs in Black ghetto neighborhoods of Washington, D.C., was studied via 3 sets of questionnaires designed to correlate program goals and recipient's goals. Of the 42 agency workers, 52 students and 32 community residents who received questionnaires, 21, 32 and 13 responded . . . The 3 groups of respondents had similar perceptions of the goals and objectives of the programs, and the short-term counseling approach was not highly regarded by any of the recipients. . . It is concluded that community-based prevention programs have a more positive effect than those offered in schools or agencies.

271
Dawkins, M.P., _Alcohol and the Black Community: Exploratory Studies of Selected Issues_, Saratoga and Palo Alto, California: Century Twenty One Publ., Div. of R and E Research Assocs., 1980, 110 p.

Quantity, quality, and utility of alcohol-related research studies on Blacks are examined. A brief critique of the alcohol and Black literature is provided, and some directions for further study are offered. A few social factors related to alcohol are briefly explored in order to provide some insight into the role alcohol plays in shaping conditions of life in the Black community. Impact of alcohol-related crime on Blacks, and the use of alcohol in adolescence are examined. Drinking and alcohol knowledge as reflected in a survey of Blacks attending college are discussed. Some policy issues on alcohol abuse among Blacks are addressed. Recommendations for addressing the alcohol problem in the Black community are presented. A list of national organizations and agencies which provide information about alcoholism and alcohol abuse is appended.

272
Dawkins, M.P., "Alcohol Information on Black Americans: Current Status and Future Needs," Journal of Alcohol and Drug Education, 25(3): 28-40, 1980.

This paper describes the current status of information on alcohol abuse and alcoholism among Black Americans in an effort to stimulate greater interest in this problem. It is contended that there is a critical shortage of information which can be used in policy-making education, prevention and program planning. Basic data regarding alcohol abuse and alcoholism among Blacks in relation to demographic factors (e.g., sex, age, income and education) are especially lacking. Studies are needed to contribute to our understanding of the part that drinking plays in the lives of members of the Black community in such areas as childhood and adolescent development, family stability, and educational and occupational mobility. An annotated bibliography that includes selected alcohol-related studies with findings pertaining to Black Americans is included.

273
Delvillano, B.C., Miller, S.I., Schacter, L.P., Tischfield, J.A., "Elevated Superoxide Dismutase in Black Alcoholics," Science, 207(4434), 991-992, 1980.

Superoxide dismutase concentrates on lysates of erythrocytes from black alcoholics were higher than those of white alcoholics and of nonalcoholics of both races. Higher concentrations of enzyme protein, as determined by competition radioimmunoassay, correspond to proportionately higher enzyme activity. Elevated superoxide dismutase levels were not related to any other clinical, historical, or demographic variables. Increased superoxide dismutase levels may delay or prevent some of the pathological sequelae of alcoholism and may be a useful biological marker for alcohol abuse.

274
Del-Villano, B.C.; Schacter, L.P., Miller, S.I., et al. "Cupro-Zinc Superoxide Dismutase: A Possible Biologic Marker for Alcohol Abuse," Drug and Alcohol Dependence, 6(1-2): 21-22, 1980.

Levels of cupro-zinc superoxide dismutase-1 (sod-1) were determined in red blood cells (RBCs) from alcoholics and non-alcoholics by competition radioimmune assay. Black alcoholics had higher concentrations of sod-1 than White alcoholics, and Black or White non-alcoholics. . . Alcoholics differed from non-alcoholics in sgot, liver dehydrogenase, alkaline phosphatase, bun, bilirubin, and mean corpuscular volume and hemoglobin, but there was no racial difference in these values. Increased levels of sod-1 in RBCs may be a useful biological marker for alcohol abuse. Results suggest that superoxide and superoxide dismutase may be important in the pathogenesis of alcohol-related tissue injury.

275
Estes, N.J., Smith-DiJulio, K., Heinemann, M.E., "Alcohol Problems in Special Groups; Racial and Ethnic Groups, Adolescents, Multidrug Abusers." In N. J. Estes, Ed., Nursing Diagnosis of the Alcoholic Person, St. Louis: C.V. Mosby, 1980, pp. 46-72.

Expanding the appraisal process for those in special groups was discussed. The special groups discussed included Blacks, American Indians and Alaskan natives, Asian Americans, adolescents and multi-drug abusers. For each group, the causative factors leading to drinking were presented along with the consequences of drinking. Special findings for each group were described and approaches in appraisal were suggested and implications for prevention and treatment were included.

276
Fleetwood, M.A., "Significant Issues Cited by Five Women in Recovery From Alcoholism: The First and Second Years," Mount Holyoke Conference on Women and Alcohol, South Hadley, MA: 24-28, Mar 1980, 12 p.

Five women in recovery from alcoholism were interviewed in two-hour sessions. The respondents were: (1) a 19 year-old woman with a history of family violence and street experience; (2) a 42-year old man divorced single parent; (3) a 50 year-old suburban housewife and mother of two adopted children; (4) a 36 year-old career woman and self-identified lesbian; and (5) a 27 year-old black woman, head of a household with three children. . . A questionnaire containing questions pertaining to self-concept, personal identity, medical history, relationships with others, work, sexuality, and spirituality was used in taping the interviews. Significant issues or common experiences cited by the five women in early sobriety are listed. Suggestions are offered for improving the treatment of women recovering from alcoholism.

277
Fuchs, M., Iosub, S., Bingol, M., et al., "Palpebral Fissure Size Revisited," Journal of Pediatrics, 96(1): 77-78, 1980.

Palpebral fissure size is a diagnostic sign of the fetal alcohol syndrome and its normal values need to be established for Black and Hispanic newborn infants. Measurement of palpebral fissures, taken across the greatest horizontal plane of the eye from medial to lateral canthus, was performed in 120 Hispanic and 101 Black full-term infants at 3 days of age. Mean fissure sizes were 1.95 cm and 2.00 cm in the Hispanic and Black infants, compared with the 1.85 cm previously found in 200 White neonates: (White vs Hispanic and White vs Black, both p .01). It is suggested that while the short palpebral fissure in the fetal alcohol syndrome is a valuable sign, it is attributable not just to decreased eye growth but to the total growth retardation occurring in the offspring of the alcohol user.

278
Gaines, A.D., Borker, R.A., "Alcohol and Black Culture," Alcoholism- Clinical and Experimental Research, 4(2): 215, 1980.

Ethnographic research into the role of alcoholism in Black culture was examined by participant observation and interviewing. . . Results showed that alcohol use bore the impress of cultural ideology which influenced consumption patterns, problem recognition and help-seeking.

279
Gary, L.E., "Role of Alcohol and Drug Abuse in Homicide," Public Health Reports, 95(6): 553-554, 1980.

It is contended that one factor in black homicide that must receive greater priority in research, program planning, and treatment strategies is alcohol and drug abuse. . . Statistical data are presented in a discussion of the role of alcohol and drug abuse in black and white homicide. The author believes that more investigations of the economic motivation that contributes to alcoholism and to homicide in the black community are needed.

280
Globetti, G., Alsikafi, M., Morse, R., "Black Female High School Students and the Use of Beverage Alcohol," International Journal of Addictions, 15(2): 198-200, 1980.

This study deals with a population group which has been neglected in the research literature; namely, Black female high school students from rural backgrounds. Not surprisingly, the proscriptive and abstinence norms in the community resulted in drinking styles of a surreptitious nature in a setting of less restraint. Consequently, there were some signs of problems with alcohol such as experiencing complications, getting high, and drinking for utilitarian reasons. The factors which influenced the girls to drink, however, were similar to those of other studies.

281
Harper, F.D., "Research and Treatment with Black Alcoholics," Alcohol Health and Research World, 4(4): 10-16, 1980.

The author contends that to hypothesize that there are no significant differences among alcoholics of different sexes, ages, races, cultures, and social classes is illogical, and empirically unfounded. . . The question of why Blacks drink is addressed, and research problems and needs are discussed. . . Some of the author's personal observations and recommendations for the resolution or minimizing of problems related to alcoholism and alcohol abuse among Black Americans are also provided.

282
Holliday, B.G., "Advocacy for Life: Mandates, Models, and Priorities for Prevention," Public Health Reports, 95(6): 558-559, 1980.

This paper discusses the role of the Law Enforcement Assistance Administration (ADSHMA) (which has a legislation mandate to support research, demonstration projects and dissemination efforts) in preventing Black homicide. It was concluded that a model for Black homicide prevention would aid in understanding the attitudes, behaviors, critical incidents and social forces that provoke homicide as well as the forces that keep other persons at high risk of homicide from becoming perpetrators or victims.

283
"Homicide Among Black Males," (No Author(s) Listed), Public Health Reports, 95: 549-550, 1980.

Black scholars attending the Alcohol, Drug Abuse and Mental Health Administration symposium on Homicidal Violence among Black Males, attempted to determine the current knowledge base of homicides among Blacks which reached a total of 5734 during 1977 (more than the 5640 Blacks killed during the entire 9 years of the Vietnam War). They also reviewed data from the National Center for Health Statistics and discussed research findings on the major causes of homicide and the role of alcohol and drug abuse.

284
Ivens, P.E., "Test of a Sociological Causal Model of Alcohol and Deviant Drinking Patterns," Dissertation. Ann Arbor, MI: University Microfilms International, 1980.

A study was conducted to test the hypothesis that childhood socialization with respect to drinking would predict adult drinking behavior, and that when this was not the case adult social integration would be a more important predictor. This situation was closely satisfied for White women only, but analysis using both independent variables simultaneously explained little of the variance in this subsample. The greatest amount of variance was explained for Black men. It is suggested that an expanded conception of social integration and a more complex conception of socialization should be used in future studies of this nature. That is, social integration may be different for specific groups.

285
Iverson, D.C., "Homicide Prevention from the Perspective of the Office of Health Promotion," Public Health Reports, 95(6): 559-560, 1980.

A behavioral model is used, and an attempt is made through review of the literature, to identify behavioral causes of homicide among Blacks. The possible causes, for example, need for money to support drug or alcohol habits or being under the influence of alcohol, were ranked in order of importance. Identification and selection of factors affecting the behavioral causes were then attempted. . .

286
Jones, L., "The Absence of the Black Professional and Semi-Professional in the Membership of Alcoholics Anonymous." In Association of Labor-Management Administrators and Consultants, ED., Arlington, VA: ALMACA, 1980, pp. 416-431.

Approximately 7 percent of Detroit's Black population are alcoholics, but out of the 5000 Alcoholics Anonymous (A.A.) members of the city, only 10 percent are Black. Detroit has a total Black population of 35-40 percent. The absence of the professional and semi-professional Black in the A.A. program is noted. The results of 12 interviews are presented which indicate that the reason for this is the Blacks difficulty in accepting the values which A.A. advocates. The socioeconomic reasons for Blacks' rejection of A.A. values are explained.

287
Kachru, R.B., Proskey, A.J., Telischi, M., "Histocompatibility Antigens and Alcoholic Cardiomyopathy," Tissue Antigens, 15(4): 398-399, 1980.

To study the possibility of a genetic predisposition to alcoholic cardiomyopathy, HLA antigens were examined in 49 hospitalized black American alcoholics (aged 37-50; 3 women) without prior history of heart disease and 226 controls of similar ethnic background. . . It is suggested that although no strong association between alcoholic cardiomyopathy and HLA antigens was found (only 1 of the 33 antigens, i.e., AW 30, was significantly different in the 2 groups), a genetic predisposition on the basis of testing the antigens of 2 loci only canot be ruled out without further investigation.

288
Kane, G.P., Garris, A., Athanail, S., "Alcohol Withdrawal Symptoms: A Black-Hispanic Difference," Alcoholism Clinical and Experimental Research, 4(2): 220, 1980.

Of the 352 descriptions of alcohol withdrawal or delirium tremens (207 Black men, 80 Hispanic men, 54 Black women, and 11 Hispanic women) at the Dr. Martin Luther King Jr., Health Center Alcoholism Unit, most included explicit descriptions of hallucinatory experiences. Hispanic patients reported delirium tremens with hallucinations more frequently than Black patients (60 vs 41 percent; p * .005). This difference may relate to the importance of religion in Hispanic culture, and specifically, to the infouence of spiritualism in Puerto Rican culture. However, there was a nonsignificant trend in interviews of Black patients for a Hispanic interviewer to elicit reports of hallucinations more frequently than Black interviewers.

289
Karasawa, T., Kushida, T., Shikata, T., et al., "Morphologic Spectrum of Liver Diseases Among Chronic Alcoholics; A Comparison Between Tokyo, Japan and Cincinnati, U.S.A.," Acta Pathology, 30(4): 505-514, 1980.

Histopathological features of liver diseases were compared in 130 Japanese and 238 American alcoholics; 129 of the Americans were Black, 90 were White, none were Japanese. . . Although all aspects of alcoholic liver disease did exist in the Japanese sample, typical cases of acute alcoholic hepatitis with alcoholic hyalin were remarkably fewer (9.2 vs 39.5 percent) than in the U.S.A. sample, and the histopathological changes were less severe. Chronic hepatitis, however, was far more common among Japanese than Americans (46.1 vs 8.4 percent). . .

290
Kellam, S.G., Ensminger, M.E., Simon, M.B., "Mental Health in First Grade and Teenage Drug, Alcohol, and Cigarette Use," Drug and Alcohol Dependence, 5(4): 273-304, 1980.

This prospective study reports on the effects of psychological and social variables as measured by the same subjects 10 years later. The subjects lived in Woodlawn, an impoverished Black Chicago suburb; of 1242 participants in 1st grade, 705 (360 females) were reassessed at age 16-17. . . Three kinds of characteristics observable in 1st grade were associated with subsequent drug use: higher 1st-grade IQ or readiness scores predicted more frequent drug use for both sexes; boys used drugs and alcohol more often than did girls and antecedents of later drug use were clearer for boys; children rated as shy used drugs least often later while those rated aggressive by 1st-grade teachers subsequently became the heaviest drug and alcohol users. Higher levels of psychiatric symptoms in 1st grade predicted lower teenage drug use. Teen-ate antisocial behavior was an important mediator of teen-age drug use for 1st-grade shy-aggressive boys.

291
Keller, A.Z., "Epidemiology of Esophageal Cancer in the West," Preventive Medicine, 9(5): 607-612, 1980.

Incidence rates, relative frequencies, and relative risk measures are compared for sites of esophageal, oral, and pharyngeal cancer with regard to race, tobacco smoked, alcoholic beverage consumption, and combinations of these factors. Data are adapted from the Third National Cancer Survey and the 171 Veterans Administration hospitals in the United States. It was found that Blacks and Whites of the same sex are at similar risks of mouth and pharynx cancers; however, Blacks of either sex are at inordinately high risks of esophageal cancer. Both tobacco smoking and alcoholic beverage consumption were found to be associated with an increased risk of cancer of oral, pharyngeal, and esophageal sites, with only alcoholic beverages being clearly associated independently with these cancers. . . These findings indicate that behavioral characteristics associated with racial differences in drinking patterns might explain differences between Whites and Blacks in morbidity and mortality ascribed to cancer of the esophagus.

292
Klerman, G.L., "Concluding Remarks (at the Symposium on Homicidal Violence Among Black Males, Washington, D.C., May 13-14, 1980)," Public Health Reports, 95(6): 561, 1980.

In a concluding address to a symposium sponsored by ADAMHA, the role of the alcohol in homicidal violence is pointed out. Suggestions were made at the symposium for working with state departments of alcohol programs and developing some unconventional outreach programs for non-white minorities.

293
Majumdar, M.N., Bhatia, P.S., "Effective Family Position and Likelihood of Becoming an Alcoholic," Journal of Alcohol and Drug Education, 25(2): 19-31, 1980.

Sex, birth order, number of older and younger siblings, stepsiblings, size of sibship "by whom raised" until age 15 and age of separation from parents were compared in 80 alcoholics (consecutive sample) and in 80 nonalcoholics (random sample) seen at a health care center serving an indigent black population in Cleveland, Ohio. . . The alcoholics had significantly fewer sibs than the nonalcoholics (3 vs 5; $p < .001$) and were less likely (36 vs 45 percent; $p < .1$) to be raised by both parents. Other variables did not differentiate the 2 groups from each other.

294
Mettlin, C., Nutritional Habits of Blacks and Whites," Preventive Medicine, 9(5): 601-606, 1980.

In a discussion of epidemiological evidence implication various dietary factors in the etiology of prostatic and esophageal cancer, it is pointed out that evidence from drinking surveys does not support the hypothesis that the higher incidence of esophageal cancer among Blacks than among Whites is due to heavier drinking among the former. In fact, Blacks are more likely than Whites to abstain and less likely to be heavy drinkers. It is concluded that general characterizations of the dietary habits of different groups are of limited value in explaining intergroup differences in cancer incidence.

295
Milgram, G.G., Alcohol Education Materials 1973-1978: An Annotated Bibliography. New Brunswick, N.J.: Rutgers Center of Alcohol Studies, 1980.

296
Miller, K.D., Lescault, B.A., Heller, J.E., Bernstein, B., "Differences in Demographic Characteristics Drinking History and Response to Treatment of Black and White Women Seen at an Alcohol Detoxification Center," Focus on Women: Journal of Addictions and Health, 1(2): 136-144, 1980.

This study demonstrates that black and white women alcoholics differ with respect to demographic characteristics, response to alcoholism treatment, family history and drug usage. In addition, it was found that age and income source defined subgroups of women within each racial group on many of the varibles studied. The significance of these differences is to serve as a reminder that women alcoholics entering treatment comprise a very heterogeneous group, whose economic, cultural, and living sitautions vary significantly. As a result, the problems encountered in their treatment and aftercare may be quite different.

297
National Council on Alcoholism, Inc., New York, NY. Position Paper on Alcoholism and Racial Minorities Developed by the Minority Affairs Committee of the National Council on Alcoholism, Inc., New York, NY, 1980.

With an increasing need for alcoholism programs to serve racial minorities, the National Council on Alcoholism's (NCA) Minority Program and the Minority Affairs Committee decided to respond to the expanding demand for greater knowledge in this area. MCA's philosophy and position on racial minority alcoholism are exemplified, and the scope of the problem is highlighted, placing greater emphasis on issues expressed by professionals, laymen, individuals, local, state, and national organizations.

298
Panepinto, W., Galanter, M., Bender, S.H., et al., "Alcoholics' Transition from Ward to Clinic; Group Orientation Improves Retention," Journal of Studies on Alcohol, 41(9): 940-945, 1980.

To encourage alcoholics to make the transition from inpatient treatment to outpatient care, an experimental program at the Bronx Municipal Hospital Center in New York City required all inpatients to attend 10 orientation sessions stressing the importance of aftercare and describing medical, social and psychological aspects of alcoholism. . . To test the effectiveness of this program, outpatient clinic attendance by all inpatients admitted during a 6-month period when the program was in effect was compared with outpatient attendance by all inpatients admitted during a 6-month period in the previous year (controls). Of 313 alcoholics who were inpatients during the experimental period, 71 percent returned to the outpatient clinic during the first 30 days after discharge, versus 53 percent of 257 controls. Blacks, Hispanics, patients under age 30 and 1st admissions showed significant increases (p * .01) in clinic attendance after the experimental program was initiated. . .

299
Peteroy, E.T., "Prediction of WAIS Scores from Quick Test Scores for White and Black Patients at a Mental Health Center," Psychological Reports, 47(1): 259-262, 1980.

When the responses to Quick Test Forms, 1, 2, and 3 and the Wechsler Adult Intelligence Scale (WAIS) of 32 White and 20 Black adult inpatients and outpatients treated at a mental health center for psychoses (41 percent), drug and alcohol abuse (23 percent), transient situational disturbances (15 percent), personality disorders (13 percent) and other problems (8 percent) were subjected to regression analyses, Quick Test Form 1 best predicted WAIS Full Scale IQs for the White, Black and combined data. No significant differences in IQs were found between White and Black subjects on any of the 4 tests administered.

300
Porter, R., Allen, L., Rogers, E.A., "Prevention Strategies for High Risk Minority Populations." In R. Faulkinberry, Ed., Problems of the 70's; Solutions for the 80's, Lafayette, LA: Endac/Print Media, 1980, pp. 91-97.

The authors contend that stereotypical drug abusers have changed, and that stereotypical approaches to drug abuse have proven ineffective as well as inappropriate. This presentation is mainly concerned with the substance (including alcohol) abuse patterns of minorities, specifically rural

Blacks, and the development of an effective program for treating and counseling them. . .

301
Robins, L.N., and Ratcliff, K.S., "Childhood Conduct Disorders and Later Arrest." In L.N. Robins, et al., Eds., Social Consequences of Psychiatric Illness. New York: Brunner/Mazel, 1980, pp. 248-263.

Several previous research studies on the concept of a single syndrome comprising a broad variety of antisocial behaviors arising in childhood and continuing into adulthood are cited and discussed. In one study conducted in 1965-1966, the possible relationship between childhood conduct disorders and certain types of adult crime was explored. Subjects in this study were young Black men, 30-35 years of age. With respect to arrests for disturbance of the peace and drunkenness, no effect of early childhood behavior or early drinking was found.

302
Rutgers University. Center of Alcohol Studies. Recent Topics in Alcohol Studies - Minorities. A050. Piscataway, N.J., 1980.

A bibliography covering epidemiological, clinical, treatment and prevention studies published since 1977 on alcohol use and alcohol problems among American Indians, Blacks, and Hispanics. For updates and other related bibliographies please write to: Information Services Division; Center for Alcohol Studies; Rutgers University, P.O. Box 969; Piscataway, N.J. 08854.

303
Starland, V.D., "Education Program Module: For Blacks Concerned with Alcohol and Drug Abuse." In R. Faulkinberry, Ed., Problems of the 70's; Solutions for the 80's. Lafayette, LA: Endac/Print Media, 1980, pp. 296-300.

The author contends that substance (including alcohol) abuse among black individuals is a social problem as well as a medical problem, and that, regardless of the type of problem identified, one step in solving or minimizing a given problem is securing knowledge (understanding) of that problem. An education program module for persons concerned with alcohol and drug abuse is presented.

304
United States. Alcohol, Drug Abuse, and Mental Health Administration's Fiscal Year 1980 Annual Report of the Alcohol, Drug Abuse, and Mental Health Administration's Minority Advisory Committee, Rockville, MD, 1980, 29p.

A summary is presented of selected program and policy initiatives undertaken by the Alcohol, Drug Abuse, and Mental Health Administration's (ADAMHA) Minority Advisory Committee (MAC) in Foscal Year 1980 (1 October 1979 to 30 September 1980). Major initiatives and activities related to minority alcohol, drug abuse, and mental health matters are emphasized. Background information on the MAC is also provided, including committee functions, membership, meetings and staff support.

305
United States. Alcohol, Drug Abuse, and Mental Health Administration, Office of Public Liaison, Implementation of recommendations formulated at the 1978 National Conference on Minority Group Alcohol, Drug Abuse, and Mental Health Issues, Denver, Colorado: Final progress report, Rockville, MD, 1980, 39p.

A conference was held to discuss alcohol, drug abuse, and mental health (ADM) issues and policies of concern to minorities, develop recommendations and strategies for their implementation, and establish linkages between the ADAMHA Minority Advisory Committee (MAC) and key minority ADM Organizations. Forty recommendations are presented concerning ADAMHA, MAC, treatment, prevention, manpower, research, and specific minority. . .

306
United States. Department of Health, Education and Welfare, "Alcohol Use in Special Population Groups." In D.A. Ward, Ed., Alcoholism: Introduction to Theory and Treatment, Dubuque, IA: Kendall/Hunt, 1980, pp. 119-128.

Alcohol use in special population groups such as women, the elderly, American Indians, Spanish-speaking persons and Blacks is discussed; it is concluded that they should be considered discrete sociocultural units with unique needs for prevention and treatment. Among all special population groups, American Indians have the highest reported frequency of problems associated with drinking acculturation stress may be partly to blame for the high rates of alcoholism among Spanish-speaking people. Black women who drink have a greater proportion of heavier drinkers than white women who drink.

307
United States. National Institute on Alcohol Abuse and Alcoholism. Alcohol Topics in Brief. _Alcohol and Blacks_. Rockville, Maryland: National Clearinghouse for Alcohol Information, 1980, pp. 1-3.

There is an increasing recognition that the Nation's alcohol problems affect every segment of our society. The black community represents the largest ethnic minority in the United States, and alcohol use and abuse is perceived to be one of the most significant health, social, and mental health problems within that population. Despite the apparent need, a review and analysis of available information reveals that few studies exist on the subject of alcohol and blacks... The bulk of identified research focuses on the black male in urban communities, with little attention being given to women and to rural populations... This article looks at the problems as associated with alcohol use and abuse among blacks from the following perspectives: (1) historical perspectives, (2) patterns of black alcohol use, (3) problems of rehabilitation and (4) what the future holds.

308
United States. National Institute on Drug Abuse. _Drug Abuse Patterns Among Young Polydrug Users and Urban Appalachian Youths_, Rockville, MD, 1980, 34p.

Two separate but related studies on the nature and patterns of drug use (including alcohol) among youths are presented. The National Youth Polydrug Study (NYPS), conducted by the Philadelphia Psychiatric Center in 1976 and 1977, presents findings from a nationwide study of youths, 18 years old and younger, who were treated in drug programs. The other study, conducted by the National Center for Urban Ethnic Affairs in 1975 and 1976, focuses on a particular ethnic population: youngsters who migrated or whose parent(s) and/or grandparent(s) migrated from the federally defined Appalachian region. This study was conducted in ethnic communities in four cities: Baltimore, Detroit, Cincinnati, and Providence.

309
Weller, R.A., Halikas, J.A., Darvish, H.S., "Alcoholism in Black Male Heroin Addicts," British Journal of Addiction, 75(4): 381-388, 1980.

From 1973 through 1974, 192 black male heroin addicts (age range of 18-50 years, mean age of 28.7 years) were interviewed in St. Louis, Missouri. Of these 192 addicts, 24 percent were diagnosed as alcoholics, and 13 percent as probable alcoholics. An additional 19 percent reported isolated problems with alcohol; thus, 56 percent of these addicts had experienced some problem because of alcohol. . . It is concluded that a sizeable portion of the herion addict population is having problems from the use of two drugs: heroin and alcohol.

310
Williams, G., "Eleventh Street: Soulful Scenes," Magazine of the Texas Commission on Alcoholism, 6(3): 11-13, 1980.

This article is part of a data summary from an anthropologist's point of view about the ritual functions drinking serves in Rosewood, a black community in east Austin. The author relates his experiences on a weekend afternoon and evening as an observer of and participant in the drinking ritual of community members at various establishments along Rosewood's Eleventh Street. . . It is suggested that to the extent that the enthnographer is pursuing a particular configuration and the role alcohol plays in the dynamic of community life, his observations necessarily must include the places and people within which and from whom the data come alive.

311
Williams, L.T., "Janusian System: A New Vision of the Minority Family in Distress (As a Result of Drug or Alcohol Abuse)," 13th Annual Eagleville Conference on Substance Abuse: The Family in Trouble, Eagleville, PA: 15-16 May 1980, pp. 254-268.

The author contends that the basic practical dilemma constantly faced in trying to understand a social problem is how to adjust social theories to reality. This paper is devoted to the formulation and application of a conceptual framework which is suitable to the study of minority families in distress because of alcohol and drug abuse. . .

## 1981

312
Adickes, E.A.; Shuman, R.M. "Human Fetal Alcohol Myopathy: An Animal Model." Journal of Neuropathology, 40: 422, 1981.

Infants born to confirmed and committed alcoholic mothers often show fetal alcohol myopathy. In a population of American Indians, Blacks and Caucasians, 10 percent in a 3 year sample of 60 biopsies from hypotonic children less than 3 years old had this disorder. Fiber Type 1 disproportion with variable atpase and oxidative enzyme activities, central nuclei and hypotrophic/atrophic sarcoplasm was seen... An experiemental model is being developed for the Sprague-Dawley rat to study muscle biopsies from infant pups of alcoholic mothers.

313
Agarwal, D.P.; Meier-Tackmann, D.; Harada, S.; Goedde, H.W., "Search for the Indianapolic-Variant of Human Alcohol Dehydrogenase in Liver Autopsy Samples from North Germany and Japan." Human Genetics, 59(2): 170-171, 1981.

Human liver alcohol dehydrogenase (ADH) variants were screened in random autopsy specimens from 53 North German and 34 Japanese individuals. Based on pH activity profile and electrophoretic pattern, only ADH2 and ADH3 variants were detected... The recently reported new molecular forms collectively called ADH-Indianapolis could not be demonstrated... Results support the hypothesis that the ADH-Indianapolis variant is confined to the American Black population.

314
Andrews, T., A Bibliography of Drug Abuse - Supplement 1977-1980. Littleton, Colorado: Libraries Unlimited, Inc., 1981.

This is a companion volume to Bibliography of Drug Abuse, Including Alcohol and Tobacco (Libraries Unlimited, 1977). The 1977 bibliography contained 725 annotated references, and this 1981 one contained 741 items. One chapter that may be of assistance is Chapter 11 "Drugs and Other Special Groups" (pp. 139-152). For general reference works see Part I (pp. 3-47).

315
Arevalo, R. "Training Program for Social Work Students Targeted at Alcohol Abuse Services for Special Populations." _NIAAA Hispanic Alcoholism Manpower/Training Workshop._ San Antonio, TX: Aug. 1981, pp. 33-35.

The purpose of the social work school training program at San Jose State University (California) is to train undergraduate and graduate social work students in the area of alcohol abuse with a particular focus on minority populations: Chicanos, Blacks, and women. The training program provides students with curriculum content relating to alcoholism, its causes, diagnostic assessment, and intervention. The goals, objectives, and content of the training program are outlined.

316
Arevalo, R., and Minor, M., Eds., _Chicanas and Alcoholism: A Socio-Cultural Perspective of Women._ San Jose State University, School of Social Work, San Jose, CA., 1981, 55 p.

This monograph focuses on the training activities and research conducted by the Clinical Alcoholism Project of the School of Social Work at San Jose State University. Its purpose was to develop curriculum in the field of alcohol abuse in relation to Chicanos, Blacks, and women, and to promote the entry of social workers into the field of alcoholism. Papers written as a part of this clinical training grant from the National Institute on Alcohol Abuse and Alcoholism (NIAAA) are presented...

317
Bachman, J.G.; Johnston, L.D.; O'Malley, P.M., "Smoking, Drinking, and Drug Use Among American High School Students: Correlates and Trends, 1975-1979," _American Journal of Public Health_, 71(1): 59-69, 1981.

Findings from five nationally representative surveys of high school seniors from 1975 through 1979 were used to examine the correlates of licit and illicit drugs, and to consider whether recent changes in youthful drug use are linked to any changes in the correlates... It is suggested that the kinds of young people most at risk remain much the same, while the types and amounts of substances they use shift somewhat from year to year.

318
Barnes, G.M.; Welte, J.W. "Alcohol Use Among New York State College Students," *Alcoholism Clinical and Experimental Research.* 5(1): 143, 1981.

A questionnaire was administered to 7700 full-time undergraduate students randomly selected from 22 colleges in New York State. Men were twice as likely than women to be classified in the heavy drinking category (more than 1 oz of absolute alcohol/day). Younger men were heavier drinkers than older men students. White men were heavier drinkers than Black, Hispanic or Oriental students. Significant number of students reported problems associated with drinking and significant relationships existed between alcohol use and geographic region, context of drinking and other social factors.

319
Baskin, D.; Bluestone, H.; Nelson, M., "Ethnicity and Psychiatric Diagnosis," *Journal of Clinical Psychology,* 37(3): 529-537, 1981.

Diagnostic differences between Black, White, and Hispanic-American patients (N=1968) seen in psychiatric outpatient clinics of a large hospital in the South Bronx, New York City, were investigated. The five most prevalent diagnoses were nonpsychotic disorders, alcoholism, transient situational disorders, schizophrenia, and depressive/affective disorders. The Black patients had a higher proportion of alcoholism and schizophrenia, while Hispanic-American patients were diagnosed more frequently as having depressive/affective disorders, transient situational disturbances, and nonpsychotic disorders... Clinician's ethnicity was found to be a significant influence on the diagnostic labels used by the clinicians. In light of the fact that diagnostic differences exist among various ethnic groups of patients and that diagnosticians from different ethnic groups make significantly different diagnoses, greater attention should be paid to how the clinician is perceiving patients' thoughts, feelings, and behavior.

320
Bell, P., and Evans, J., "Alcohol Use and Abuse in Black America: Part I," *Black Bag* : *Journal of the Student National Medical Association*, Special Issue: 18-21, April 1981.

Part I of a two-part series is presented. An historical perspective of blacks and alcohol use and abuse is provided, including a definition of alcoholism...Generalizations that have emerged from the ethnographic literature on drinking are enumerated, and are correlated with alcohol use and abuse in black Americans. The impact of alcoholism on the black community is discussed, and an example of behavioral change in alcohol use patterns which was brought on by changing the environment in which that behavior takes place is also presented...

321
Bell, P., and Evans, J., _Counseling the Black Client: Alcohol Use and Abuse in Black America_, Center City, MN: Hazelden Educational Services, 1981, 43 p.

This booklet is divided into two parts. In the first part, the use and abuse of alcohol by black Americans is examined from an anthropological perspective, and alcoholism's impact on the black community is described. In the second part, the following topics are discussed: (1) white and black counseling styles when interacting with black clients; (2) heterogeniety in the black community; (3) cultural defense systems; (4) the concept of black double-consciousness; (5) general guidelines and questions for effective counseling; and (6) alcoholism service gaps in the black community and programming ideas to fill them.

322
Benjamin, R., and Benjamin, M., "Sociocultural Correlates of Black Drinking: Implications for Research and Treatment," _Journal of Studies on Alcohol_, Supplement No. 9: 214-245, 1981.

Findings from several studies are cited in a discussion of sociocultural correlates associated with drinking among Blacks...It is contended that, to study Blacks and alcohol, more attention needs to be given to: (1) measures of alcohol use and misuse from Black minority group perspectives; (2) the impact of alcohol overuse; (3) the management of alcohol-overusing family members and friends; and (4) intra-racial comparisons of perception of alcohol misuse, the impact of and management strategies for alcohol- misuse.

323
Beverly, C.C., "Psycho-Social Research and its Application to Alcohol and Drug Addiction Programs," _National Institute on Alcohol Abuse and Alcoholism Skills Development Workshop...Agenda for Black Alcoholism Programs_, Jackson, MS: 15-17 July 1981,24p.

It is stated that the basic principle of the psychosocial research model rests on the assumption that performance in social functioning is fundamentally tied to intrapsychic processes and is therefore minimally influenced by socioeconomic factors...In this paper the author calls for a reversal of the psychosocial model to a socioeconomic model under the assumption that the latter holds greater promise in the fight against substance abuse in Black communities.

324
Bland, J., "Working with State Governments," _National Institute on Alcohol Abuse and Alcoholism Skills Development Workshop... Agenda For Black Alcoholism Programs_. Jackson, MS: 15-17, 1981, 11 p.

The author believes that the agenda for Black alcoholism programs today is to survive, and that working with State government, including both the executive and the legislative branches, is now and increasingly will prove to be important strategies to insure the continuation of Black alcoholism programming...

325
Bohtemps, P., "Past, Present, and Future of Black Alcoholism Programs," _National Institute on Alcohol Abuse and Alcoholism Skills Development Workshop... Agenda for Black Alcoholism Programs_, Jackson, MS: 15-17, 1981, 6 p.

A general historical account of Black drinking practices is provided, describing cultural and social factors which have contributed to this behavior. The author believes that ways must be found to convince Blacks that prevention efforts are not simply echoing moralistic teachings of the Puritans and other temperance crusaders, but are concerted efforts to improve the quality (and the length) of life for Blacks.

326
Caldwell, F.J., "Alcoholics Anonymous as a Viable Treatment Resource for Black Alcoholics," National Institute on Alcohol Abuse and Alcoholism Skills Development Workshop...Agenda for Black Alcoholism Programs, Jackson, MS: 15-17, July 1981, 29 p.

In this paper, Alcoholics Anonymous (AA) is described as a very effective and economical voluntary resource for the treatment of alcoholism and a highly personal experience of which understanding is best achieved through subjective involvement; its essence cannot be adquately understood using traditional social science methods. The philosophy, psychology, and politics of AA are discussed, and cultural differences are addressed...

327
Carroll, J.F.X., Malloy, T.E., Roscioli, D.L., et al. "Personality Simmilarities and Differences in Four Diagnostic Groups of Women Alcoholics and Drug Addicts," Journal of Studies on Alcohol, 42(5): 432-440, 1981.

The Personality Research Form (PRF) was administered to 225 women alcoholics and drug addicts at the Eagleville Hospital and Rehabilitation Center. The women were grouped into 4 diagnostic categories: A, alcohol misuse only; D, drug misuse only; A + D, alcohol and secondary misuse only; D + A, drug and secondary misuse of alcohol... Significant differences on 9 prf scales were attributed to race. The White women scored significantly higher ($p < .01$) than the Blacks on the Affiliation, Impulsivity, Play and Sentience scales, whereas the Black women scored significantly higher than the Whites on the Aggression ($p < .01$), Cognitive structure ($p < .03$), Dominance ($p < .01$), Harmavoidance ($p < .01$) and Understanding ($p < .05$) scales.

328
Carter, J.H., "Treating Black Patients: The Risks of Ignoring Critical Social Issues," Hospital and Community Psychiatry, 32(4): 281-282, 1981.

The risks of ignoring critical issues while treating Black patients suffering from mental illnesses, such as alcohol and drug abuse, are discussed.

329
Carter, R.M., "Strategy for Mobilizing In-Kind Contributions for a Community Alcoholism Program," _National Institute on Alcohol Abuse and Alcoholism Skills Development Workshop...Agenda for Black Alcoholism Programs_, Jackson, MS: 15-17, July 1981, 19 p.

The necessity for local programs to secure in-kind contributions for ongoing or new alcoholism projectsdesigned to serve minority populations is emphasized, focusing on those straegies developed by the Broward County (Florida) Alcohol and Drug Abuse Services Division Outreach Program.

330
Chatham, L.R., "Opening Remarks Presented at National Institute on Alcohol Abuse and Alcoholism Skills Development Workshop," _National Institute on Alcohol Abuse and Alcoholism Skills Development Workshop...Agenda for Black Alcoholism Programs_, Jackson, MS: 15-17, July 1981, 6 p.

Opening remarks by the author to the National Institute on Alcohol Abuse and Alcoholism NIAAA Skills Development Workshop are presented.

331
Crawford, P.M., "Feasibility of Increased Private Resources for Black Alcoholism Program Financing and Services Delivery," _National Institute on Alcohol Abuse and Alcoholism Skills Development Workshop...Agenda for Black Alcoholism Programs_, Jackson, MS: 15-17, July 1981, 25p.

The feasibility of increased private resources for Black alcoholism program financing and services delivery is addressed ina discussion of the following topics: (1) three perspectives of the independent sector; (2) private philantrophy; (3) volunteerism; and (4) self-help organizations. Issues that may be addressed as a part of future Black alcoholism program research endeavors are enumerated.

332
Davis, W.H., "Working with Black Owned Business and Black Employee Populations," _National Institute on Alcohol Abuse and Alcoholism Skills Development Workshop...Agenda for Black Alcoholism Programs_, Jackson, MS: 15-17, July 1981, 11 p.

The author contends that, in Black owned businesses nd organizations employing a significantnumber of Blacks, the sociocultural aspects of Blacks aflicted with alcohol-related problemsmust be addressed with dispatch...Some of the key issues that must be explored if Black businesses or organizations with Black employees are truly concerned about their employees are listed...

333
Dawkins, M.P., Alcohol and Drug Survey Among Youth and Adolescents in Washington, D.C. Report 1: A Descriptive Summary, Washington Area Council on Alcoholism and Drug Abuse, Inc., Washington, DC: 1981, 35 p.

The first in a series of reports on alcohol and drug related experiences of young people in Washington, D.C. is presented, based on a city-wide survey (N=1,095) conducted in the summer of 1980...A descriptive summary is provided of findings based on responses of participants to a wide range of questions about alcohol and drugs. These findings indicate that youth and adolescents in the District of Columbia follow some of the patterns reported in national studies in terms of the more frequent use of alcohol and marijuana in comparison to other substances, and tend to be corroborated by data reported in crime, health, and social service statistics with respect to problems related to the use of these two drugs.

334
Dennis, R.E., "Self-Definition, Self-Determination, Self-Solution: Agenda for Black Alcoholism Programs," National Institute on Alcohol Abuse and Alcoholism Skills Development Workshop...Agenda for Black Alcoholism Programs, Jackson, MS: 15-17, July 1981, 9 p.

In this paper, the heterogeneity of alcoholism is emphasized, as opposed to the difference between Black and White alcoholics, and the diverse nature of the alcoholic as noted in treatment modalities and resources is discussed...

335
Durant, A.D., "Treatment of Alcoholism Among Blacks: Toward a Comprehensive Approach," National Council on Alcoholism, 13 April 1981, 21 p.

A historical background is traced of Black drinking behavior and Black alcoholics' adaptation in a hostile environment. Factors influencing the thoughts, feelings and behavior of Blacks are explained for the benefit of helping persons.

336
Everette, L.H., and Bennett, D.R., "Program Evaluation: More Now Than Ever Before," National Institute on Alcohol Abuse and Alcoholism Skills Development Workshop...Agenda for Black Alcoholism Programs, Jackson, MS" 15-17, July 1981, 50 p.

It is stated that formalized evaluation has often been a "sore spot" for program people, i.e., program directors and especially line staff feel threatened by the concept of having someonemake judgment with regard to the quality of their performance. The author contends that program people should utilize evaluation asa viable management tool...It is suggested that evaluation beviewed as a tool for measuring internal proficiency resulting in improved service provision to Black alcoholics and their families. The Rubicon Alcoholism Program's Discrepancy Evaluation Model is described and offered as an example of a modified evaluation system.

337
Ferguson, L. Black Clients in National Institute on Alcohol Abuse and Alcoholism Funded Categorical Programs: Calendar Year 1979, United States Alcohol, Drug Abuse, and Mental Health Administration, Information Systems and Evaluation Branch, Rockville, MD: 1981, 16 p.

Data, collected through the National Alcoholism Program Information System (NAPIS), concerning Black clients in treatment programs funded by the National Institute on Alcohol Abuse and Alcoholism (NIAAA) during Calendar Year 1979 are reviewed...Data are examined with respect to program activity, characteristics, type of care received, and changes in drinking patterns after six months of treatment. Recommendations for improving treatment programs for Blacks are presented.

338
Floyd, L.L., "Principles and Techniques of Alcohol/Drug Training," National Institute on Alcohol Abuse and Alcoholism Skills Development Workshop...Agenda for Black Alcoholism Programs, Jackson, MS: 15-17 July 1981, 43 p.

This position paper provides information on the fundamental principles and techniques of drug and/or alcohol training.

339
Gay, J.E., "Alcohol and Metropolitan Black Teenagers," Journal of Drug Education, 11(1): 19-26, 1981.

Data comparing adolescents who drink and those who do not with regard to both physical and emotional health are presented from a study of adolescent health in Baltimore, Maryland. Personal interviews were conducted with 728 young black people, between the ages of eleven and sixteen years, over a six month period in 1978. It was found that drinkers were more likely to report health problems, including more incidences of sleep disturbance. This correlation between drinking and poor health was most significant among young males and older females. Tobacco use was found to be the most positive predictor of drinking among males and pregnancy for females.

340
Heath, D.B. and Cooper, A.M., Alcohol Use and World Cultures: A Comprehensive Bibliography of Anthropological Sources, Bibliographic Series No. 15. Toronto, Ontario, Canada: Addiction Research Foundation, 1981.

This bibliography contains 1398 references. The listing under "Blacks" can be found on pp. 219-220.

341
Holliday, B.G., "Making the Best of a Bad Situation: Pragmatic Planning Strategies for Black Alcohol Prevention Efforts in the 1980s," National Institute on Alcohol Abuse and Alcoholism Skills Development Workshop...Agenda for Black Alcoholism Programs, Jackson, MS: 15-17 July 1981, 15 p.

It is stated that the current ideological climate dictates that Black communities must adopt more pragmatic approaches to issues of social services and social policy. Doctrines of pragmatism indicate that greater emphasis must be placed on conceptions of problemsand issues, the role of research, and selection of program evaluation criteria...

342
Horowitz, B., and Wolock, I., "Material Deprivation, Child Maltreatment, and Agency, Interventions Among Poor Families," In L.H. Pelton, Ed., Social Context of Child Abuse and Neglect, New York, NY: Human Sciences Press, 1981, pp. 137-184.

Research literature on poor families and abuse or neglect of children is cited and briefly discussed. Results from a study designed to examilne the role of material and social deprivation in child maltreatment and patterns of agency intervention are presented...The following findings are reported: (1) case record data analysis revealed that alcohol was a serious problem for approximately 50 percent of the families; (2) alcohol abuse was not related to material level of living butwas related to ethnicity, with white parents more likely to be identified as having a drinking problem (74 percent) than black parents (54 percent); and (3) the greater incidence of alcohol abuse among whites fits a pattern of factors associated with child maltreatment in which greater interpersonal and intrapersonal behavior difficulties are prominent. Recommendations for intervention and/or prevention are enumerated.

343
Jackson, N., Carlisi, J., Greenway, C., Zalesnick, M. "Age of Initial Drug Experimentation Among White and Non-White Ethnics," International Journal of the Addictions, 16(8): 1373-1386, 1981.

A 196 item questionnaire on ethnic background and drug use patterns was administered to 1414 students in inner city communities of Baltimore, Detroit, Cincinnati, and Providence...Results revealed significant differences in actual age of experimentation among ethnic groups, as well as differences in other general patterns relating to age of first drug use. A comparison of Whites to non-Whites showed little difference in ages of initial drug experimentation. Polish, Italian, German, and Black youth tended to try most drugs at a later age than average, whereas Native Americans and Mixed Race youth (those whose parents were of different races) tended to try drugs at an earlier age.

344
Kalish, H.I., "Operant Conditioning and the Behavior Disorders," In H.I. Kalish, Ed., From Behavioral Science to

Behavior Modification, New York, NY: McGraw-Hill, 1981, 436 p. (pp. 155-183).

In this chapter, behavior under the control of addictive reinforces, specifically alcohol and drugs, is described. The following myths about alcohol-related behavior are dispelled: (1) the belief that some individuals are more susceptible than others to excessive drinking because of their "addictive" or "prealcoholic" tendencies; and (2) the "craving hypothesis," i.e., that, even when sober, all alcoholics will crave a drink and that one drink will inevitably lead to more and, ultimately, to complete intoxiction. Alcoholism in relation to "good feeling" and social learning is discussed.

345
Kane, G.P.,, Inner-City Alcoholism: An Ecological Analysis and Cross-Cultural Study, New York, NY: Human Sciences Press, 1981, 263 p.

Theories on alcoholism and its causes, particularly among inner city residents, are reviewed. Sociocultural aspects of alcoholism among American Black and Hispanic individuals are examined. Extensive data are presented from an epidemiological study of Black and Hispanic alcoholics in the South Bronx section of New York City. Planning and evaluation of treatment and prevention programs are discussed, and an attempt is made to establish a link between the etiology of alcoholism and the use of the medical model for describing alcoholism as a disease.

346
Keller, A.Z., "Alcohol and Tobacco Use Among Cirrhotic and Non-Cirrhotic Males with Cancer," Progress in Clinical and Biological Research, 53: 213-223, 1981.

The anatomical site distributions of cancers among 474 Black cirrhotics and noncirrhotics with cancer were studied using data from 171 veterans hospitals for the 6-year priod, July 1, 1969 to June 30, 1975. Also compared were 305 Blacks and 370 Whites, with cancer but without liver cirrhosis, by cancer site distributions, tobacco use and alcohol consumption in an attempt to explain racial differences in cancer risks...The overall relative risk of multiple primary cancers was 3.2 times greater for cirrhotics than for noncirrhotics. Blacks and Whites had similar relativce frequencies and incidence rates of mouth and pharynx cancers, but skin and lip cancers were common among Whites and rare among blacks. Prostate and gastrointestinal cancers were high among blacks. Even when levels of tobacco use and alcohol consumption for the races were the same blacks manifested a higher rate of pancreatic esophageal and gastric cancers...

347
Kidane, A., "Self-Definition, Self-Determination, Self-Solution: Economic Issues of Black Alcoholics," National Institute on Alcohol Abuse and Alcoholism Skills Development Workshop...Agenda for Black Alcoholism Programs, Jackson, MS: 15-17 July 1981, 10 p.

Economic issues of alcoholism among Blacks are discussed.

348
Kittrell, R.C., and Miller, L.P., Don't Feel Rained On, North Carolina Department of Human Resources, 1981, 12 p.

Information is provided about alcohol, its use and abuse. This booklet is geared specifically to black youth. Sources of referral are given, as well as suggestions on how family members can cope with the problems brought about by living with an alcoholic.

349
Lipscomb, W.R., "Study of Drinking Practices of Black Americans," 27th International Institute on the Prevention and Treatment of Alcoholism, Vienna, Austria: International Cohncil on Alcohol and Addictions, 15-20 June 1981, pp. 193-205.

In this paper, the Black Drinking Practices Study Project, designed, schedules, and in the process of being conducted in two predominantly black neighborhoods in San Francisco, California is described. The historical background of this project is traced, and some hypothesis generators which have been developed over the first 20 months are presented.

350
Lipscomb, W.R., and Trocki, K., Black Drinking Practice Study, SOURCE, Inc., Berkeley, CA: 1981, 114 p.

Results are presented from a two-year study (1979 through 1981) designed to investigate drinking patterns and practices of Blacks in two areas of San Francisco, California. It was found that: (1) Blacks exhibit a high level of denial of their drinking problems, i.e., they do not readily identify their own or others' problem drinking, nor do they demonstrate a clear agreement about the consequences of problem drinking; (2) appropriate treatment and counseling establishments, which are shamefully few in number, are little understood and employed by Blacks, whose alcohol-related problems need remedial services; and (3) there is a need to develop and employ a maximum of preventive efforts, especially directed at Black youth. Recommendations for alcoholism treatment and prevention among Blacks are provided, and a copy of the household survey questionnaire is appended.

351
Littles, R.T., "Medicaid-Medicare: Third Party Funding for Black Alcohol Programs?," _National Institute on Alcohol Abuse and Alcoholism Skills Development Workshop...Agenda for Black Alcoholism Programs_, Jackson, MS: 15-17 July 1981, 7 p.

Proceedings from the position that most, if not all, publicly supported Black Alcoholism programs provide treatment to Blacks who for the great part represent the categorically needy and the medically indigent, the history of Medicaid and Medicare, operational constraints and current legislative mood as applicable to Black alcoholism programs, is briefly addressed. The author calls for maximum utilization of Medicaid options and political pressuring, if these programs are to benefit financially from third party payments.

352
Malezer, L., "Impact of Drugs and Alcohol Use on Aboriginals: Alcohol Prevention," _First Pan-Pacific Conference on Drugs and Alcohol_, Canberra, Australia: 26 February - 5 March 1980, pp. 150-151.

The impact and prevention of drug and alcohol use on the Aborigines of Australia is described.

353
Megargee, E.I., and Zager, L.D., "Seven MMPI Alcohol and Drug Abuse Scales: An Empirical Investigation of Their Interrelationships, Convergent and Discriminant Validity, and

Degree of Racial Bias," Journal of Personality and Social Psychology, 40(3): 532-544, 1981.

Results are presented from an empirical investigation designed to assess five Minnesota Multiphasic Personality Inventory (MMPI) alcohol scales and two drug scales, their interrelationships, convergent and discriminant validity, and degree of racial bias. Subjects (N=1,048, mean age 22.3 years) entering the Federal Correctional Institute in Tallahassee, Florida, between 3 November 1980 and 2 November 1972, were administered a battery of psychological tests including the MMPI, and an interview that included a number of questions related to patterns of alcohol and drug use. Five scales indicated some degree of convergent or discriminant validity, and racial differences were observed on five scales, with Blacks scoring lower on all of these scales except one. These results indicate that those currently utilizing alcohol or drug abuse scales with youthful samples or with a criminal offender must do so with caution, and the racial identity of the respondent should be taken into consideration in interpreting the results and assigning cutting scores.

354
Minnesota Institute on Black Chemical Abuse, Minnesota Institute on Black Chemical Abuse Annual Report. Minneapolis, Minnesota, 1981, 23 p. (No authors listed).

In this annual report, steps aken by the Minnesota Institute on Black Chemical Abuse (MIBCA) to provide quality service are described, and questions pertaining to the operation of the MIBCA are answered. Statistical data on new client demographics are provided, including data which summarize MIBCA program goals...

355
Miranda, V.L., "Black Alcohol Prevention Programming Past, Present, Future," National Institute on Alcohol Abuse and Alcoholism Skills Development Workshop...Agenda for Black Alcoholism Programs, Jackson, MS: 15-17 July 1981, 35 p.

Past developments in the prevention and education fields, initiated and funded by the National Institute on Alcohol Abuse and Alcoholism (NIAAA) are described, including strategies that have been incorporated into three model programs targeted at youth ranging from elementary to college age. The author contends that much of what has been done in prevention has not looked closely at the inherent cultural differences between Black and White alcohol abuse; however, although the effort is late, work is being done in the area of Black alcohol problem prevention through a publication called "A Guidebook for Planning Alcohol Prevention Programs with Black Youth," which details community action strategies...

356
Monroe-Scott, B., and Miranda, V., Guidebook for Planning Alcohol Prevention Programs with Black Youth. United States Alcohol, Drug Abuse, and Mental Health Administration, National Institute on Alcohol Abuse and Alcoholism, National Clearinghouse for Alcohol Information, Rockville, MD: 1981, 130 p.

In this guidebook, ideas for starting programs to prevent alcohol abuse among black youth are provided. The following beginning steps are described: (1) mobilizing interested groups; (2) obtaining multiple agency support throughnetworking; (3) finding out what youth and alcohol issues are of concern to the individual community; (4) writing a grant proposal; (5) obtaining funding support; (6) conducting a prevention workshop; and (7) involving youth as partners in programs that encourage independent decision making about alcohol.

357
National Black Alcoholism Council, Inc. Abscess: Blacks and Sedation, Detroit, MI, 1981, 60 p., (No authors listed).

This document is the result of a literature search and formal discussion among selected members of the National Black Alcoholism Council, Michigan Chapter. A hypothesis regarding problem drinking and/or alcoholism among Blacks is presented.

358
Nebraska Division on Alcoholism, Department of Public Institutions. Discussion of the Data on Black Admissions to Alcoholism Treatment in Nebraska, Lilncoln, Nebraska, 1981, 11 p. (No authors listed).

Information obtained from the Nebraska Division on Alcoholism and Drug Abuse Management Information System (NDADA-MIS) is presented. A comparison is made between certain characteristics of Black Americans and other racial and/or ethnic groups admitted to alcoholism treatment during Fiscal Year 1980.

359
New York City Task Force on Women and Alcoholism. Women and Alcoholism: Public Hearing Testimony, New York, NY, 1981 (No authors listed).

Testimonies from participants at the Women and Alcoholism Public Hearing, sponsored by the New York City Task Force on Women and Alcoholism held 17 February 1981 are presented. The following topics are addressed: (1) women in the workplace; (2) women in the correctional system [prisons]; (3) the woman affected by another's alcoholism; (4) displaced homemakers; (5) prenatal needs; (6) residential and child care needs; (7) special needs; (8) intervention and prevention issues; and (9) advocacy issues.

360
Nobles, J.L., "MMPI and Drinking Pattern Differences Among Black/White Male Alcoholic Rehabilitation Patients," Dissertation. Ann Arbor, MI: University Microfilms International, 1981.

A study was conducted to determine the ways in which a number of dependent variables and 91 self report MMPI scale scores were related to the two independent variables of race (Black/White) and level of alcohol abuse (high/low), after the variance accountable to eight demographic/personality variables were partialled out...A sizeable portion of the variance was accounted for by certain MMPI scales that each accounted for one percent or more of the variance. Four such scales were found able to predict subjects' race: (1) tension, worry, and fear; (2) inferiority/personal discomfort; (3) psychoticism; and (4) persecutory ideas. All four sales were significantly higher for Blacks. Six scales were found to predict alcohol abuse level, including: (1) brooding; (2) manifest anxiety; (3) inferiority/personal discomfort; (4) mental dullness; (5) repression/sensitization; and (6) repression. All except the latter were significantly higher for high abusers.

361
Novy, C., Gadsen, R.H., and Quinn, L., "Appearance of a Sixty Lactate Dehydrogenase Isoenzyme (LDH6) in a Previously Healthy Patient," Stanford Medical Journal, 74: 507-508, 1981.

The case of a 36 year old Black man with marked metabolic acidosis secondary to alcohol ingestion (blood alcohol level 338 mg/dl) is reported...After massive administration of bicarbonate, the acute alcohol intoxication and severe metabolic acidoses slowly resolved but renal shutdown ensued and the patient became increasingly obtunded. The marked elevation of ldh (1540 IU, normal 100 to 230), especially ldh5 (44 percent of total ldh) and recurrent hypotension were suggestive of liver damage with associated passive hyperemia. Necrosis or damage occurring in multiple organ systems was also indicated. The patient died 78 hours after hospital admission.

362
Patterson, E.T., Charles, H.L., Woodward, W.A., et al., "Differences in Measures of Personality and Family Environment Among Black and White Alcoholics," Journal of Consulting and Clinical Psychology, 49(1): 1-9, 1981.

The Black-White differences in the Minnesota Mutiphasic Personality Inventories (MMPIS) were explored in alcoholics (272 White, mean age 46.64 years and 56 Blacks, mean age 41.34 years) admitted between October 1978 and May 1980 to an alcohol dependence treatment program at a Veterans Administration medical center...Blacks scored significantly lower on a few MMPI scales (e.g., hysteria), but profile differences were not clinically meaningful, particularly when controlled for age, education, and socioeconomic status. Blacks differed considerably on the Family Environment Scale, rating social climates more positively than Whites.

363
Porche, M., "Alcohol Abuse Concerns and Needs of Minority Populations," National Council on Alcoholism 29th Annual Forum, New Orleans, LA: 12 April 1981.

The social correlates of alcohol abuse in relation to minority populations are described. These minority populations include Blacks, females, teenagers, elderly, Spanish speaking individuals, and Native American Indians. Topics covered in this paper include demographic characteristics, incidents and outcomes, unique needs and concerns, treatment modalities, preventive measures, and research findings.

364
Pottern, L.M., Morris, L.E., Blot, W.J., Ziegler, R.G., and Fraumeni, J.F., "Esophageal Cancer Among Black Men in Washington, D.C. Part I: Alcohol, Tobacco, and Other Risk Factors," Journal of the National Cancer Institute, 67(4): 777-783, 1981.

Results are presented from a case-control study designed to identify risk factors that may be responsible for the high mortality rates from esophageal cancer found among Black male residents of Washington, DC...Findings indicate that alcoholic beverage conumption was the major factor responsible for the high age-adjusted annual death rate for nonwhite males (1970 through 1975) in Washington, DC, with an estimated 81 percent of the esophageal cancers attributed to its use; high use of alcoholic beverages was also found among the controls. While the relative risk increased with amount of ethanol consumed and was highest among drinkers of hard liquor, the risk was also elevated among consumers of wine and/or beer only.

365
Redd, B., "Working with Local Governments and Institutions," National Institute on Alcohol Abuse and Alcoholism Skills Development Workshop...Agenda for Black Alcoholism Programs, Jackson, MS: 15-17 July 1981, 12 p.

The impact of poverty program legislation of the late 1960s on the development of the current substance abuse strategies is analyzed, describing the way in which these new "systems of the seventies" have been implemented and their impact upon minoriries. Empowerment, through building networks that include professionals and consumers, is seen as the key to the development of self-sufficiency in minority communities.

366
Reed, S.W. "Toward a Model for Alcohol Rehabilitation of Urban Minorities," In A.J. Schecter, Ed., Drug Dependence & Alcoholism, Vol. 2: Social & Behavioral Issues. New York, NY: Plenum Press, 1981, pp. 11-13.

The alcoholism treatment program at West Side Veterans Administration Hospital serves a basically Black, inner city population. The program attempts to address problems related to the patients' poorly developed social support systems in several ways...An attempt has also been made to counter the powerful support system developed by drinking companions, by establishing a social crisis intervention center...

367
Rivers, W.L., "Is There a Relationship Between Drug Use and Academic Achievement?", Journal of School Health, 51(3): 171-174, 1981.

A survey was conducted during the academic year 1977-1978, on 250 full time students enrolled at an urban community college in the Sheepshead Bay section of Brooklyn, New York, to determine the nature and extent of drug and alcohol use, and to ascertain the relationship, if any, between the use of drugs and alcohol and academic success. These students represented a cross section of the student population in terms of sex, ethnicity, class rank, and age...It is concluded that most students do not suffer a drug problem of the magnitude alleged by many in educational, medical, and legal circles.

368
Roizen, J., "Alcohol and Criminal Behavior Among Blacks: The Case for Research on Special Populations," In J.J. Collins, Ed., Drinking and Crime. New York, NY: Guilford Press, 1981, pp. 207-252.

This chapter reviews some of the empirical research on the drinking behavior of Blacks, in terms of its adequacy and its relevance to understanding criminal events and criminal careers...The chapter is organized to answer the following questions: (1) what contributions can the study of special populations make to understanding the role of alcohol in criminal behavior; (2) what is the empirical evidence for an "alcohol explanation" of criminal behavior among Blacks; (3) do available data and theories support subcultural or demographic explanations? If so, which populations deserve special status and for what reasons; and (4) what are the gaps in existing literatures on drinking patterns and criminal behavior of Blacks as well as in the literatures asserting a putative relationship between the two.

369
Rosemon, W.F., "Working with Unions from a Black Perspective," _National Institute on Alcohol Abuse and Alcoholism Skills Development Workshop...Agenda for Black Alcoholism Programs_, Jackson, MS: 15-17 July 1981, 26 p.

Oral interviews conducted with a staff member from each of four alcoholism treatment facilities, to determine the participation of Blacks as clients or staff members, are reported. Treatment facilities included: Raleigh Hills and Hermann Hospitals (Houston, Texas); Baptist Hospital of Southeast Texas (Beaumont); and Memorial Hospital (Gardena, California). Past developments and current major activities of employee assistance programs (EAP), and how alcoholism among Blacks is being ignored are discussed, including some major barriers in future development of these areas...

370
Royce, J.E., "Special Groups," In J.E. Royce, Ed., _Alcohol Problems and Alcoholism: A Comprehensive Survey_. New York: The Free Press, 1981.

The alcohol problems of women, youth, the elderly, racial minorities (American Indians, Blacks, Hispanics, Asian-Americans), the military, Skid Row Alcoholics and other special groups (physicians, clergy) are discussed...

371
Rutgers University. Center of Alcohol Studies. _Alcohol Studies: Retrospective Bibliographies - Black, U.S._ B015. Piscataway, N.J., 1981.

This bibliography includes epidemiological, clinical, treatment and prevention studies on Black alcoholism. For current updates or more information please write to: Information Services Division; Center of Alcohol Studies; Rutgers University, P.O. Box 969; Piscataway, N.J. 08854.

372
Saunders, M., "Double Bind: Minority Women," In P. Russianoff, Ed., _Women in Crisis_. New York, NY: Human Sciences Press, 1981, pp. 49-55.

Problems associated with being a minority woman, specifically a Black woman, in society, and with substance abuse treatment are discussed, including the background that the Black woman brings into any treatment program.

373
Scott, B.M. "Alcohol Prevention for Black Communities," Alcoholism in the Black Community Seminar, Newark, NJ: 3 October 1981, 14 p.

Cultural considerations in developing and implementing alcoholism preventionprograms for the Black community, and for Black youth in particular, are examined. Efforts by the National Institute on Alcohol Abuse and Alcoholism (NIAAA) through the Natinal Clearinghouse for Alcohol Information (NCALI) in the area of alcohol problem prevention are highlighted.

374
Simmons, L., and Williams, C., "Credentialing as a Strategy for the Survival of the Black Alcoholism Counselor," National Institute on Alcohol Abuse and Alcoholism Skills Development Workshop...Agenda for Black Alcoholism Programs, Jackson, MS: 15-17 July 1981, 15 p.

The development of Black alcoholism counselors is traced. The authors describe how the "new" profession of alcoholism counselors precipitated the credentialing process, and how this process affects Black alcoholism counselors.

375
Smith, E., "Public Information Systems and Community Education Programs Utilizing the Media," National Institute on Alcohol Abuse and Alcoholism Skills Development Workshop...Agenda for Black Alcoholism Programs, Jackson, MS: 15-17 July 1981, 3 p.

The utilization of the mass media by public information systems and community education programs to disseminate information concerning alcoholism and alcohol abuse is discussed.

376
Sullivan, N.R., "Self-Definition, Self-Determination and Self-Solutions for Alcohol Problems of Black Americans: Idealistic Conception and Pragmatic Constraints for Planning

and Administration: A Position Statement," *National Institute on Alcohol Abuse and Alcoholism Skills Development Workshop...Agenda for Black Alcoholism Programs*, Jackson, MS: 15-17 July 1981, 16 p.

Past developments in administration and planning of alcoholism programs are reviewed, considering factors which historically precluded the provision of services to Blacks. Current activities and practices are examined, including pertinent administrative and planning mechanisms at the federal, state and local levels...The author attempts to show how this theme provides a lofty and even admirable idea, but concludes that, in the absence of "definitions of the situation" that are inclusive of the need for empowerment of Blacks, self-determination and self-solutions are not likely to be forthcoming.

377
United States. Alcohol, Drug Abuse, and Mental Health Administration, National Institute on Alcohol Abuse and Alcoholism, *Skills Development Workshop.* *"Self-Definition, Self-Determination, Self-Solution: Agenda for Black Alcoholism Programs,"* Rockville, MD, 1981, 470 p.,

Papers presented at the Skills Development Workshop, entitled "Self-Definition, Self-Determination, Self-Solution: Agenda for Black Alcoholism Programs," sponsored by the National Institute on Alcohol Abuse and Alcoholism (NIAAA) in Jackson, Mississippi, 15-17 July 1981, are provided...

378
United States. National Institute on Alcohol Abuse and Alcoholism. *Alcohol Health and Research World* 5(3): 24-33, 1981. "Social Implications of Alcohol Abuse."

This special issue of this journal is devoted to summaries of *The Fourth Special Report to the U.S. Congress on Alcohol and Health*. This section on social implications of alcohol abuse includes sections on special populations, including Black Americans (pp. 27-28).

379
United States. National Institute on Drug Abuse. *Bibliography on Multicultural Drug Abuse Prevention Issues*. Rockville, Maryland, 1981. DHHS Publication No (ADM) 81-1086.

This bibliography contains over 280 references divided into four subject categories: 1. Primary Prevention of Drug Abuse for Multicultural Communities (pp. 3-21); 2. Bicultural Women and Substance Abuse (pp. 23-36); 3. Program Processes in Multicultural Drug Abuse Prevention (pp. 37-55); 4. Spanish and Bilingual Materials on Drug Abuse Prevention (pp. 57-64).

380
United States. National Institute on Drug Abuse. _A Guide to Multicultural Drug Abuse Prevention_. Rockville, Maryland, 1981. DHHS Publication Nos. (ADM) 81-1121 - 81-1126 (six booklets).

Booklet 1 - Introduction (ADM) 81-1121; Booklet 2 - Needs Assessment (ADM) 81-1122; Booklet 3 - Strategies (ADM) 81-1123; Booklet 4 - Resources (ADM) 81-1124; Booklet 5 - Funding (ADM) 81-1125; Booklet 6 - Evaluation (ADM) 81-1126.

381
Van-De-Merwe, T.J. "'n Detoksifikasie-eenheid Vir Volwasse Swartmans Met 'n Gestandaardiseerde Behandelingsregimen." Translated Title, "Detoxication Unit for Adult Black Males with a Standard Treatment Regimen," _South African Medical Journal_, 59(13): 443-447, 1981.

A special detoxication unit was established in 1975 because of a high rate of mortality (9.29 percent of 398 patients) during the preceding 6-month period among young South African Black men with toxic psychosis due to alcoholism, complicated by pellagra, malnutrition or pneumonia. Of the 615 high-risk patients treated in this unit with a standard regimen in 2.5 years, 33 (5.36 percent) died, which corresponds to 1.57 percent of the total number (4065) with alcohol- induced toxic psychosis.

382
Watts, C.D., "Health Insurance Coverage for Underserved Populations," _Alcohol Health and Research World_, 5(4): 35-36, 1981.

Problems associated with health insurance coverage for alcoholism for minorities are briefly discussed. The author feels these problems can be addressed only by first getting at their roots, the economic problems.

383
Winbush, R.A., and Henderson, P.S., "We May as Well Try This": Some Reflections on Alcoholism Services Research in the African-American Community," _National Institute on Alcohol Abuse and Alcoholism Skills Development Workshop...Agenda for Black Alcoholism Programs_, Jackson, MS: 15-17 July 1981, 15 p.

The authors contend that a lack of definitive research on Black alcoholism exists, rendering any conclusion concerning its causes, incidence, and treatment at best tentative and at worst misleading.

384
Winn, D.M., Blot, W.J., Shy, C.M., et al. "Snuff Dipping and Oral Cancer Among Women in the Southern United States," _New England Journal of Medicine_, 304(13): 745-749, 1981.

A North Carolina case-control study involving 255 women (15 percent Black, 85 percent White; 72 percent aged 60 or older) with oral or pharyngeal cancer and 502 controls matched for age, race, residence and source of ascertainment (hospital or death certificate) revealed that the high mortality from this cancer among White women in the South is due to snuff dipping. In the absence of snuff dipping, oral and pharyngeal cancer was associated mainly with the combination of drinking and cigarette smoking. Drinking was a risk factor only among smokers.

385
Wright, E.J., "Counseling from a Cultural Perspective: Requisites for Working with Black Clients," _National Institute on Alcohol Abuse and Alcoholism Skills Development Workshop...Agenda for Black Alcoholism Programs_, Jackson, MS: 15-17 July 1981, 19 p.

It is stated that counseling from a cultural perspective is a redefined concept that has significant implications for the development of alcoholism treatment services that are responsive to the needs of Black clients...In this paper, it is presupposed that the need for alcoholism services in minority communities has always existed, but that too often culturally unacceptable treatment approaches and counseling strategies were deterrents to minority participation in alcohol programs. Two issues are explored: (1) the importance of counselor awareness of cultural differences in the therapeutic process; and (2) the need for differential treatment approaches that reflect cultural realities of Black alcoholic clients.

386
Yamamoto, J., and Steinberg, A. "Ethnic, Racial, and Social Class Factors in Mental Health," Journal of the National Medical Association, 73(2): 231-240, 1981.

A review of the literature on ethnic, racial and social factors in mental health shows that Blacks and other minorities have generally been excluded from the scholarly evaluation of social class factors in alcoholism, drug abuse, and mental illness...Better studies are needed of Blacks, Hispanics, Native Americans, Asian and Pacific Island minorities, and all lower-class patients, particularly in epidemiology, diagnosis, treatment and prevention...

## 1982

387
Barnes, G.M., comp., with assistance from Robert J. Brown, *Alcohol and Youth: A Comprehensive Bibliography*. Westport, Connecticut: Greenwood Press, 1982.

4,666 total citations are included here. References to Black youth can be found on p. 426 in the Index.

388
Belcastro, P.A., and Nicholson, T., "Chemical Foreplay Among Black and White Students," *Journal of Drug Education*, 12(4): 373-384, 1982.

Results are presented from a study designated to determine whether individuals who use alcohol and/or marijuana prior to coitus do not. A sample of 1,090 white and black students enrolled in health education courses at a midwestern university was surveyed, using the Belcastro Sexual Behavior Inventory (BSBI). Findings indicate that: (1) for this population, experimentation with alcohol and marijuana prior to coitus was not typical; (2) for black students, the pattern of sexual behaviors was not very dissimilar between those who did and did not use alcohol and marijuana prior to coitus; and (3) white females who used alcohol and marijuana prior to coitus had a sexual behavior profile which was in sharp contrast to those females who did not use these drugs prior to coitus. . .

389
Carroll, J.F.X., Malloy, T.E., Rosciolo, D.L., et al., "Similarities and Differences in Self-Concepts of Women Alcoholics and Drug Addicts," *Journal of Studies on Alcohol*, 43(7): 725-738, 1982.

To examine the similarities and differences in self-concepts of women alcoholics and drug addicts, 200 (White, 103; Black 97) first-time admissions to Eagleville Hospital and Rehabilitation Center were studied. . . The Tennessee Self Concept Scale (TSCS) was administered to all women between the 10th and 14th day. Analysis of covariance results revealed significant differences due to diagnostic category on 7 of the TSCS scales; these scales, however, are significantly intercorrelated. Adjusted mean scale scores of the 4 diagnostic groups indicate that all suffered from low levels of self-esteem. Black women tended to be more confused, contradictory and conflicted in self-perception and manifested more signs of serious emotional distress than their White counterparts.

390
Carter, J.H., "Alcoholism in Black Vietnam Veterans: Symptoms of Posttraumatic Stress Disorder," Journal of the National Medical Association, 74(7): 655-660, 1982.

An alarming increase in alcoholism has been found in black Vietnam veterans and is believed to be an attempt to reduce the feelngs of inadequacy, pessimis, and uncontrollable rage that accompany both the stresses of war and of racism. Two cases are described that illustrate the posttraumatic stress disorder and alcoholism in these men. A brief discussion of salient issues that are crucial to diagnosis and treatment is presented.

391
Caution, G., Ethnic Drinking Patterns. South Carolina State College, Department of Psychology, Orangeburg, SC., 1982, 63 p.

The existing research on alcohol consumption patterns of Jewish Americans, Black Americans, and Native Americans is reviewed. Arrest rates, health related issues, sex differences, and age patterns, as well as other methodological and theoretical issues, are examined. It is contented that the major difficulties in existing literature lie in the propensity which researchers have, to view ethnic groups as homogenous, and therefore neglect to control for the differences within a particular ethnic group. The largest predictor of alcohol abuse within an ethnic group appears to be social stability in terms of family stability, the presence or absence of alcoholic parents, and job opportunities enabling an adequate and stable income...

392
Corrigan, E.M., and Anderson, S.C., "Black Alcohol Women in Treatment," Focus on Women: Journal of Addictions and Health, 3(1): 49-58, 1982.

Black and white women who entered treatment for alcoholism, particularly those background factors associated with their drinking, are compared, and the results of their treatment are analyzed. A number of implications for treatment emerge from the findings, including the fact that black women are more likely to give social reasons for drinking and seem to ahve very little support or incentive to alter their drinking behavior. Because of this lack, the burden of support necesarily falls back on the treatment setting. This also makes clear the need for the variety of social ties between women in the black community. The strong concern black women have for their physical weel being and less for their emotional state may also be a clue for the direction which needs to be taken to increase the likelihood of a positive treatment outcome for this population.

393
Edwards, D.W., and Letman, S.T., Eds., Alcoholism in the Urban Community. Chicago, IL: Loyola University, 1982, 97 p. Monograph.

Theoretical and planning issues concerning alcoholism in the urban community are discussed, i.e., alcoholism models and associated theories, defining alcoholism and examining its causes, and planning and organizing alcoholism services. The relationship between the use and abuse of mood-altering substances, particularly alcohol, and the work performance of employees is examined, including Irish, Jewish, and Black Americans drinking patterns. Alcohol abuse among women and teenagers is also examined...

394
Gary, L.E., "Substance Abuse, Homicide and the Black Male," Black Caucus Journal, 13: 13-18, 1982.

395
Gary, L.E., and Leashore, B.R., "High-Risk Status of Black Men," Social Work, 27(1): 54-58, 1982.

Data are presented from a variety of sources that indicate that black men bear the brunt of the inequalities in the American social, economic, and health systems. It is reported that: (1) alcohol abuse is estimated to be a factor in more than 10 percent of all deaths in the U.S., and has been associated with cirrhosis and cancer of the liver, with nonwhite men being more likely to die from these illnesses than white men; and (2) homicide among black men (more than six times that of white men) has been linked to alcohol and drug abuse. It is concluded that the social work profession can play a larger role in helping to reduce the high-risk status of black men by encouraging support networks in community groups.

396
Gillum, R.F., and Grant, C.T., "Coronary Heart Disease in Black Populations. Part II: Risk Factors," American Heart Journal, 104(4, Part 1): 852-864, 1982.

The authors discuss alcohol consumption as one of the risk factors associated with coronary heart disease (CHD) found among Blacks. Some findings from drinking studies are cited, indicating that middle-class Blacks would be at higher risk for CHD than Whites on the basis of alcohol intake.

397
Gomberg, E.L., "Special Populations." In E.L. Gomberg, et al., Eds., Alcohol, Science and Society Revisited. Ann Arbor, MI: University of Michigan Press, 1982, pp. 337-354.

The author contends that the definition of "special populations," i.e., those groups who have special treatment needs and who have been underserved, represents some real progress in recognizing the complexities of alcohol problems; although the differentiations made among alcoholics in Alcohol, Science and Society (published in 1945) are valid and important, the recognition of unique issues relating to alcoholics in different age, racial, and gender groups is useful and good. In this chapter, literature is cited in a discussion of the diagnostic features of alcoholism and social class differences used to classify special populations (young, elderly, women, and minority groups). A brief summative description of the state of knowledge about the drinking patterns and problems of each of these groups is presented...

398
Goodwin, D.W., "Alcoholism and Suicide: Association Factors." In E. Pattison, and E. Kaufman, Eds., Encyclopedic Handbook of Alcoholism. New York, NY: Gardner Press, 1982, pp. 665-662.

The author contends that an association between alcoholism and suicide can be studied by either examining the drinking habits of suicide victims and suicide attempters, or by determining how many alcoholics die by suicide or attempt suicide. In this chapter, findings from both kinds of studies are reviewed, and tentative explanations are provided for race, age, and sex differences in alcoholic suicides...

399
Inciardi, J.A., Pottiger, A.E., Faupel, C.E., "Black Women, Heroin and Crime: Some Empirical Notes," Journal of Drug Issues, 12(3): 241-250, 1982.

Data are presented from a study of self-reported drug use and criminal involvement of 63 black female heroin users in Miami, Florida. These data indicate a wide variety of drug use and criminal involvement. It was found that: (1) the first substance typically used was alcohol at a median age of 14.6 years, followed by marijuana (15.5 years), barbiturates (17.3 years), heroin (18.3 years), cocaine (19.3 years), and illegal methadone (20.9 years); (2) criminal involvement typically began significantly prior to expensive durg use, which raise serious questions concerning the causal relationship between drugs and crime; and (3) only a small percentage of these women relied heavily on a single type of criminal activity for income as defined by a particular activity constituting over 50 percent of their total offenses.

400
Kalow, W., "Ethnic Differences in Drug Metabolism," Clinical Pharmacokinetics, 7(5): 373-400, 1982.

The literature concerning ethnic differences in drug metabolism is reviewed... Many studies with probe drugs comparing different populations have given results that are equivocal in terms of the nature/nurture interplay. However, a set of data with antipyrine has pointed to environmental factors as the principal determinant of differences in metabolizing capacity, while data with debrisoquine indicate monogenically controlled variation of one facet of the cytochrome P-450 system. In several instances, statistically significant differences between population means have been established by testing small numbers of subjects, numbers insufficient to establish distribution patterns that would allow recognition of genetic polymorphism...

401
King, L.M., "Alcoholism: Studies Regarding Black Americans 1977-1980." In _Alcohol and Health Monograph No. 4: Special Population Issues_. Washington, D.C.: U.S. Government Printing Office, 1982, pp. 385-407.

The growth in knowledge and action made in alcoholism studies among black Americans since the _Third Special Report on Alcohol and Health_ (U.S. Department of Health, Education, and Welfare, 1978) are examined... This review is organized under the following five major topics: (1) theoretical preamble, which includes key findings from questions raised by prior research, operational definitions of concepts, and a working model for analysis of the published literature; (2) research issues, which focus primarily on analysis of the published literature in the areas of diagnosis, epidemiology, drinking characteristics, etiology, and related issues; (3) response to the problem, which explores social actions in the area, including treatment, prevention, and professional concerns; (4) methodological issues; and (5) implications and conclusions, which address present concerns and directions for future action. It is concluded that, since the last report to the U.S. Congress, the problems and consequences of black alcoholism have become more serious and very little is being done to address them.

402
Luepnitz, R.R., Randolph, D.L., Gutsch, K.U., "Race and Socioeconomic Status as Confounding Variables in the Accurate Diagnosis of Alcoholism," _Journal of Clinical Psychology_, 38(3): 665-669, 1982.

Results are presented from a study designed to determine if race and socioeconomic status of patients are confounding variables in the accurate diagnosis of alcoholism by psychology students... Results indicate that race and socioeconomic status had differential effects on the diagnosis of alcoholism, with a significant interaction between the two. It was found that lower socioeconomic status individuals, whether black or white, were diagnosed correctly for alcoholism more often than were upper socioeconomic status individuals. Diagnostic and treatment implications of these findings are discussed.

403
McAdoo, H.P., "Demographic Trends for People of Color," Social Work, 27(1): 15-23, 1982.

Statistical data on population trends, income, employment, education, and physical and mental health for people of color are presented. It is reported that: (1) diagnoses of schizophrenia and alcohol-related problems were the most prevalent for inpatients in all groups except majority (white) females; and (2) birth defects among minorities, the second most frequent cause of death, are related to pollution in the parents' workplace, poor nutrition, and the consumption of drugs and alcohol during pregnancy. These data are discussed in relation to the changing needs of individuals and families that must be addressed by those who design, implement, and evaluate programs for people of color.

404
Nurco, D.N., Cisin, I., and Balter, M.B. "Trends in the Age of Onset of Narcotic Addiction," Chemical Dependencies, 4(3): 221-228, 1982.

Results are presented from a study designed to investigate a community-wide population of narcotic users in Baltimore, Maryland. Data were obtained from a police roster of male narcotic abusers first known to the Baltimore City Police Department between the years 1952 and 1971. A total of 252 subjects were interviewed, and were classified into five cohorts based on the year first regular drug use began, i.e., 1937 through 1949, 1950 through 1954, 1955 through 1959, 1960 through 1964, and 1965 through 1971... It seems that the group who became addicted to narcotic drugs at an early age are a unique product of the ready availability of narcotic drugs, a reduction in countervailing forces, and an increase in personal susceptibility.

405
Penk, W.E., et al., "MMPI Differences of Black and White Male Polydrug Abusers Seeking Treatment," Journal of Consulting and Clinical Psychology, 50(3): 463-465, 1982.

Minnesota Multiphasic Personality Inventory (MMPI) profiles of Black and White male polydrug abusers seeking treatment were compared. The Black males (N=159) reported significantly less psychopathology than the White males (n=494). Black polydrug abusers scored lower on the Psychopathic Deviate subscale;

and, when controlled for age, education, socioeconomic status, and intelligence, they scored lower on Depression, Hysteria, Psychasthenia, and higher on scale L (a validity scale). The findings do not support the notion of ethnic bias in the MMPI. Rather, the results underscore the need for identifying moderator variables that differentially interact to produce (in comparison to Whites) lower Black profiles among substance abusers but higher Black profiles among psychiatric patients...

406
Pittman, D.J., "Primary Prevention of Alcoholism and Alcoholism Related Damage: New Directions." In E.J. Tongue, Ed., _28th International Institute on the Prevention and Treatment of Alcoholism_. Lausanne, Switzerland: International Council on Alcohol and Addictions, 1982, pp. 222-234.

It is contended that primary prevention of alcoholism and alcohol abuse programs will be most effective in culturally pluralistic societies (e.g., United States, Canada, and Western Europe) if emphasis is placed on two primary prevention models: the educational model and the social structural model. These two models are described, noting their effectiveness in altering the fundamental drinking patterns of high risk and cultural groups.

407
Ralston, L., _Alcohol in a Carribbean Perspective: A Case Study of the Role of Beverage Alcohol in Nevis, West Indies_. San Francisco, CA: Alcohol Research Group, 1982.

An original ethnographic study incorporating historical and ethnographic analysis.

408
Small, J., "Minority Volunteers Focus of Task Force," _Alcohol Health and Research World_, 6(3): 57-58, 1982.

Efforts by the Black Task Force of the North Carolina Council on Alcoholism (NCCA) to recruit Black volunteers to the alcoholism field are described.

409
United States. Alcohol, Drug Abuse, and Mental Health Administration, National Institute on Alcohol Aubse and Alcoholism. Alcohol and Health Monograph No. 4: Special Population Issues, Rockville, MD, 1982, 446p.

Research papers are presented on the unique problems of special population groups whose need for alcoholism and alcohol abuse programs has been underserved. It is demonstrated that a base of scientific knowledge exists on prevalence, incidence, and nature of alcohol-related problems of special population groups defined by sex, age, race, and ethnicity.

410
Watson, D.W., and Sobell, M.B., "Social Influences on Alcohol Consumption by Black and White Males," Addictive Behaviors, 7(1): 87-97, 1982.

The effects of a heavy drinking model (experimental accomplice) on alcohol consumption in a co-action (simultaneous drinking) condition were investigated among Black and White males, 18 to 30 years old. Thirty-two Black and 32 White Male normal drinkers participated in a beer tase test either simulatneously (co-action condition) with a heavy drinking Black or White experimental accomplice or while the accomplice completed an art rating task (control observer condition)... Subjects in the co-action condition drank significantly more beer than subjects in the control observer condition, regardless of their race or the race of their accomplice... The mechanism underlying the robust co-action facilitation effect on drinking, now demonstrated in several studies and extended to Black males in the present study, remains unexplained...

411
Westermeyer, J., "Alcoholism and Psychiatry: A Cross-Cultural Perspective." In J. Solomon, Ed., Alcoholism and Clinical Psychiatry. New York: NY: Plenum Medical Book, 1982, pp. 35-47.

A cross-cultural perspective of alcoholism and psychiatry is presented. The following topics are discussed: (1) what culture is; (2) contributions of cultural studies to theories about alcoholism; (3) effects of alcoholism on ethnicity; (4)

the role of ethnicity in treatment; and (5) the relationship between culture and primary prevention.

412
Westermeyer, J., "Alcoholism and Services for Ethnic Populations." In E. Pattison and E. Kaufman, Eds., *Encyclopedic Handbook of Alcoholism*. New York: NY: Gardner Press, 1982, pp. 709-717.

The author describes some of the demographic and clinical variations found among various ethnic groups, and discusses the factors that influence their access to treatment for alcoholism. Treatment methods used with ethnic groups are also discussed, including treatment outcome. It is concluded that in the treatment of ethnic groups: (1) class factors may masquerade as ethnic factors; (2) ethnicity may influence the kind of alcohol-related problems that come to treatment; (3) ethnic bias is most manifest in regards to access to treatment programs, i.e., economically disadvantaged minorities are admitted to treatment less often than epidemiologic findings would warrant, but once in treatment, however, they generally have full availability of services, they persist in treatment, and their outcome is comparable to that of others; and (4) ethnically oriented programs appear more effective in facilitating entry into treatment among socioeconomically disadvantaged groups.

413
Williams, M., "Blacks and Alcoholism: Issues in the 1980s," *Alcohol Health & Research World*, 6(4): 31-40, 1982.

Issues addressed at a workshop sponsored by the National Institute on Alcohol Abuse and Alcoholism (Jackson, Mississippi, 1981) concerning blacks and alcoholism are discussed.

## 1983

414
Anderson, R., and Maypole, D.E., "Minority Alcoholism Programs: Issues in Service Delivery Models," International Journal of the Addictions, 18(7): 987-1001, 1983.

One metropolitan community program established for the treatment of Black alcoholics is described. The effort is analyzed from direct service and administrative perspectives. This program failed, and an alternative model was developed. The two programs are compared, and an integrated model for minority community alcoholism services is proposed.

415
Austin, D.J., "Blues in a Bottle," Essence, 14(4): 88, 90, 122, 124, 131, 1983.

The story of a black woman who triumphed over alcoholism.

416
Bell, P., and Evans, J., "Counseling the Black Alcoholic Client." See Watts and Wright, 1983, pp. 100-121 and Bell, P., and Evans, J., 1981.

417
Beverly, C.C., "Psychosocial Research and its Application to Alcohol and Drug Addiction Programs." See Watts and Wright, 1983, pp. 184-197 and Beverly, C.C., 1981.

418
Bosron, W.F., Magnes, L.J., Li, T.K., "Human Liver Alcohol Dehydrogenase: ADH Indianpolis Results From Genetic Polymorphism at the ADH 2 gene locus," Biochemical Genetics, 21(7/8): 735-744, 1983.

The identification of subunits making up newly discovered molecular forms of human liver alcohol dehydrogenase, collectively designated ADH subscript Indianapolis (ADH subscript Ind), is reported. Human liver specimens were obtained at autopsy from 135 healthy persons who had suddenly died... It is concluded that ADH subscript Ind results from polymorphism at the ADH subscript 2 locus, with the variant ADH superscript IND subscript 2 allele coding for the beta subscript Ind subunit. The frequency of ADH superscript Ind subscript 2 was 0.16 in black Americans; this allele was not observed in any of the 63 livers from white Americans. The frequency of the ADH superscript 1 subscript 3 and ADH superscript 2 subscript 3 alleles also differed in these two populations.

419
Caldwell, F.J., "Alcoholics Anonymous as a Viable Treatment Resource for Black Alcoholics." See Watts and Wright, 1983, pp. 85-99 and Caldwell, F.J., 1981.

420
Charlotte Drug Education Center, _Overview of Key Findings_. Charlotte, N.C.: 1983. (No authors listed).

Statistical data on drug and alcohol use among junior and senior high school students in Mecklenburg County, North Carolina are provided. These data indicate that: (1) as of 1983, the most widely used drug was alcohol; (2) in terms of daily usage, cigarettes are the most widely used followed by mairjuana, chewing tobacco, alcohol, amphetamines, and inhalants; (3) more than 33 percent of these students, whose population at risk is about 12, 766, are current users of alcohol...

421
Dawkins, M.P., "Critical Issues in Alcoholism Research on Blacks." In Proceedings: _First Annual Wisconsin AODA Research Conference: "Critical Issues in Alcoholism Research and Treatment._ Milwaukee, WI: University of Wisconsin, 8 April 1983.

Some of the critical issues in assessing alcohol research needs related to the study of alcohol problems among Black Americans are highlighted. It is contended that research should have theoretical significance to contribute to understanding of the causes of alcohol abuse and alcoholism among Blacks, and it should have practical significance to guide practitioners who must directly confront alcohol problems at the community level. A review is presented on the availability of studies on alcohol and Blacks in terms of the extent to which research has fulfilled this dual function.

422
Dawkins, M.P., "Policy Issues." See Watts and Wright, 1983, pp. 206-220.

This chapter explored several questions based on a nonrandom sample of alcoholism specialists in community-based programs. Questions included one on whether black alcoholics have sufficient access to the treatment system, another on where blacks turn for help with their alcohol problems, another on what ways can the black community be used in the effective prevention and treatment of alcohol problems, another on whether blacks can counsel black alcoholics more effectively than whites, and another on whether traditional white agencies, organizations and programs have been effective in treating black alcohol problems. Also examined here are the policy implications of alcohol assessibility, studied through a description of the distribution of liquor licenses in an urban setting.

423
Dawkins, R.L., and Dawkins, M.P., "Alcohol Use and Delinquency Among Black, White and Hispanic Adolescent Offenders," Adolescence, 18(72): 799-809, 1983.

Results are presented from a study designed to examine the relationship between drinking and criminal behavior among Black, White, and Hispanic adolescent criminal offenders. Data were collected by means of questionnaires administered to 342 residents of a public juvenile facility in the summer of 1979. Using simple data correlation, it was found that drinking is strongly associated with minor juvenile offenses among each subgroup; however, the correlation between drinking and serious offenses is strong only for Blacks and Whites. Multiple regression analysis revealed that, relative to other background and behavioral factors, drinking is the strongest single predictor of criminal offenses among Blacks, with less importance for Whites, and little importance for Hispanics. Implications of these findings for prevention are discussed.

424
Dawkins, M.P., and Harper, F.D., "Alcoholism among Women: A Comparison of Black and White Problem Drinkers," International Journal of the Addictions, 18(3): 333-349, 1983.

Factors associated with female problem drinkers in selected studies are reviewed. Specifically, results are presented from a study designed to examine the extent to which race (singularly and in combination with other factors) affects alcohol-related experiences of female problem drinkers... Findings indicate some similarities and important differences between Black and White women in terms of selected factors. When social background factors (e.g., income, education, community size) are held constant, race continues to be a significant predictor of selected drinking behavior factors. These differences tended to support previous research which indicates that Black women are younger at onset of alcoholism, but less likely than White women to drink heavily because of psychological reasons such as loneliness, lack of hope, and personal misfortune... Implications for improving alcoholism prevention and treatment services for women are discussed.

425
DeRisi, W., and Vega, W.A., "Impact of Deinstitutionalization on California's State Hospital Population," Hospital and Community Psychiatry, 34(2): 140-145, 1983.

Results are presented from two surveys (1980 and 1982) designed to assess the demographic characteristics, psychiatric diagnosis, health status, and behavioral traits of California State hospital patients. The most significant variation found between ethnic groups was for substance (including alcohol) use: 9.5 percent of Hispanics were found in this diagnostic category, but only 2.5 percent of blacks and 2.2 percent whites.

426
Evans, J., See Bell, P., and Evans, J., 1983, and Bell, P., and Evans, J., 1981.

427
Galizio, M., and Stein, F.S., "Sensation Seeking and Drug Choice," International Journal of the Addictions, 18(8): 1039-1048, 1983.

Findings from studies of the association between sensation seeking and drug use are summarized, indicating that subjects' sensation seeking scores (SSS) were positively related to their drug and alcohol use. Specifically, results are presented from a study designed to reexamine this relationship, using a detailed analysis of SSS of four groups of chronic drug abusers: comparable groups of Blacks and

Whites whose major drug problem was either heroin (including other opiates, or depressants) or was multiple drug (including alcohol) use... It was found that polydrug users scored higher in sensation seeking than depressant users, and that this effect was independent of demographic differences between groups...

428
Gary, L.E., "The Impact of Alcohol and Drug Abuse on Homicidal Violence." See Watts and Wright, 1983, pp. 136-151.

This chapter describes and assesses the literature on the role of substance abuse in homocide among black people (with a focus on black men, but with applicability to black women). Some emphasis is placed on identifying factors that account for the problem of substance abuse and homicide in black communities, and limitations of research conducted in this area.

429
Goldstein, G., Tarter, R.E., Shelly, C., Alterman, A.I., & Petrarulo, E., "Withdrawal Seizures in Black and White Alcoholic Patients: Intellectual and Neuropsychological Sequelae," Drug and Alcohol Dependence, 12(4): 349-354, 1983.

The effect of withdrawal seizures on neuropsychological and intellectual capacity was studied in black and white alcoholics. Subjects were 42 male inpatient alcoholics, of whom 22 were white and 20 black. Half of the subjects in each group had had at least one withdrawal seizure, while the other half had verified seizure-free histories. The four groups were equated for age and education; none had a history of neurological disorder. The subjects were administered a modified vesion of the Halstead-Reitan neuropsychological test battery, including the full Wechsler Adult Intelligence Scale (WAIS). Race was significant in half of the subtests... It is concluded that blacks who suffer from withdrawal seizures develop more severe neuropsychological sequelae than whites. Some possible explanations cited include that blacks have a greater vulnerability to alcohol's effects and that economic privation may result in consumption of lower grade beverages with toxic congeners.

430
Harper, F.D., "Alcohol Use and Alcoholism Among Black Americans: A Review." See Watts and Wright, 1983, pp. 19-36.

This chapter presented a brief review of the quantity and quality of literature on alcohol use and alcoholiism among black Americans, with an outline, summary and analysis of research findings and theories.

431
Harper, F.D., "Alcoholism Treatment and Black Americans: A Review and Analysis." See Watts and Wright, 1983, pp. 71-84, and Harper, F.D., 1979.

This chapter defined, described and examined alcoholism treatment and its implications for black Americans. It discussed cultural and personality factors related to treatment, reviewed literature on black alcoholism treatment, presented issues and concerns from the field, and a summary and analysis of the literature and issues presented.

432
Harper, F., and Dawkins, M., "Alcoholism Among Women: A Comparison of Black and White Problem Drinkers," _International Journal of the Addictions_, 183:333-349, 1983.

Results are presented from a study examining the extent to which race affects alcohol-related experiences of female problem drinkers. Findings suggest that race is a significant predictor of differential drinking behavior. Implications for improving alcoholism prevention and treatment services for women are discussed.

433
Henderson, P.S., See Winbush, R.A. and Henderson, P.S., 1983, and Winbush, R.A., and Henderson, P.S., 1981.

434
Herd, D.A., _Migration, Cultural Transformation and the Rise of Black Cirrhosis_. Medical Research Institute of San Francisco, Alcohol Research Group, Berkeley, CA, June, 1983, 22p.

The newness of the Black cirrhosis epidemic and the discrepancy between reported consumption patterns and mortality rates indicate that current cirrhosis rates probably result from complex changes in Black drinking patterns over time... Epidemiological data on cirrhosis, dating from the 1930s through the mid-1970s, are presented, demonstrating the importance of both strong "cohort effects" and regional differentiation in the current distribution of cirrhosis mortality. These findings are interpreted from a socio-historical perspective which argues that there has been a profound shift in the place of alcohol in Black culture that, in conjunction with massive waves of migration and urbanization, underlies the present epidemic of non-White cirrhosis mortality.

435
Herd, D.A., "Prohibition, Racism, and Class Politics in the Post-Reconstruction South," Journal of Drug Issues, 13(1): 77-94, 1983.

The virulent racism associated with the southern prohibition movement in the late 19th and early 20th century is practically invisible in literature on the history of alcohol reform movements. This paper explores the rise of racist ideology in the anti-liquor movement and its particular relationship to political factionalism and class conflict in the Post-Reconstruction South. The analysis suggests that the strong role of the anti-liquor movements in campaigns for black disfranchisement and Jim Crow legislation was tied into broader struggles for economic control and political power in an era of socio-economic crisis. In the wake of a prolonged period of radical reform and labor protests, the prohibition movement played an increasingly important role in the political and economic repression of both blacks and lower class whites.

436
Holliday, B.G., "Making the Best of a Bad Situation: Pragmatic Planning Strategies for Black Alcohol Prevention Efforts in the 1980s." See Watts and Wright, 1983, pp. 152-161, and Holliday, B.G., 1981.

437
Humphrey, J.A., Stephens, V., Allen, D.F., "Race, Sex, Marihuana Use and Alcohol Intoxication in College Students," Journal of Studies on Alcohol, 44(4): 733-738, 1983.

Undergraduate college students from two state supported universities in the southeastern United States were surveyed to determine the effect of race and sex on the frequency of alcohol intoxication and marijuana use during a typical month. Alcohol intoxication was found to be more frequency in men than in women, in Whites than in Blacks, and in White women than in Black women. The difference between White and Black men regarding alcohol intoxication was negligible. Findings indicate that intoxicated Whites also tend to smoke marijuana more than intoxicated Blacks; intoxicated women were slightly more likely to use marijuana than intoxicated men. White men were the most common users of both alcohol and marijuana, followed, in descending order, by Black women, White women, and Black men. Although Black women's use of both drugs was generally below average, if they used one intoxicant, they were pront to use both...

438
Isralowitz, R., and Singer, M., Eds., Adolescent Substance Abuse: A Guide to Prevention and Treatment. New York: NY: Haworth Press, 1983.

The problem of adolescent substance (including alcohol) abuse and addiction is examined as a cultural phenomenon, rooted in childhood. Special consideration is given to this problem as it relates to Black and Hispanic youth, and the developmental disabled. Suggestions for the development of adolescent substance abuse services for youth offered, and implications for practice in these services are also examined.

439
Kellam, S.G., Stevenson, D.L., Rubin, B.R., "How Specific are the Early Predictors of Teenage Drug Use?," National Institute on Drug Abuse Research Monograph 43, April 1983, pp. 329-334.

Results are presented from a followup study designed to examine the specificity of certain early predictors of teenage alcohol and drug use. All of these predictors (shyness, aggressiveness, underachievement, and readiness for school and intelligence quotient) were behavioral responses rated by first grade teachers, or scored on test of specific classroom tasks demands set for children by teachers... Results indicate that: (1) aggressiveness in first grade males predicts heavy drug, alcohol, and cigarette use as well as delinquency, but does not predict these outcomes for females; (2) shyness predicts an inhibition of both substance use and delinquency, but also predicts higher anxiety levels in adolescents; (3) higher first grade scorers use more drugs and alcohol, and at an earlier age, while low scorers report more symptoms of distress as teenagers. Implications of these findings for prevention of teenage alcohol and drug use are discussed.

440
Kilty, K.M., "Styles of Drinking and Types of Drinkers," Journal of Studies on Alcohol, 44(5): 797-816, 1983.

It is contended that a general taxonomy of drinking behavior could be useful in explicating what alcoholism and alcohol misuse are, what varieties they have, and how they are different from and similar to normal kinds of drinking. An attempt is made to develop such a general typology, emphasizing normal drinking, by focusing on the interrelationships among drinking situations or settings (drinking styles) and on the interrelationships or clustering of respondents (types of drinkers). Data were collected on 197 subjects, "normal" drinkers ranging in age from 21 to 50 years, in a medium-sized city in northeastern Pennsylvania, using an inventory of drinking behavior... Four drinking styles and six types of drinkers were differentiated. The four drinking styles reflected the use of alcohol in convivial drinking, as a beverage (or thirst quencher), as an expression of lifestyle, and to change one's mood. The six types of drinkers were those who use alcohol to alter their moods, light drinkers who dislike the taste of alcohol, light drinkers who use alcohol as an occasional thirst quencher, new middle-class men beer drinkers, new sophisticated middle-class women drinkers, and moderate social drinkers. In illustrating the multifaceted nature of drinking in the United States, these results were inconsistent with traditional assertions that each culture has one predominant drinking style.

441
King, L.M., "Alcoholism: Studies Regarding Black Americans - 1977-1980." See Watts and Wright, 1983, pp. 37-63, and King., L.M., 1982.

This research review examined mainly the literature on black alcoholism published between 1977 and 1980. Only articles published in 1977 or later were included (with the exception of Harper, (1976)). The purpose of this review was that of examining implications of this literature for the quality of life of black Americans.

442
Klatsky, A.L., Siegelaub, A.B., Landy, C., Friedman, G.D., "Racial Patterns of Alcoholic Beverage Use," Alcoholism Clinical and Experimental Research, 7(4): 372-377, 1983.

Data were collected from ambulatory persons who had multiphasic health examinations at the Kaiser-Permanente Medical Center in Oakland, California from January 1978 through March 1980. The proportions reporting drinking among self-classified racial groups were: White, 89 percent; Latin, 84 percent; Japanese, 81.9 percent; Black, 79.8 percent; Chinese, 68.1 percent; and Filipino, 63.9 percent. Reported use of three or more drinks daily was found to be similar in Whites, Latins, and Blacks, but was much lower in the Asian groups. Men of all races reported more drinking than women. A larger proportion of drinkers in all race and sex subgroups reported using small amounts of alcohol, with most nondrinkers reporting lifelong abstinence... A comparison of these data with those collected 15 years earlier reveal a substantial decline in reported proportions of abstainers and heavier drinkers, as well as an apparent narrowing of race and sex differences.

443
Lee, L.J., "Reducing Black Adolescents' Drug Use: Family Revisited," In R. Isralowitz and M. Singer, Eds., Adolescent Substance Abuse: A Guide to Prevention and Treatment. New York, NY: Haworth Press, 1983, pp. 57-69.

Primary prevention and reduction of drug and alcohol abuse by Black adolescents are discussed, focusing on a review of research findings intimately related to adolescent drug and alcohol use and Black family issues... It is contended that the family is an underutilized and minimally acknowledged resource in drug and alcohol abuse prevention efforts. It is argued, therefore, that a national family policy is needed in support for all American families; now and in the future, the American family represents the best primary prevention program available.

444
Lewis, C., "Individual Treatment is Key, Counselor Says," _National Leader_, 6 Oct., 1983, p. 22.

Ronnie Colcher, a therapist at the Vally Forge Medical Center and Hospital in Norristown, Pennsylvania, argues that, while there are some basic similarities in all people, it is the differences that make them individuals, and that alcoholism treatment for Blacks must be individually designed.

445
Lewis, C.E., Cloninger, C.R., Pais, J., "Alcoholism, Antisocial Personality and Drug Use in a Criminal Population," _Alcohol and Alcoholism_, 18(1): 53-60, 1983.

In 1974, a sample of the criminal population (N=340) on probation and parole in Missouri was interviewd as a pilot project for a comprehensive family study designed to investigate the interaction of alcoholism, antisocial personality, and drug use. Since white and black men comprised 91 percent of this sample, only data on these men are provided. It was found that: (1) men with antisocial personality had higher rates of alcoholism and illicit drug use than men without; and (2) both antisocial symptomatology and degree of illicit drug use added independently to the predictability of alcoholism. The investigative importance of the relationship between these three disorders is discussed.

446
Lowman, C., Harford, T.C., Kaelber, C.T., "Alcohol Use Among Black Senior High School Students," _Alcohol Health and Research World_ 7(3): 37-46, 1983.

Findings from previous research studies on alcohol use among Black and White high school students are briefly reviewed. Specifically, findings are summarized from a 1978 survey conducted by the Research Triangle Institute (RTI) on stylistic differences in the use of alcohol among Black and White senior high school students. Some background information on alcohol problems among Black adults is presented, providing a matrix within which these findings on Black senior high school students may be evaluated.

447
Mathews, R.L., "Personality Characteristics of Black and White Male Alcoholic Veterans," Dissertation. Ann Arbor, MI: University Microfilms International, 1983.

A study was conducted to examine the test results of Black and White male alcoholic veterans for information on personality factors and profile types which may be related to treatment issues. Personality test data and demographic characteristics of 459 alcoholics (382 Whites and 77 Blacks) and 53 psychiatric patients (controls) from the Veterans Administration Hospital in Gulfport, Mississippi were examined... It was found that alcoholics differed from controls in terms of mean personality results; controls were more likely to be severely disturbed and to exhibit symptoms of labile and/or inappropriate affect, plus possible hallucinations or other thought disturbances. Alcoholics as a whole did not demonstrate lower self-esteem on the self-acceptance scale of the CPI, but did exhibit lower socialization than the normative sample on the CPI. Black alcoholics did not show lower self-esteem than Whites on the Self-acceptance scale of the CPI. Significant differences between Black and White alcoholics were found, however, on some of the CPI scales measuring aspects of socialization, providing evidence for differences in the interpersonal functioning of members of these two groups.

448
Maypole, D.E., and Anderson, R., "Alcoholism Programs Serving Minorities: Administrative Structures and Problems," National Council on Alcoholism Forum. Houston, TX: 14-17 April, 1983, 18 p.

Findings from previous studies of alcoholism services provided to minorities are summarized. Specifically, preliminary findings are reported from a research project designed to study the delivery of services to minorities in an upper midwestern State... A summary description for each of the seven agencies studied is provided, and problem areas found within these agencies are described. Minority administrators' relationship problems are enumerated, and community program administrators' recommendations are presented, including the views of State agency administrators. Implications of these findings are discussed.

449
McClain, J.W., "Black Alcohol-Involved Criminal Offender and the Criminal Justice System: New Solutions for an Old Problem." Dissertation. Ann Arbor, MI: University Microfilms International, 1983.

A study was conducted to identify differences between Black alcohol-involved criminal offenders who successfully completed and those who dropped out of a court clinic alcohol treatment program, to identify those key independent variables that appear to either frustrate or enhance the desired outcome of a criminal justice system policy to motivate Blacks to remain in treatment. These independent variables were subsumed under the broad categories of predisposing factors (age, level of education, prior felonies, and social and/or family relations) and policy levers (probation status, charges dropped, and continuance prior to arraignment). Only the predisposing factors were found to be significantly related to treatment outcome... It is recommended that cluster-specific treatment models be developed to improve success in treatment.

450
Miranda, V.L., "Black Alcohol Prevention - Past, Present, Future." See Watts and Wright, 1983, pp. 162-173, and Miranda, V.L., 1981.

451
Morgan, P. "Alcohol, Disinhibition and Domination: A Conceptual Analysis," In R. Room, and G. Collins, Eds., Alcohol and Disinhibition: ... Washington, D.C.: U.S. Government Print. Off., 1983, pp. 405-436.

In any society where there is an unequal distribution of resources and power among its members, systems of domination exist which act symbolically or substantively to reinforce that domination. It is contended that, much as religion was used in the sixteenth and seventeenth centuries to foster and legitimate class struggles over political and economic power, the effects and characteristics associated with alcoholic beverages ae used both symbolically and instrumentally to promote systems of subordination and domination. The nature of belief systems which link alcohol and disinhibition to relationships of domination are examined. This link is analyzed through examples of their institutional manifestations...

452
National Leader, "Alcoholism: The Silent Sickness," 6 Oct. 1983, p. 16, (No Author Listed).

Reference is made to an article by J. Reichwein, entitled "Alcoholism: A Staggering Black Problem" (The National Leader, 6 October 1983). Alcohol abuse and alcoholism among Blacks is described as an especially tragic problem because very little reliable information is available about it, even though it is regarded as the number one health problem of Black Americans.

453
Petitti, D.B., and Siegelaub, A.S., "Interrelationships of Heavy Use of Coffee, Alcohol and Cigarettes in Individuals," Meeting of the American Public Health Association, Dallas, TX: 13-16 November 1983, 11 p.

Statistical data are presented from a survey of the use of coffee, alcohol, and cigarettes (alone and in combination) among 66,868 White and Black males and females taking multiphasic health check-ups at Northern California Kaiser-Permanente Facilities in Oakland and San Francisco... These data indicate that: (1) similar percentages of White females are heavy users of cigarettes, alcohol, and coffee at each group; (2) heavy use of these three substances follows a similar pattern, rising from the age of 25, reaching a peak at 45 to 49 years-of-age, and then declining; and (3) this pattern of use which increases with age to the late 30s, mid-40s, and declining thereafter is observed with a number of addictive drugs, including heroin. It was found that, when two of these substance use behaviors were used to predict the third behavior, they were significantly related to the third behavior, independent of age, sex, and race. Implications of these findings are briefly discussed.

454
Reichwein, J., "Alcoholism: A Staggering Black Problem," National Leader, 6 October 1983, pp. 1, 8-9, 20-22.

The National Black Alcoholism Council (NBAC) contends that alcoholism is the number one social problem in Black America, and that alcohol has been so ingrained in Black American culture that its impact and role have been overlooked. Statistical data on alcoholism and alcohol abuse among Blacks are provided in a discussion of what alcoholism is, its symptoms, the damages it causes, what is being done about it, and what the prospects are for a cure and recovery by the problem drinker. The need for treatment of minorities by counselors who are culturally aware is also discussed, including the perspective of the Black middle class that alcoholism is a problem affecting the poor...

455
Roberts, T.W., "Patterns of Esophageal Carcinoma in a Black Community," Urban Health, 12(11): 33-37, 1983.

Heavy alcohol consumption has long been considered an etiologic factor in the development of esophageal cancer. However, in parts of North China (where the prevalence of esophageal cancer is particularly high), India, and Iran, no relationship between alcohol and esophageal cancer has been found. It has been suggested that, it is perhaps not the alcohol but contaminants which are more significant... It is general knowledge that inexpensive wines are popular intoxicants in the inner-city and ghetto community. As such, this opens a completely new potential source of carcinogens.

456
Senay, E.C., "Special Populations," In E.C. Senay, Ed., Substance Abuse Disorders in Clinical Practice. Boston, MA: John Wright, 1983, pp. 175-189.

The term "special populations" has been coined to indicate that substance (including alcohol) abusers, in a given group, have unique characteristics that, for best results, must be taken into account in diagnosis and treatment...

457
Smith-Peterson, C. "Substance Abuse Treatment and Cultural Diversity," In G. Bennett, et al., Eds., Substance Abuse: Pharmacologic, Developmental, and Clinical Perspectives. New York, NY: John Wiley & Sons, 1983, pp. 370-382.

This chapter has been organized to address the frequent omission of cultural variables in the consideration of treatment approaches and prevention strategies. It is based on the belief that past failures to acknowledge important cultural and ethnic differences in substance abuse problems and patterns in the United States have perpetuated problems in stereotyping, misunderstanding, and program effectiveness.

Accordingly, the patterms and specific characteristics of substance abuse and related problems are considered in ethnic populations, including Black Americans, Native Americans, and Hispanics. While the focus is on alcohol use patterns within a cultural context, anthropologic and sociologic perspectives are considered, with many of these concepts applying to the cultural context of other types of substance use and abuse...

458
United States. National Institute on Alcohol Abuse and Alcoholism. _A Growing Concern: How to Provide Services for Children from Alcoholic Families_. Rockville, Md., 1983. DHHS Publ. No. (ADM) 83-1257. See Chapter IV "The Role of Cultural Issues in Service Delivery to Children of Alcoholic Families" (pp. 26-39).

This chapter examines the role of cultural issues in service delivery to children of alcoholic families, focusing on what function alcohol serves in cultural groups, how cultural groups regard alcoholism, and what role do the members of the family and cultural community play in the treatment or prevention of alcoholism.

459
United States. National Institute on Alcohol Abuse and Alcoholism, "Major Research Models," See Watts and Wright, 1983, pp. 129-135.

Approaches to the prevention of alcohol-related problems have been derived from three seminal models, each of which is discussed here: (1) the public health model, (2) the distribution of consumption model, and (3) the sociocultural theoretical model.

460
United States. National Institute on Alcohol Abuse and Alcoholism. _National Drug and Alcoholism Treatment Utilization Survey, Comprehensive Report-1982_. Rockville, MD, 1983. 103 pp.

A general compendium of statistical information concerning the use of drug and alcohol treatment facilities. Includes data on the race or ethnicity of staff and clients in both drug and alcohol units and alcohol-only units. Also relates these data to sources of program funding.

461
van der Burgh, C., "Drinking Patterms in Multiethnic South African Society," Journal of Studies on Alcohol, 44(3): 446-459, 1983.

Alcohol consumption by the various ethnic groups (Whites, Blacks, Coloreds, and Indians) in South Africa is discussed. Results from studies conducted in 1975 through 1977 concerning alcohol consumption by these ethnic groups are presented as they relate to drinking status, types of alcoholic beverages consumed mostly, and drinking frequency... It is contended that drinking can be regarded as a social act imbedded in a context of values, attitudes, and conceptions of reality often varying from one cultural and population group to another; drinking patterns are significantly affected in this way as well as by social context in which alcohol consumption takes place.

462
Waite, B.J., and Ludwig, M.J., Growing Concern: How to Provide Services for Children from Alcoholic Families. U.S. Alcohol, Drug Abuse, and Mental Health Administration, Rockville, MD., 1983, 52 p.

To enlighten caregivers on how to identify, intervene with, treat, and prevent further problems of children of alcoholic parents, the National Institute on Alcohol Abuse and Alcoholism (NIAAA) has sponsored the development of resource materials on issues and service needs of this population. The purpose of this publication is to provide caregivers with such information. Problems and needs of children of alcoholics are outlined, and appropriate approaches for meeting these needs are described, including the role of caregivers. Organizational issues and the role of cultural issues in the provision of services to these children are discussed...

463
Walters, G.D., Jeffrey, T.B., Kruzich, D.J., Green, R.L., Haskin, J.J., "Racial Variations on the MacAndrew Alcoholism Scale of the MMPI," Journal of Consulting and Clinical Psychology, 51(6): 947-948, 1983.

The effect of race on the MacAndrew Alcoholism Scale (MAC) performance of alcoholic and nonalcoholic inpatients in an active duty military sample was investigated. Black and White alcoholics performed similarly on the MAC in terms of mean score and accuracy of identification by cutting scores. Black nonalcoholics scored significantly higher on the MAC than White nonalcoholics. It was discovered that the MAC discriminated successfully between White alcoholics and nonalcoholics, but not between Black alcoholics and Black nonalcoholics in an active duty military sample suggests caution in its use with Black patients in this setting.

464
Watts, T.D., and Wright, R., Eds., _Black Alcoholism: Toward A Comprehensive Understanding_, Springfield, IL: Charles C. Thomas, 1983, 252 p.

A comprehensive overview of alcoholism among Blacks is presented. Etiological perspectives of Black alcoholism are examined, including the nature and extent of this problem. Research on the treatment of Black alcoholics is reviewed, i.e., what appears to work and not to work, and the treatment of Black alcoholics in the environment in which they live and work. Difficult problems associated with the prevention of alcoholism among Blacks are described, and the relationship of alcohol abuse and alcoholism to the criminal justice system and to mental health is also examined in the context of prevention efforts. Alcohol policy, research, and practice implications are discussed. A resource listing of programs, organizations, and materials concerned with alcohol abuse among Blacks and other ethnic groups (Asian Americans, Hispanics, American Indians, Alaskan Natives, and Jewish Americans) is appended.

465
Wilson, P.W.F., et al., "HDL-Cholesterol in a Sample of Black Adults: The Framingham Minority Study," _Metabolism_, 32(4): 328-332, 1983.

Plasma lipids, general health status, and cigarette and alcohol consumption were studied in a group of 100 adult Black residents of Framingham, Massachusetts, and compared with those of White residents of Framingham.... Investigations of lipid levels and heart disease in Black populations should consider that Blacks among middle and upper socioeconomic subgroups may have lipoprotein profiles that differ from those reported in lower socioeconomic subgroups.

466
Winbush, R.A., and Henderson, P.S., "'We May as Well Try This': Some Reflections on Alcoholism Services Research in the African-American Community." See Watts and Wright, 1983, pp. 198-205, and Winbush, R.A., and Henderson, P.S., 1981.

467
Yu, M.C., Mack, T., Hanisch, R., Peters, R.L., Henderson, B.E., and Pike, M.C., "Hepatitis, Alcohol Consumption, Cigarette Smoking, and Hepatocellular Carcinoma in Los Angeles," Cancer Research, 42(12, Pt. 1): 6077-6079, 1983.

As part of a larger case-controlled study being conducted in Los Angeles County (California), 79 Black and White patients (50 males and 28 females, 70 years or younger at diagnosis) with primary hepatocellular carcinoma (PHC) were interviewed, along with 78 controls matched for age, sex, and race. Information was obtained on dietary and drinking habits, cigarette smoking habits, prior medical conditions, including a history of hepatitis, prior exposure to blood products, and occupational history. It was found that cigarette smoking and alcohol consumption were both significantly related to PHC, even after allowing for the effect of the other; individuals who drank 80 grams or more of ethanol per day had a relative risk of 4.2 compared to those who drank less than 10 grams per day. It was also found that among current smokers of more than one pack per day, heavy drinkers had a 7.8 fold risk of PHC compared to more moderate drinkers with similar smoking habits.

## 1984

468
Austin, G.A., and Prendergast, M.L., Eds., Drug Use and Abuse: A Guide to Research Findings. Santa Barbara, CA: ABC-Clio Information Services, 1984.

125 lengthy abstracts in Volume I: Adults. Digests and reproduce information, tables, findings, and comprehensive indexes. Abstracts are arranged by topics within six categories. Volume II: Adolescents bring together research findings unique to the teenage drug scene. 113 abstracts divided into four sections. Both volumes contain abstracts relating to drug use among ethnic minority adults and adolescents.

469
Battle, C., Coleman, S.A., Morris, V.E., and Womble, M.E., Eds., Resource Guide To Alcohol Abuse Prevention Materials for Black and Hispanic Populations: A Review of Current Literature and Audio-Visuals. Springfield, IL: A.H. Training and Development Systems, Prevention Resource Center, 1984, 66 pp.

470
Beaubrun, M.H., "Problem of Alcoholism in the Commonwealth Carribean," West Indian Medical Journal, 33(1): 1-2, 1984.

The problems alcoholism and alcohol-related health and social problems pose for the Commonwealth Caribbean, which includes the Bahamas, Bermuda, the U.S. Virgin Islands, Trinidad, Tobago, Barbados, and Jamaica are discussed. It is contended that alcohol is the chief drug undermining the health and productivity of the Commonwealth Caribbean.

471
Burke, A.W., "Cultural Aspects of Drinking Behaviour Among Migrant West Indians and Related Groups." In A.W. Burke, Ed., Alcohol Related Problems: Room for Manoeuvre. New York: N.Y.: John Wiley and Sons Ltd., 1984. pp. 197-205.

The effects of migration on black alcoholism is discussed with reference to West Indians. Previous studies have indicated a preference of the West Indian male for marijuana over alcohol.

A similar trend has developed in the British West Indians. It has been suggested that sociocultural factors are significant determinants in the response to alcohol abuse by blacks... Unlike black Americans, black West Indians do not use drugs other than marijuana and have little incidence of alcohol or drug-related suicide... These findings suggest that despite the probability that personality disorder and chronic alcoholism are similarly distributed among ethnic groups in North America, there is no similar evidence among West Indians in Britain. Mental hospital admissions among West Indians in Britain for alcoholism and affective disorders are 2 to 3 times greater than in the West Indies. In conclusion, it is suggested that the deprivation and discrimination experienced by West Indian immigrants may be having the effect of preventing manifest alcoholism...

472
Byram, O.W., and Fly, J.W., "Family Structure, Race and Adolescents' Alcohol Use: A Research Note," _American Journal of Drug and Alcohol Abuse_, 10(3): 467-478, 1984.

Family structure is related to adolescents' drinking behavior differently for Blacks than Whites. Black adolescents were more likely to be heavy alcohol users when both natural parents were present, but the opposite was true for the whites. Only when non-White adolscents were in families with both parents, and the father had at least a high school education, did they drink near the rate of White adolescents. There was support of social learning theory.

473
Caetano, R., "Ethnicity and Drinking in Northern California: A Comparison Among Whites, Blacks and Hispanics," _Alcohol and Alcoholism_, 19(1): 31-44, 1984.

This survey of 1,206 Blacks (468 males, 738 females), 2,327 Whites, (1,047 males, 1,280 females) and 634 Hispanics (279 males, 355 females) living in northern California studied their drinking patterns and alcohol-related problems. Results indicated that both Black and Hispanic females had higher rates of abstention than White females, and that the drinking patterns of males were similar across ethnic groups. Among Whites, the prevalence of alcohol-related problems decreased from the 18-29 to the 30-39 year old age group, a trend that was reversed for Blacks and Hispanics. Demographic correlates of both number of drinks consumed per month and number of alcohol-related problems differend among ethnic groups. Both Blacks and Hispanics had more liberal attitudes toward alcohol use than Whites.

474
Caetano, R., and Herd, D.A., "Black Drinking Practices in Northern California," American Journal of Drug and Alcohol Abuse, 10(4): 571-587, 1984.

The data for this research come from three independent community surveys conducted between 1979 and 1980 in the San Francisco Bay Area. All surveys followed the same sampling plan and only probability techniques were employed. Of a total of 4,150 adult respondents, 1,206 identified themselves as Blacks and are analyzed in this report. A total of 29% of the females and 16% of the males are abstainers. Frequent heavier drinkers comprise 22% of the males but only 6% of the females. Among males, heavier drinking and alcohol problems are highest among those in their thirties and, therefore, cannot be associated with a youthful lifestyle as it happens in the United States general population. Characteristics such as income, employment status, and education are not associated with drinking. Religion, however, is associated with drinking patterns, and Fundamentalists have significantly more abstainers and light drinkers than other religious groups. These findings are also discussed in the light of Black culture and minority status. It is suggested that drinking patterns among Blacks are influenced more by internal norms originated from common cultural and socio-political characteristics than from norms associated with class affiliations in the larger society.

475
Gary, L.E., and Berry, G.L., "Some Determinants of Attitudes Toward Substance Abuse in an Urban Ethnic-Community," Psychological Reports 54(2): 539-545, 1984.

Personal interview responses of a stratified random sample of 411 non-institutionalized black adults, 18 years of age and older, residing in a large northeastern U.S. city, showed marital status, age, sex, racial consciousness, community involvement and religious involvement as significantly related to attitudes toward substance abuse. Women, persons 65 years of age and older, and married respondents were less tolerant of substance use than males, persons less than 25 years of age, and those who were single. Educational status was not an important predictor of attitudes. Respondents who had a high level of racial consciousness and those involved in church and community activities were more likely to express intolerant attitudes toward substance abuse than those not so involved or aware. The authors discuss the significance of these findings and implications for substance abuse prevention programs.

476
Herd, D.A., _A Review of Drinking Patterns and Alcohol Problems Among U.S. Blacks_. San Francisco, CA: Alcohol Research Group, 1984.

Prepared for the U.S. Department of Health and Human Service Task Force on Black and Minority Health.

477
Herd, D.A., "The Paradox of Temperance: Blacks and the Alcohol Question in 19th Century America." Paper presented at the conference on _Social History of Alcohol: Drinking and Culture in Modern Society_. Alcohol Research Group, Berkeley, California, January 2-5, 1984.

The symbolic characterization of beverage alcohol and race came together in quite dramatic ways in the 19th century anti-alcohol movements. They gave rise to the dualistic image of "alcohol the enslaver" versus "alcohol the disinhibitor." The first summarized the addiction concept of man as a victim of a powerful temptor and master; the second focused on the power of alcohol to release the violent, uncivilized savage within. This paper looks at the ideological and social contexts which gave rise to these stereotypes. It also examines the instrumental functions associated with these images, taking Cohen's thesis that symbols act to influence "the distribution, maintenance and exercise of power." Additionally, it looks at how the stereotypes became associated with various types of social action, both from the dominant classes and from blacks themselves. It analyzes the way stereotypes functioned at different times as symbols of humanistic social change and as instruments of social domination.

478
Kail, B.L., and Lukoff, I.F., "The Black Female Addict's Career Options: A Typology and Theory," _American Journal of Drug and Alcohol Abuse_, 10(3): 39-52, 1984.

Female addicts are typically treated as one group with similar needs and experiences. This is particularly true for Black female addicts. This study of Black men and women entering an inner-city methadone maintenance treatment program attempts to delineate (1) how Black women differ from Black men in their heroin-using careers and (2) differences among Black women in their integration of drug use and lifestyle. Findings show men and women do develop different patterns of criminal activity, drug use, family ties, and labor force participation. Further analysis using multiple discriminant techniques indicates that Black female addicts are not one homogeneous group. Conclusions based on these findings suggest that role expectations may structure heroin use. Other social locators such as age may also delimit available career paths, lending further support to the theoretical framework employed here.

479
Leland, J., "Alcohol Use and Abuse in Ethnic Minority Women." In S.C. Wilsnack and L.J. Beckman, Eds., Alcohol Problems in Women: Antecedents, Consequences, and Intervention. New York, NY: The Guilford Press, 1984, pp. 66-96.

The purpose of this chapter is to use the available information, scanty as it is, to describe and analyze differences and similarities among women of the principal American Ethnic groups: Whites, Blacks, Hispanics and, to the degree that the data permit, Asians and Indians... The author concludes that the consequences of drinking appear to be more severe for ethnic-minority women than for White women by wider margins than their relative heavy drinking or alcohol-dependence rates in national surveys predict... Culture-specific programs are necessary to attract minority women into treatment... In addition, observational studies to determine how programs are actually tailored to each ethnic group and the relative success of different methods are needed to share prevention and treatment efforts... Overall, we need a great deal more basic data about the drinking behavior of women of all ethnic groups, with particular attention to within group variability, as a basis for more definitive suggestions for prevention and treatment.

480
Lipscomb, W.R. and Goddard, L.L., "Black Family Features and Drinking Behavior," Journal of Drug Issues 14(2): 337-347, 1984.

The structural features of the Black family are explored here. The features of Black family life, as well as the pattern of drinking behavior, are unique, and this uniqueness derives from the cultural world-view of Black people. It is suggested here that current Black drinking patterns are a product of historical traditions originating from the African continent, which have been modified by the concrete historical experience of Blacks in America.

481
Lipscomb, W., and Trocki, K., "An Ethnographic Study of Black Drinking Practices," In Brill, L., and Winick, C., Eds., _Yearbook of Substance Use and Abuse_, Volume 3. New York: Human Sciences Press, 1985.

Presents results of a 2-year study of drinking patterns and practices of blacks in two areas of San Francisco. Among the findings are that blacks exhibit considerable denial of their drinking problems, both as individuals and as a community; that appropriate treatment establishments are few in number and underutilized; and that intensive prevention efforts directed at black youth are needed.

482
McCalep, S.T., "Career Maturity of Selected Black High School Senior Drug/Alcohol Users and Nondrug/Alcohol Users." Dissertation. Ann Arbor, MI: University Microfilms International, 1984.

The effects of drug use upon the degree of career maturity among selected Black high school seniors (N=201) was investigated. The career maturity of these students was determined in terms of Career Maturity Inventory Attitude Component Scale: decisiveness, involvement, independence, orientation, and compromise to career decision making. Data obtained from these students were used to analyze those on the local sample, and to compare local scores to those scores on the national level. Comparing scores of alcohol and drug users with those who did not use alcohol or drugs, a statistical difference was found in the categories of decisiveness, independence, orientation, and compromise, but no significant difference was found in the area of involvement. The local sample (both users and nonusers) scored lower than the national sample in career maturity...

483
McClean, V. and Willis, W., "Alcoholic Intoxicants in the Slave Community: Evidence from the Narratives." Paper delivered at The Association for the Study of Afro-American Life and History Annual Meeting, Washington, D.C., October, 1984.

The authors conclude that "it was not until after slavery that alcoholism was abused in any significant measure in the black community," and that alcohol was often used as a means of social control.

484
Morgan, M.C., Wingard, D.L., and Felice, M.E., "Subcultural Differences in Alcohol Use Among Youth," Journal of Adolescent Health Care, 5(3): 191-195, 1984.

A survey was made of 335 adolescents in the San Diego Job Corps Center to determine patterns among ethnic groups. There were 67 Caucasians, 65 Blacks, 111 Hispanics, 69 Indochinese, and 23 others. Eighty-five percent of the youths reported drinking alcohol one to five times weekly during the previous 6 months, and 14 percent reported average weekend binges of more than 20 drinks. Sixty percent of the youths reported medical, legal, or vocational problems caused by drinking. Striking differences were noted in the drinking habits of the four major ethnic groups: Caucasian males began serious drinking at an earlier age than black, Hispanic, or Indochinese youths; more Hispanic youths used drugs in addition to marijuana, which was commonly used by all adolescent drinkers; and recently immigrated Indochinese youths drank in order to forget past experiences. In addition, it was found that young men and women drank the same amount.

485
Nace, E.P., "Epidemiology of Alcoholism and Prospects for Treatment," Annual Review of Medicine, 35:293-309, 1984.

Current American drinking patterns and the prevalence of problems resulting from alcohol use were reviewed. Sophisticated epidemilogical methodology provides data that document drinking practices across decades and indicate no marked changes in drinking practices for the past decade... When subgroups within the population were examined, women were found to have a lower rate of alcoholism than men. There are indications that blacks and Hispanics exceed the general population in prevalence of alcoholism although the data are incomplete in this regard... The prospects for treatment are highly favorable, with no data to suggest clearly that any one of the above subgroups is at a relative disadvantage.

486
Newman, R., comp., _Black Access: A Bibliography of Afro-American Bibliographies_. Westport, Connecticut: Greenwood Press, 1984.

This is an exhaustive compilation of the many bibliographies on black subject areas published (beginning with the first, compiled by W.E.B. DuBois). This can be very helpful to the researcher on black alcoholism, in that a thorough search can be launched, employing this comprehensive reference tool. into the many areas of black life touched by alcohol abuse and alcoholism, and the many areas that intersect with black alcoholism (black family life, black mental health, etc.). See references to the bibliographies of Lenwood G. Davis, and others, on the many areas of black life and thought.

487
Oshodin, O.G., "Parental Influence Upon Alcohol Use by Teenagers in Benin City, Nigeria," _Journal of the Royal Society of Health_, 104(3): 106-107, 110, 1984.

The influences of parents on the drinking patterns of teenagers in Benin City, Nigeria, were studied. A random sample of 500 secondary school students was selected with equal numbers of males and females. They were given a questionnaire with questions on background factors such as sex, age, and religion, and questions indentifying drinking patterns and practices... Some 75 percent of the students had taken their first drink when they were 16 years old or younger. Most of the students reported that their parents also drank, that they had never been in trouble with their parents after drinking alcohol, and that their parents often offered them alcohol. Approximately 60 percent of the students said they drank alcohol because they do not see anything wrong with the practice since their parents drink alcohol. Alcohol consumption had increased during the past year for 61 percent of the students, had remained the same for 15 percent, and had decreased for 9 percent. It is concluded that an alcohol education program may need to be set up for parents and students, which would cover knowledge, behavioral implications, and patterns of alcohol use and abuse.

488
Stimmel, B., Ed., Cultural and Sociological Aspects of Alcoholism and Substance Abuse. New York: The Haworth Press, 1984. This was also published as Advances in Alcohol and Substance Abuse, 4(1), 1984.

This volume focuses on selected aspects of the sociocultural interactions between alcoholism and substance abuse, including the role of ethnicity in substance abuse, sex-role values and bias in treatment personnel, and the influence of the family and religion on long-term outcomes among addicts.

489
United States. National Institute on Alcohol Abuse and Alcoholism. Fifth Special Report to the U.S. Congress on Alcohol and Health. Rockville, MD: 1984, 146 pp.

This is the most official and prominent statement of the federal government on alcohol abuse and alcoholism. It is not a report on black alcoholism, per se, but is a good research starting point for anyone interested in black alcoholism. The five special reports were published in 1971, 1974, 1978, 1981, and 1984.

490
Watts, T.D., and Wright, R., "Some Reflections on Black Alcoholism Treatment," Journal of the National Medical Association, 76(2): 101-102, 1984. Guest Editorial. From Watts, T.D. and Wright, Jr., R., Eds., Black Alcoholism: Toward a Comprehensive Understanding. Springfield, Ill.: Charles C. Thomas, Publ., 1983. Revised slightly from the original "Discussion" (pp. 66-70) (introduction to Section II of the book).

The possible contributing factors that must be addressed in treating alcoholism among Blacks are discussed. These factors include poverty and racism, the lack of available information on alcoholism among Blacks, the underutilization of treatment facilities by Black alcoholics, and questions that arise concerning treatment of Black alcoholics.

## 1985

491
Amin, R., Alexis, R., Korzis, J., "Fatal Ruptured Duodenal Varix: A Case Report and Review of Literature," American Journal of Gastroenterology, 80(1):13-18, 1985.

A case is reported of a 35-year-old black male who died of severe upper gastrointestinal bleeding from a ruptured duodenal varix located in the second portion of the duodenum. The patient had a 17-year history of chronic alcoholism, consuming 6 cans of beer or 1½ pints of vodka daily, and had been drinking heavily for the previous 5 years . . . From all of the possible causes of duodenal varix, chronic liver disease, mainly cirrhosis, was the predominant etiological factor, accounting for 30.7 percent of reported cases.

492
Avery, R.S., "A Survey of Blacks Toward Alcohol and Drug Use and Abuse." Paper presented at the 12th Annual Meeting of the Mid-South Summer School on Alcohol and Drug Problems, June 2-7, 1985, Fayetteville, Arkansas. Co-sponsored by the Arkansas Office on Alcohol and Drug Abuse Prevention and the University of Arkansas at Little Rock, Graduate School of Social Work.

493
Bell, C.C., "Alcohol Related Organic Brain Syndromes: Frequently Misdiagnosed as Schizophrenia." Bulletin of the New York State Chapter of the National Black Alcoholism Council, 4(1): 3-4, 1985.

The misdiagnosis of alcohol related organic brain syndromes, also known as alcoholic psychoses, such as schizophrenia, is frequently found in black males. It is contended that part of the cause of misdiagnosis of alcoholic psychoses lies in culturally biased diagnostic criteria which is accepted as the standard for various cultural and ethnic groups. This cause for misdiagnosis is compounded by a lack of recognition that there are different cultural drinking patterns and a lack of recognition of what impact these different patterns have on the course of alcoholism. Other cultural or socioeconomic parameters such as diet, poor nutrition, unavailability of medical services, etc., also are not considered in how the course of alcoholism may develop. Because treatment approaches are different for schizophrenia and alcohol related organic brain disorders, and especially since the true schizophrenic has a poorer prognosis (for both health and employment rehabilitation), it is important that alcohol related psychoses be recognized as a mimic of schizophrenia.

494
Bennett, L.A., and Ames, G.M., Eds., _The American Experience With Alcohol: Contrasting Cultural Perspectives_. New York: N.Y.: Plenum Press, 1985, 490 pages.

This is a comprehensive examination of alcohol and American society and culture. Two chapters of particular interest for those interested in the study of blacks and alcohol are by D. Herd and A.D. Gaines (see references to some).

495
Bertolucci, D., Noble, J., and Dufour, M., "Alcohol-Associated Premature Mortality: United States-1980." _Morbidity and Mortality Weekly Report (MMWR)_, 34(32): 493-494, 1985.

Race- and sex-specific rates of years of potential life lost (YPLL) due to alcohol abuse, dependence, cirrhosis and other cirrhoses are shown in table form. Native Americans have the highest rate, followed by blacks. Males of all races have a higher rate for each mortality cause than females. However, Native American females have a higher rate of deaths attributable to alcohol cirrhosis than either black or white males.

496
Beverly, C., "Limitations of Prevention in Addiction Services," In Roosevelt Wright, Jr., and Thomas D. Watts, Eds., _Prevention of Black Alcoholism: Issues and Strategies_. Springfield, IL: Charles C. Thomas Publisher, 1985, pp. 65-88.

It is argued that prevention as a goal of intervention with blacks is insufficient and that the goal of intervention should be social development. Prevention is reclassified as an objective necessary to achieve in pursuit of social development as a goal. A synthesis of addiction services is provided. Physiological, psychological, and sociological dimensions are discussed.

497
Brisbane, F.L., "Understanding the Female Child's Role of Family Hero in Black Alcoholic Families: The Significance of Race, Culture, and Gender," Bulletin of the New York State Chapter of the National Black Alcoholism Council, Inc., 4(1): 5-8, 1985.

The eldest or only black female children are more likely than their brothers to be cast into the survival role of family hero. Because of their constant giving and assuming responsibility for others, and receiving praise from immediate and extended family members for doing so, black female family heros are unlikely to seek help for their problems. What little self-esteem they have is related to the efficient way they manage the family hero role and acknowledgement of this by others.

498
Brisbane, F.L., and Womble, M., Eds., Treatment of Black Alcoholics. New York, NY: Haworth Press, 1985. Also published as Alcoholism Treatment Quarterly, 2(3) Summer, 1985.

A book exploring the policies, programs, and personnel needed to meet the treatment needs of Black alcoholics. A distinguished roster of authorities in their fields discuss such issues as Black and Employee Assistance Programs, the application of psychoanalytically oriented psychotherapy in treating Black substance abusers, working with middle-class Black families, cultural factors in the treatment of Black families, etc.

499
Chambers, C.D., "Epidemiology of Narcotic Abuse Among Blacks in the United States: 1935-1980," In Leon Brill and Charles Winick, Eds., Yearbook of Substance Use and Abuse: Volume III. New York, N.Y.: Human Sciences Press Inc., 1985, pp. 307-343.

The findings are reported of a series of analyses and a review of existing studies conducted in an attempt to continue the evolutionary monitoring of the incidence, prevalence, and descriptive character of black drug abuse and to provide a description of the contemporary abuser.

500
Combs-Orme, T., Taylor, J.R., and Robins, L.N., "Occupational Prestige and Mortality in Black and White Alcoholics," Journal of Studies on Alcohol, 46(5): 443-446, 1985.

Mortality was examined in 1289 Black and White alcoholics. The overall proportion of mortality over 5-9 years was 22.0%. No overall differences were found between Black and White mortality rates by crude death proportions or standardized mortality ratios. Blacks were significantly younger at death than were Whites and were also significantly younger than Whites at admission to treatment. Occupational prestige was examined in the 374 Whites and 270 Blacks for whom an occupation was known, prestige being divided here into high, medium and low categories. Whites suffered significantly higher mortality in the high prestige group. Alcoholics in the high prestige group suffered slightly greater mortality than alcoholics in the middle and lower groups. The results here would appear to indicate that although occupational prestige is an important variable in mortality among alcoholics, other variables that were not controlled in these analyses may also be important.

501
Diehl, A.M. et al., "Effect of Parenteral Amino Acid Supplementation in Alcoholic Hepatitis," Hepatology, 5(1):57-63, 1985.

The effect of administration of a parenteral amino acid/glucose solution for 1 month on nutritional, clinical, biochemical, and histological parameters was studied in 15 patients with biopsy-proven alcoholic hepatitis. The patients ranged in age from 32 to 61 years, with a mean age of 45 years; 12 were male and 3 female. All were of low socioeconomic status and 14 of 15 were black . . . It is concluded that the clinical syndrome of alcoholic hepatitis is heavily influenced initially by metabolic consequences of alcohol consumption, and that it is the resolution of this alcohol effect that is most influenced by parenteral amino acid supplementation.

502
Edwards, D.W., "Investigation of the Use and Abuse of Alcohol and Other Drugs Among 50 Aged Male Alcoholics and 50 Aged Female Alcoholics," Journal of Alcohol and Drug Education, 30(2):24-30, 1985.

The use and abuse of alcohol and other drugs among Americans aged 55 years and older were studied in 50 male alcoholics and 50 female alcoholics. Findings suggest that the marital and family support system is more at risk among aged female alcoholics than that of males. Because most of the aged alcoholics drink primarily at home or alone, the significance of early identification and intervention becomes even more important, as well as being more difficult. It is concluded that more innovative and effective strategies need to be developed for use in both anticipating and responding to the needs and problems of the aged who may abuse alcohol and other drugs.

503
Einstein, S., "Drug Use Intervention with and for Special Populations," _The International Journal of the Addictions_, 20(1):1-12, 1985.

Introductory essay for a special anniversary issue of the _International Journal of the Addictions_ entitled "Drug Use Intervention with and for Special Populations." The collection of articles in this thematic volume is the outcome of a meeting sponsored by the Institute for the Study of Drug Misuse (ISDM). This meeting, the first of an annual series, was developed in order to explore generic critical issues which affect the planning and/or carrying out of necessary substance use/misuse intervention programs, projects, policies, methods, models, etc. The author concludes that "if, indeed, special populations is not simple a didactic concept, but is rather a dynamic series of structures and systems, which may or may not be related, we will be challenged to develop specific intervention models which are suitable to and for specific populations, at specific points/phases in time within a particular milieu."

504
Fernandez-Pol, B., Bluestone, H., Missouri, C., Morales, G., and Mizruchi, S., "Inner City Drinking Patterns: A Study of Black Americans and Puerto Ricans," _Journal of Studies on Alcohol_, forthcoming issue.

505
Gaines, A.D., "Alcohol: Cultural Conceptions and Social Behavior Among Urban Blacks." In L.A. Bennett and G.M. Ames, Eds., _The American Experience with Alcohol: Contrasting_

<u>Cultural Perspectives</u>. New York, N.Y.: Plenum Publ. Corp., 1985, pp. 171-197.

This chapter examines the problem of variation in beliefs and practices in respect to alcohol use among urban blacks. Variation "among people assigned the social classification 'Black' were discerned through a symbolic, interpretative approach... there is no unitary 'black experience' (or 'family') common and unique to all people in America with African ancestry." Two levels of folk theories are discussed here, those of the bureaucratic, social scientific professionals (and their systems of social classification), and those of the people so classified by the first group. This chapter considers how "folk theory, in both science and society, contributes to the ethnography of alcohol and the anthropology of science."

506
Gary, L.E., and Berry, G.L., "Predicting Attitudes Toward Substance Use in a Black Community: Implications for Prevention," <u>Community Mental Health Journal</u>, 21(1): 42-51, 1985.

This study identified those demographic and sociocultural factors that best predict the attitudes of black adults toward substance use. Data were collected by survey research methods from a probability sample of 411 black adults who resided in an urban community. The study found that racial consciousness was the best predictor of substance use attitudes and that gender, age, church involvement, and marital status were other significant predictors.

507
Hall, W.D. (M.D.), Saunders,E. (M.D.) and Shulman, N.B. (M.D.), See Thomson, G.E. (M.D.)

508
Hanson, B., "Drug Treatment Effectiveness: The Case of Racial and Ethnic Minorities in America - Some Research Questions and Proposals," <u>The International Journal of the Addictions</u>, 20(1):99-137, 1985.

This paper is concerned with the following issues and goals:

1. To describe specific areas of recently completed and ongoing research pertaining to the treatment effectiveness for a specific type of special population; namely, minority drug misusers
2. To point out the major findings and knowledge gaps emerging from these studies
3. To encourage the development of much needed (and long overdue) systematic, integrated, and practically useful treatment, and outcome research by suggesting a tentative research framework
4. Formulating relevant research questions withing the framework
5. Presenting an outline of two potential large-scale research projects . . .

The upshot of what has been discussed is that, for whatever reasons, we simply do not know very much about how to provide effective treatment for minority group members. We do not know if different minority groups have special (and different) treatment needs, and, if they do, we don't know what these needs are or how they might influence the treatment process. Further, we still don't know what techniques would help us address minority members' needs during treatment and aftercare or what overall service delivery system will work best for which minority group. If there is one underlying or central message in this paper, it is that researchers must develop new and productive avenues of inquiry which are oriented around issues and variables (e.g., powerlessness, the counselor-client relationship, social growth, and value-change treatment criteria) sensitive to minority people's perspectives regarding the special circumstances of minority drug abusers in America.

509
Harford, T.C., "Alcohol Use Among Black Teenagers and Young Adults," Paper presented at the National Institute on Alcohol Abuse and Alcoholism, Conference on the Epidemiology of Alcohol Use and Abuse Among U.S. Ethnic Minority Groups, September 11-14, 1985, Bethesda, Maryland.

This paper describes drinking patterns and alcohol-related problems among Black teenagers and young adults. Surveys of high school students indicate that alcohol abstinence rates are higher for Black than for non-Black teenagers and that lower proportions of Black teenagers are heavy drinkers. The 1978 national survey of senior high school students revealed that the lower prevalence of heavier drinking among Black teenagers persisted when relevant demographic variables were controlled. The findings further suggested that the onset of drinking among Black teenagers, relative to other students, appears to be delayed. Drawing upon both the 1978 national survey and a recent household survey conducted in Baton Rouge, Louisiana, data are presented with respect to several measures of alcohol use, the contexts in which alcohol is used, and attitudes related to alcohol use.

510
Harford, T.C., "Drinking Patterns Among Black and Non-Black Adolescents: Results of a National Survey." See Wright and Watts, 1985, pp. 122-139.

This chapter examined factors predictive of differential alcohol use among black and nonblack students. Using multivariate analytic procedures on data from a national probability sample of junior and senior high school students (grades 7-12), the author found that both demographic varibles associated with social class and variables associated with exposure to and involvement with alcohol significantly differentiated black and nonblack drinkers. Environmental variables associated with the use of alcohol did not significantly differentiate these two groups. The author suggests that future studies need to identify environmental factors which delay exposure to a more extensive network of peer drinking models and access to alcohol among black students. A major implication of this chapter is that the distinctive pattern of alcohol use among black youth is indicative of the need for broad-based and culturally sensitive programs that integrate alcohol abuse prevention measures with academic and vocational training.

511
Harvey, W.B., "Alcohol Abuse and the Black Community: A Contemporary Analysis," _Journal of Drug Issues_, 15(1):81-91, 1985.

The thrust of current social thought on the prevalence and contributing factors of alcoholism in black Americans and the resultant treatment approaches is examined. The provision of indigenous and culturally sensitive methods for combatting the problem is supported.

512
Herd, D.A., "Alcohol Use and Alcohol Problems: A Review of the Literature on American Blacks," Paper Presented at the National Institute on Alcohol Abuse and Alcoholism, Conference on the Epidemiology of Alcohol Use and Abuse Among U.S. Ethnic Minority Groups, September 11-14, 1985, Bethesda, Maryland.

This paper examines the literature on Blacks and alcohol use in the Post WWII period. Areas covered in the review include epidemiological, clinical, social survey and ethnographic findings. The focus of the review is on the prevalence and patterns of alcohol-related problems and alcohol consumption. In the area of alcohol-related problems, several areas of research are discussed. First, epidemiological trends on liver cirrhosis and esophageal cancer morbility and mortality are explored. Second, indicators of psychosocial/behavioral problems such as arrests for public drunkenness, arrests for drinking and driving, and hospital admissions statistics are examined. Third, self-reported social problems related to alcohol use from surveys of the general population are described. The discussion of drinking patterns reviews the findings from both ethnographic and survey studies of drinking patterns. Recent findings from a national survey of Black and Hispanic drinking patterns are highlighted. This part of the paper focuses on the sociocultural aspects of drinking patterns, including demographic correlates of alcohol use, norms and attitudes towards alcohol beverages, and social contexts of drinking. The final section of the paper compares and contrasts findings about alcohol consumption and alcohol-related problems described in the literature. Areas of agreement and disagreement, including reasons for any conflicting findings, are explored and discussed. Based on this discussion, gaps in the literature and the needs for future research on Blacks and alcohol are identified.

513
Herd, D.A., "Ambiguity in Black Drinking Norms: An Ethnohistorical Interpretation." In L.A. Bennett and G.M. Ames, Eds., The American Experience with Alcohol: Contrasting Cultural Perspectives. New York: Plenum Publ. Corp., 1985, pp. 149-170.

This chapter "examines the problem of ambiguity and cultural conflict in drinking norms among present-day blacks from an ethnohistorical perpective." Black Americans were heavily involved in the anti-alcohol movements of the 19th century - facilitating a major black temperance movement and a network of "dry" religious and social organizations. Ambivalence around alcohol use in the black population, as in the general American population, is the product of complex historical changes. In the early part of the 19th century, alcohol was looked upon more favorably, but not so in the antebellum period. Alcohol re-emerged in a more favorable light in the 20th century. Nevertheless, ambivalence is also characteristic of this period.

514
Herd, D.A., "Migration, Cultural Transformation and the Rise of Black Liver Cirrhosis Mortality," British Journal of Addiction, Forthcoming, 1985.

Social, historical and epidemiological cohort analysis.

515
Herd, D.A., "We Cannot Stagger to Freedom: A History of Blacks and Alcohol in American Politics." In L. Brill and C. Winick, Eds., Yearbook of Substance Use and Abuse, Vol. 3. New York, NY: Human Sciences Press, 1985.

This paper traces the history of blacks and alcohol in the American temperance and prohibition periods. Black attitudes concerning alcohol have been heavily influenced by the overriding political issues of freedom and the attainment of social equality. Thus in the 1830's when the temperance movement and the anti-slavery campaigns overlapped, blacks spearheaded a major temperance movement and there was a strong commitment to personal abstinence in the black community. In the wake of this, cirrhosis mortality and other alcohol problems among blacks seem to have been extraordinarily low throughout the 19th century. In contrast, in the period of southern white reaction after the Civil War, the prohibition movement became associated with white supremacy and black disfranchisement. Prohibitionists urged the passage of Jim Crow laws, advocated stripping blacks of their voting rights, and condoned anti-black terrorism. Consequently, black political leaders lost interest in alcohol issues and efforts to control liquor consumption greatly diminished in black communities. Blacks became noted as small-time traders and large-scale consumers of illegal alcohol. The long range results of these trends have seen an extraordinarily high rate of cirrhosis mortality among certain groups of black males. The paper concludes that the upturn in black drinking problems at the aggregate level is more related to patterns of racial oppression and economic exploitation stemming from the prohibition era, rather than to weak cultural norms or the psychological problems that are often hypothesized in other studies. Efforts to prevent and minimize alcohol problems in the black community must take into account the general interest among blacks in political and socio-economic betterment, rather than exclusively focusing on clinical and individual level solutions to alcohol problems.

516
Illes, R.W., Mill, W. B., Roy, T.S., "Current Management of Squamous Cell Carcinoma of the Esophagus," Missouri Medicine, 82(5):255-259, 1985.

A retrospective study of 19 patients at St. Louis University Hospital with squamous cell carcinoma of the esophagus were reviewed with respect to management of their condition and the results of treatment . . . Mean age of the patients was 63.6 years. Sixty-five percent of the patients were male. Blacks outnumbered whites 15 to 5. Seventy percent of the patients were heavy smokers (greater than 50 packs per year) and 60 percent consumed more than the equivalent of 16 ounces of alcohol per week -- two major predisposing factors, with incidence of esophageal carcinoma increasing with their increasing use. A review of survival rates by clinical stage and treatment modality demonstrated no significant differences. All patients in the study died, median survival for the group being 5.5 months. It is believed that new methods of management must be found . . .

517
International Journal of the Addictions, 20(1), 1985. "Special Anniversary Issue: Intervening with Special Populations." A publication developed from a meeting sponsored by The Institute for the Study of Drug Misuse.

Several articles in this special issue deal with minorities and substance abuse.

518
Johnson, R.L., "Black Adolescents: Issues Critical to Their Survival," Journal of the National Medical Association, 77(6):447-448, 1985.

The rates of illness and death among adolescents are increasing due to accidents, especially motor vehicle accidents, and homicide and suicide. Violence threatens the survival of the black teenager in America -- he is more likely to be killed or injured due to self-inflicted violence (alcohol, marijuana, cigarettes, and angel dust) or violence inflicted by peers or society. Racism, poor education, lack of employment, poverty, and a lack of opportunity impede his progress and generate hoplessness, anger, and depression leading to homicide, suicide, drug/alcohol abuse, early parenthood, academic failure, and delinquency. Holistic care of the black adolescent is advocated.

519
Kail, Barbara, L., "The Black Woman, Alcohol and Prevention: An Empirical Exploration." See Wright and Watts, 1985.

This study suggests that there may be some differences between black and white women as hosts, in their access to alcohol, and the environmental context in which alcohol is used. Black women in this sample are more likely to abstain and are less likely to be aware of community resources for treatment. Black respondents also seem to have less access to alcohol--they are less likely to go to social functions where alcohol is served and less likely to drink in public. Black women in this sample are more likely to see alcohol as a drug. Implications for prevention are discussed.

520
Kelly, J., "Alcohol Use and Abuse Among Black Youth," Health Education, 16(3): 27-29, 1985.

Black children often have bleak and unhappy experiences with school and the job market; their family life is often disorganized. While many blacks drink without significant problems, alcohol misuse and abuse are two of the major problems threatening their future. There is an alarming need for more research data on black youth, not confined to the disease or potential for alcoholism, but on cultural norms, values, beliefs, and socioeconomic and regional differences.

521
King, L., "Biobehavioral Indices of Alcoholism in a Black Community: Research Findings," Paper Presented at the National Institute on Alcohol Abuse and Alcoholism, Conference

on the Epidemiology of Alcohol Use and Abuse Among U.S. Ethnic Minority Groups, September 11-14, 1985, Bethesda, Maryland.

This paper examines the current research on the biobehavioral indices of alcoholism among Black Americans. An examination of this literature is evaluated via a biobehavioral model developed in 1982 by King and his colleagues which evaluates a set of complex relationships (biological, economic, social, and cultural) to derive various degrees of development and underdevelopment. Alcoholism is viewed as an outcome of underdevelopment. Further, the paper discusses the design of a new study which focuses on deriving biobehavioral indices of alcoholism in a selected Black community. Using data collected among a group of 300 Black twins between the ages of 15 and 55, multivariate analyses are used to isolate factors which best predict alcohol-related problems among the twins. The initial hypothesis is that alcoholism is a specific multivariate syndrome with both biological and social parameters.

522
King, S.W., "Black Females and Alcoholism Prevention Strategies." In Roosevelt Wright, Jr., and Thomas D. Watts, Eds., Prevention of Black Alcoholism: Issues and Strategies. Springfield, IL: Charles C. Thomas Publ., 1985, pp. 89-107.

Black female alcohol abuse and alcoholism is examined through (1) a review of available literature on blacks and alcoholism and on women and alcoholism; (2) a discussion of the implications and explanatory nature of the literature as it relates to black females and alcohol abuse and alcoholism among this high risk subgroup.

523
Kirsch, R.E., Ed., Alcoholic Liver Disease: Pathobiology, Epidemiology and Clinical Aspects, New York, N.Y.: Wiley-Medical, 1985.

A review of the literature summarizes data on drinking patterns and the epidemiology of alcoholic liver disease in the Republic of South Africa. Approximately 70 percent of South Africans are black, 20 percent of European extraction, 9 percent mixed ("colored"), and 3 percent Asian. Drinking patterns and consequences of alcohol abuse in white South Africans are similar to those seen in England, Europe, or North America. However, several aspects of alcohol use and abuse among black or brown South Africans differ from those seen in whites and in other geographic regions. Clinical features of alcoholic liver disease are complicated by the high incidence of malnutrition, siderosis, and hepatitis B virus infection in the black population. Cutaneous and endocrine symptoms of alcoholic cirrhosis commonly seen in Europe and North America are rarely seen in black South Africans, although they are present in racially mixed patients. Histological patterns are similar in blacks, whites, and colored patients. However, the presence of fat is less common in colored patients than in whites, and is rare in blacks. This may reflect the predominant consumption by blacks of home-brewed high-iron, low-alcohol sorghum beer. This beverage also causes iron overload which results in a high incidence of siderosis and high hepatic rion concentrations in blacks. With increasing amounts of iron, there is a greater chance of protal tract fibrosis and micronodular cirrhosis. The common association of siderosis with micronodular cirrhosis suggests a direct relationship between iron, hepatic fibrosis, and cirrhosis. One of the clinical features associated with iron overload is a high incidence of porphyria cutanea tarda (PCT). PCT appears to be more common in black and colored patients than in whites. The finding of siderosis in nearly all patients suggests a direct relationship between iron and defective porphyrin metabolism. It appears that the precipitating factors of alcohol abuse and/or iron overload are necessary to produce overt disease. Although the exact relationship of PCT to iron and alcohol is not clear, PCT cases respond dramatically to withdrawal from alcohol and venesection.

524
Kline, R.B., Snyder, D.K., "Replicated MMPI Subtypes for Alcoholic Men and Women: Relationship to Self-Reported Drinking Behaviors," _Journal of Consulting and Clinical Psychology_, 53(1):70-79, 1985.

The relationship of replicated Minnesota Multiphasic Personality Inventory (MMPI) subtypes for inpatient alcoholic men and women to self-reported drinking behaviors was investigated . . . The results yielded significant differentiation by alcohol-use scales among the MMPI subtypes for women only. Increasing psychopathology as measured by the MMPI was clearly predictive of increasing intake of alcohol and other substances of abuse, obsessive preoccupation with alcohol consumption, and associated affective and physiological disturbances related to drinking consequences for female alcoholic inpatients. In contrast, there was relatively poor differentiation among subtypes of men by these measures. The implications of the findings for future alcoholic-personality assessment and drinking-style assessment are discussed.

525
Lewis, C.E., Robin, L., Rice, J., "Association of Alcoholism with Antisocial Personality in Urban Men," Journal of Nervous and Mental Disease, 173(3):166-174, 1985.

The association between alcoholism and antisocial personality (ASP) in urban black men was investigated. Antisocial and social alcoholics were compared . . . In a sample of urban black men, it was found that those with antisocial personality had a higher rate of alcoholism than those without. In addition, a family history of problem drinking, low educational level, and excessive irritability were also closely associated with alcoholism. The clinical, genetic, and neurophysiological implications of these findings are discussed. It is concluded that both antisocial personality and a family history of alcoholism were highly predictive of alcoholism . . .

526
Linsky, A.S., Straus, M.A., Colby, J.P., Jr., "Stressful Events, Stressful Conditions and Alcohol Problems in the United States: A Partial Test of Bales's Theory," Journal of Studies on Alcohol, 46(1):72-80, 1985.

The hypothesized relationship between stress or tension levels within social structures and heavy drinking or alcoholism as formulated by Bales in 1946 was examined as a means of explaining variations in the levels of alcoholism in the 50 States. Two types of social stress were conceptualized and measured at the State level . . . Both stressful events and stressful conditions correlated with all indicators of alcoholism at the State level, 19 of 20 correlations being in the theoretically expected direction. Correlations were enchanced when age, urbanicity, the percentage of blacks, low income, and education were controlled for. The three macro measures of stress taken together explain 27 percent of the variation in cirrhosis death rates,, 14 percent of the variation in alcoholism and alcoholic psychosis death rates, and 47 percent of the variation in alcohol consumption rates.

527
Lipscomb, W.R., "Ethnographic Study of Black Drinking Practices." In Leon Brill and Charles Winick, Eds., Yearbook of Substance Use and Abuse: Volume III. New York, N.Y.: Human Sciences Press Inc., 1985, pp. 283-306.

A study concerning black drinking practices, conducted during 1979 and 1980, is reported. The study utilized an ethnographic research approach to explore the role of alcohol in the lives of black community residents in San Francisco (CA). The treatment implications of the findings, preliminary conclusions, and recommendations are discussed.

528
Livingston, I.L., "Alcohol Consumption and Hypertension: A Review with Suggested Implications," Journal of the National Medical Association, 77(2):129-135, 1985.

Evidence that substantiates a relationship between alcohol consumption and hypertension is presented, along with a brief overview of the individual areas of alcohol use and abuse and hypertension. Data suggests that compared with the general U.S. population, black Americans are disproportionately afflicted with both hypertension and alcoholism. Prevention and treatment implications in high-risk groups are emphasized. It is suggested that health care providers and other related personnel should become more cognizant of various treatment, management, and prevention implications associated with hypertension, especially for high-risk groups. Specific examples are outlined using Black Americans as a representative high-risk group.

529
Martin, C.H., "Relationship Between Level of Self-Concept and Drinking Patterns of Black Youths." Dissertation. Ann Arbor, MI: University Microfilms International, 1985.

The relationship between self-concept and drinking patterns of black youths is examined in a sample of 121 black youths aged 12 to 17. Three hypotheses are tested: (1) there is no significant relationship between socioeconomic status and patterns of drinking for black youths; (2) there is no significant relationship between the level of self-concept, frequency of use, and socioeconomic status; and (3) there is no significant difference in the relative contributions of age, sex, socioeconomic status, and level of self-concept to patterns of drinking. The data indicate there is no significant relationship between the independent variable (level of self-concept) and the dependent variable (patterns of drinking). The relative contribution of age, sex, and socioeconomic status and level of self-concept to patterns of drinking of black male and female youths is not significant.

530
Mayers, Raymond S. and Feazell, Carann S., "Prevention and Treatment of Black Alcoholism in the Workplace." See Wright and Watts, 1985.

In this chapter an overview of employee assistance programs, especially those features that could be utilized to help the black alcoholic employee, are discussed. Of particular concern are aspects of prevention and treatment in the workplace that might be applied to the black worker. A variety of strategies are discussed here within a framework of differing interpersonal lifestyles of blacks.

531
Mayet, F.G., Schutte, C.H., Reinach, S.G., "Anemia Among the Inhabitants of a Rural Area in Northern Natal," South African Medical Journal, 67(12):458-462, 1985.

Haemotological and parasitological investigations of apparently healthy subjects in a rural area of Natal (South Africa) found a high prevalence of anemia. A fair amount of alcohol is consumed by this population in the form of "palm beer", brewed from the local ilala palm. The iron content of the beer is low and does not add to the iron intake, as in the case in the diets of other blacks in South Africa.

532
Mayo, M.A., "Comparison of MMPI Diagnostic Strategies to Identify Black and White Male Alcoholics." Dissertation. Ann Arbor, MI: University Microfilms International, 1985.

MMPI diagnostic strategies were compared to assess the relative accuracy and racial bias of each strategy to differentiate alcoholics from psychiatric patients within a VA inpatient treatment setting. Diagnostic strategies included identifying alcoholics on the basis of (a) high scale 4 scores, (b) specific two-point and cluster profile types, (c) high MacAndrew alcoholism scale (MAC) scores, and (d) high scores on multiple discriminant functions derived from the MMPI clinical and validity scales, MAC and subject's age. Veterans medical records from the period of January 1975 to June 1984 were randomly selected and reviewed. Alcoholics included veterans with a valid MMPI protocol and a primary medical diagnosis of alcoholism, with no secondary diagnosis of psychosis or drug abuse. Psychiatric patients included only subjects with valid MMPI protocols and no primary or secondary alcoholism or drug abuse diagnosis. The sample included 150 white alcoholics, 150 white psychiatric patients, 40 black alcoholics, and 40 black psychiatric patients. With alcoholics and psychiatric patients obtaining similar scale 4 scores and two-point and cluster profile types, little differentiation between groups was found for either black or white samples. Consequently, it was not possible to assess racial bias for these diagnostic strategies. With separate scale cut-scores for black and white males to separate optimally alcoholics from psychiatric patients, the MAC accurately discriminated between white alcoholics and nonalcoholics (67.7% overall diagnostic accuracy) but not between black alcoholics and nonalcoholics (57.5%) Caution is suggested in applying the MAC to black samples. Black nonalcoholics score in a similarly high range as black alcoholics, which may lead to an overdiagnosis of alcoholism. Derivation of multiple discriminant functions were limited to the white sample due to small black sample size. Cross-validation of multiple discriminant analyses of MMPI scales for white males (66.0%) was not superior to results found for the MAC alone. Including the MAC and subject's age with MMPI scales in the discriminant analyses resulted in increased diagnostic accuracy (74.0%) for white males. Application of both discriminant functions to black males differentiated black alcoholics from nonalcoholics (62.5% and 63.8% respectively).

533
McBride, W., Richter, G.C., "Gastrointestinal Malignancies in Black Americans," New York State Journal of Medicine, 85(4):157-159, 1985.

The major gastrointestinal malignancies that occur in black Americans are discussed with reference to environmental or socioeconomic factors as they relate to cancer incidence rates, survival trends, and cancer prevention. Racial differences in alcohol consumption is cited as a possible contribution to the high risk of carcinoma development in black Americans.

534
McClellan, K., "Blacks and the EAP Movement," The U.S. Journal of Drug and Alcohol Dependence, 9(6):8, 1985.

The EAP movement sometimes gives the impression that it is the special preserve of White workers, as there are few Blacks, Asians, Indians or Hispanics in the EAP field. Moreover, there is little valid and reliable information concerning alcohol, drug abuse, and mental health (ADM) problems among Black, Asian, Indian, and Hispanic workers, anywhere in the world. These facts are particularly regrettable, since more than two-thirds of the world's workers are of non-European origin . . . One hopes that the EAP movement will attract Black and Brown workers, and that Third World nations will reach a stage of development where EAPs become attractive devices for improving the quality of life for their working people. However, this is unlikely to occur without research to determine and publicize the need for EAPs for all workers, and to discern the cultural variables that affect EAP and ADM treatment success.

535
McNeil, John S., "An Analysis of Models of Alcoholism and Prevention and Their Applicability to American Blacks," In Roosevelt Wright, Jr., and Thomas D. Watts, Eds., Prevention of Black Alcoholism: Issues and Strategies. Springfield, IL: Charles C. Thomas Publisher, 1985, pp. 51-64.

This chapter discusses three alcoholism prevention models, the public health model, the sociocultural model, and the distribution of consumption model, and their possible applicability or appropriateness for the study, treatment, and prevention of black alcoholism.

536
Pagan, G., "Social Influences on the Drinking Behavior of Black and White Male College Students: A Comparison of the Laboratory and the Natural Setting." Dissertation. Ann Arbor, MI: University Microfilms International, 1985.

The drinking behavior of black and white male college students was studied while they interacted with members of their own and other race in the laboratory and in the natural environment . . . The races did not differ in the overall number of glasses consumed and number of sips taken. However, blacks drank at a faster rate than did whites in dyads, and at a slower rate in groups. It is concluded that race is not a major social determinant of drinking behavior of blacks and whites, but plays a role in drinking, nevertheless.

537
Paterson, A.C. et al., "Liver Morphology in Southern African Blacks with Hepatocellular Carcinoma: A Study within the Urban Environment," Hepatology, 5(1):72-78, 1985.

Liver morphology and tumor patterns in urban South African blacks with hepatocellular carcinoma (HCC) are described, and changes in morphology of nonneoplastic liver tissue during two time periods (1956-1962 and 1977-1982) are examined . . . It is concluded that alcohol is increasing in importance as an etiologic association of HCC in urban South African Blacks, while the prevalence of macronodular cirrhosis, and of cirrhosis as a whole, in urban patients with HCC has declined.

538
Redd, M.L., "Alcoholism Treatment Outcomes." Dissertation. Ann Arbor, MI: University Microfilms International, 1985.

Alcoholism treatment outcomes were assessed for 78 respondents successfully posttested to examine the relationship between these outcomes, the type of treatment, and race (black or white). Data was gathered at the time treatment was selected and six months later. An analysis of the data found six statistically significant relationships: (1) inpatients were drinking less at following than outpatients; (2) more black inpatients than black outpatients were drinking less at followup; (3) among inpatients more blacks than whites were drinking less; (4) more white outpatients than white inpatients were abstinent; (5) more outpatients were employed than inpatients; and (6) more outpatients at posttest were employed than at pretest. Overall treatment success was minimal.

539
Robins, L., "Alcohol Abuse Among Blacks and Whites: Results From the ECA," Paper Presented at the National Institute on Alcohol Abuse and Alcoholism, Conference on the Epidemiology of Alcohol Use and Abuse Among U.S. Ethnic Minority Groups, September 11-14, 1985, Bethesda, Maryland.

This paper reports on the prevalence of diagnosis of alcohol abuse and dependence, and specific alcohol problems in Blacks and Whites. Data are gathered from a survey of respondents in the St. Louis Epidemiologic Catchment Area (ECA), one of the five collaborating field sites comprising the NIMH-sponsored ECA program. Comparative findings are presented on correlations of alcohol abuse and dependence with education, occupation, marital history, fecundity, and major life events for both groups.

540
Russell, M., "Alcohol Use in Black Gynecologic Patients," Paper Presented at the National Institute on Alcohol Abuse and Alcoholism, Conference on the Epidemiology of Alcohol Use and Abuse Among U.S. Ethnic Minority Groups, September 11-14, 1985, Bethesda, Maryland.

Drinking patterns, alcohol-related problems and sociodemographic characteristics are examined in a systematic sample of 982 Black and 985 White gynecologic outpatients. Data were gathered via self-administered questionnaires in five settings: three hospital clinics and two private practices. Findings indicate that the prevalence of heavy drinking and alcohol-related problems was similar in Blacks and Whites, but there were significantly more abstainers and fewer light and moderate drinkers among the Black outpatients. Young White women had high rates of heavy drinking which decreased with age, and young Black women had low rates which increased up through the forties, after which they fell to about the same rates as in Whites. Black housewives had high rates of heavy drinking compared to low rates in White housewives. Except among housewives, Blacks tended to have rates of heavy drinking that were about the same or lower than those among Whites having similar sociodemogrpahic characteristics. High rates of heavy drinking among Black gynecolgic patients are partially attributable to the fact that more of the Blacks had never married, were unemployed and had not completed any years of education beyond high school - all factors associated with higher rates of heavy drinking and alcohol-related problems.

541
Swift, Carolyn F., and Beverly, Sethard, "The Utilization of Ministers as Alcohol Counselors and Educators: Increasing Prevention and Treatment Resources in the Black Community." See Wright and Watts, 1985.

This chapter describes a program in which black ministers were invited to assist in attempting to provide resources to confront the problem of black alcoholism in a midwestern American community.

542
Thomson, G.E., (M.D.), "Nonpharmacologic Therapy of Hypertension in Blacks." In W.D. Hall, M.D., E. Saunders, M.D., and N.B. Shulman, M.D., Hypertension in Blacks: Epidemiology, Pathophysiology and Treatment. Chicago: Year Book Medical Publishers, Inc., 1985, pp. 159-181.

In this chapter the author states that the chronic ingestion of alcohol may have significant longitudinal effects on blood pressure. He discusses the effects of same on pp. 169-170 of this book.

543
United States. National Institute on Alcohol Abuse and Alcoholism. A Guidebook for Planning Alcohol Prevention Programs with Black Youth. Rockville, Maryland, 1981.

"Approaching the Problem" (Chapter 2) (1981). Reprinted as Chapter 8 in Wright and Watts (1985).

The purpose of this chapter is to help black youth develop positive attitudes and behaviors concerning alcohol use. Discussion focuses on what alcohol abuse prevention is, why black youth try alcohol, what a prevention strategy is, and understanding the difference between alcohol-specific and nonspecific strategies. The chapter underscores being aware of recommendations from black experts/prevention planners regarding the planning of culturally specific alcohol programs for black youth, and prevention strategies that can help youth develop more positive attitudes and behaviors about alcohol use.

"Blacks and Alcohol: Significant Dates," (1981, p. 9) (from above publication) Reprinted on p. 12 of Wright and Watts (1985).

This list of significant dates in the history of blacks and alcohol is designed to provide a brief chronological overview of the history of the experiences of blacks with alcohol in America.

544
United States. National Institute on Alcohol Abuse and Alcoholism. "Alcohol and Black Americans," Alcohol Resources: Update, September, 1985: 1-7.

No less than other Americans, blacks are seriously afflicted by alcoholism and alcohol abuse. Not only do they suffer all the usual kinds of health problems associated with excessive alcohol use, alcoholism also appears to increase the risks of cancer, severe malnutrition, hypertension, and birth defects in blacks. Cirrhosis mortality rates among black Americans have remained unusually high--nearly twice those of whites--even through the rate in the general population has been declining since 1973. The precise nature and extent of alcoholism and alcohol problems in the black community are still not thoroughly understood. Research on the subject has been relatively scarce and often deficient in methodology, e.g., in the use of small or nonrepresentative samples, or in the glossing over of culture-specific factors in treatment and prevention. But scientists are beginning to remedy some of these deficiencies. The differences in drinking patterns and practices associated with racial differences are becoming clearer, as are the racial attitudes potentially at work in the process of detecting and diagnosing alcoholism. The roots of black attitudes toward alcohol and drinking, stemming from ancient traditions as modified by historical experience, are becoming more widely recognized, and their implications for services are being considered more carefully. The resources listed in this Update are divided into three categories: Readings (books, journal articles, and other print materials), Audiovisuals, and Organizations.

545
United States. National Institute on Alcohol Abuse and Alcoholism. Alcohol Health and Research World 5(3): 33-41, 1981. "Prevention of Alcohol-Related Problems: Strategies and Activities." Reprinted as Chapter 2 in Wright and Watts, (1985).

This chapter discusses approaches to the prevention of alcohol-related problems, which have been derived from three important models discussed here, the public health model, the "distribution of consumption" model, and the sociocultural theoretical model.

546
Warheit, G.J., "Alcohol Behavior Among Southern Blacks: A Comparative Analysis," Paper Presented at the National Institute on Alcohol Abuse and Alcoholism, Conference on the Epidemiology of Alcohol Use and Abuse Among U.S. Ethnic Minority Groups, September 11-14, 1985, Bethesda, Maryland.

This paper presents preliminary findings from an epidemiologic study of alcohol use and problem drinking among differing social and demographic subgroups of the general population (N=1,063). The data are controlled for age, sex and race. Problem drinking is defined as congruent with symptoms of excess and dependence, social consequences, and physical health sequelae. It is also viewed in the context of the DSM-III criteria for alcohol abuse and dependence as determined by the Diagnostic Interview Schedule (DIS). These preliminary findings are based on responses from 296 Blacks and 767 Whites who represent approximately one-half of the field survey data which have been collected. Overall, the data showed a higher proportion of Black abstainers than White ones. The highest prevalence rates of current alcohol use were found among White males 18-29 (94.3%); the lowest rates were discovered among Black females 60 or older (15.7%). Blacks tended to begin drinking at a later age than Whites in most age cohorts. In addition, more males then females of both races were found to be consumers of alcohol. The lowest current prevalence rates of alcohol abuse and/or dependence as determined by the DIS were found among Black females under 60 years of age; the highest rates were found among White males 18-29 and Black males 30-59. However, the small cell sizes dictate caution in interpreting the latter finding. Of particular significance is the observation that alcohol abuse and/or dependence occurred at some time in the lives of approximately 25 percent of both White and Black males; the rates for White and Black females were much lower.

547
Watts, T.D., Wright R., Jr., "Some Notes on Black Alcoholism Prevention," Journal of Alcohol and Drug Education, 30(2):1-3, 1985. From Thomas D. Watts and Roosevelt Wright, Jr., Eds., Black Alcoholism: Toward A Comprehensive Understanding. Springfield, IL: Charles C. Thomas Publ., 1983. Revised slightly from the original "Discussion" (pp. 125-128) (introduction to Section III of the book).

Black alcoholism is a complex, environmental, physiological, health, and mental health problem. Prevention efforts must correlate to the wide ranging complexity of the problem. Some suggestions for black alcoholism prevention are presented.

548
Weiss, K.J., Rosenberg, D.J., "Prevalence of Anxiety Disorder Among Alcoholics," Journal of Clinical Psychiatry, 46(1):3-5, 1985.

A preliminary study was conducted to assess the prevalence of DSM-III anxiety disorders in a group of inpatients being treated for alcohol detoxification. Subjects were 84 hospital inpatients (74 men and 10 women; 30 white and 54 black) who had volunteered to participate and had completed the acute phase of detoxification. A data base consisting of sociodemographic data and the details fo each patient's psychiatric, medical, and substance use history was established . . . It is concluded that a significant number of alcoholism patients have concurrent anxiety disorders and that attention should be given to associations between anxiety patterns and drinking behavior. Emphasis should be put not only on discovering the etiology of alcoholism, but also on identifying, among alcoholics, patients with otherwise treatable psychiatric problems. The potential may exist for preventing alcoholism in some patients with treatable phobic and anxious states.

549
Williams, M., "Alcohol and Ethnic Minorities: Black Americans - An Update," Alcohol Health and Research World, 9(3):52-54, 1985.

This brief report updating information on the alcohol problems of ethnic minorities in the United States is the second in a series to be featured in Alcohol Health and Research World... The reports are based on reviews of the NCALI data base.

550
Williams, M., "Blacks and Alcoholism: Issues in the 1980s." See Wright and Watts (1985). For the abstract, see Williams, 1982.

551
Williams, M., "Special Populations," Alcohol Health and Research World, 9(3):13-14, 1985.

Outlined are the goals, methods, and resasons for a national probability study of the drinking practices of Hispanic and black Americans, a current project of the NIAAA Alcohol Research Center at the Medical Research Institute in San Francisco.

552
Wright, Jr., R., and Watts, T.D., Eds., Prevention of Black Alcoholism: Issues and Strategies. Springfield, IL: Charels C. Thomas Publishers, 1985, 213 pp.

This book focuses on the prevention of alcohol abuse and alcoholism among American Blacks... Assessments are made of the strengths and weaknesses of contemporary preventive efforts and new directions for the future are explored. Chapters by Millree Williams on black alcoholism issues in the 1980s, NIAAA on prevention, John S. McNeil on models, prevention and black alcoholism, Creigs Beverly on the limitations of prevention and black alcoholism, Shirley W. King on black female alcoholism, Barbara L. Kail on black female alcoholism, Thomas C. Harford on black adolescent alcoholism, NIAAA on approaching the problem, Raymond S. Mayers and Carann S. Feazell on black alcoholism prevention and treatment in the workplace, and Carolyn F. Swift and Sethard Beverly on the utilization of ministers as black alcoholism prevention and treatment resources.

553
Young, Jr., J.L., "The Incidence of Alcohol-Related Cancers in U.S. Minorities," Paper Presented at the National Institute on Alcohol Abuse and Alcoholism, Conference on the Epidemiology of Alcohol Use and Abuse Among U.S. Ethnic Minority Groups, September 11-14, 1985, Bethesda, Maryland.

Epidemiological studies have shown the intake of alcohol to be associated with cancers of the oral cavity, larynx, esophagus, stomach, rectum and liver. Alcohol has also been suggested as a risk factor for cancer of the pancreas and prostate but the association is weak, and the increased risk, if any, is small. No association has been shown between consumption of alcohol and cancers of the urinary system. Data for the time period 1978-81 from the Surveillance, Epidemiology, and End Results (SEER) Program of the National Cancer Institute were examined for these cancer sites to contrast the risk in incidence between Whites, Blacks, Chinese, Japanese, Filipinos, Hawaiians, American Indians and Hispanics in New Mexico and

Puerto Rico. With the exception of cancers of the gall bladder, males experience an excess risk of incidence of these alcohol-related cancers. For cancers of the oral cavity and esophagus, Blacks, Chinese and Puerto Ricans experienced the highest risks. For cancer of the stomach, all minority groups except for the Chinese and Filipinos experienced a higher risk than Whites. For cancers of the rectum, Japanese were the only minority at an increased risk. Both Blacks and Hispanics experienced an increased risk of pancreatic cancer, while Blacks, Hawaiians, and Hispanics were at an increased risk to laryngeal cancer. Five-year relative survival rates for these cancer sites were also examined for the various ethnic groups except Puerto Ricans. In general Blacks and American Indians had lower survival rates while Japanese had higher survival rates than Whites. Rates for Hispanics were similar to those for other Caucasians.

# APPENDIX

## ALCOHOL AND BLACK AMERICANS: RESOURCE LISTING*

### Organizations

Alcoholics Anonymous (AA), P. O. Box 459, Grand Central Station, New York, NY 10163 (212) 686-1100. A national fellowship open to anyone who wants to achieve and maintain sobriety; an important adjunct to many treatment programs. Develops and disseminates publications on alcohol abuse and alcoholism. (Also check local telephone listings under "Alcoholics Anonymous.")

Center of Alcohol Studies, Rutgers, The State University, Smithers Hall, Busch Campus, Piscataway, NJ 08854 (201) 932-2190. An internationally known center for alcoholism research, education, clinical services, and information. Annual Summer School and the Continuing Education Seminar series offer general courses on all aspects of alcoholism as well as more specialized courses on alcoholism among blacks and other minorities or subpopulations. Publishes the *Journal of Studies on Alcohol* and books, monographs and pamphlets. Center's library, among other services, distributes annually updated research bibliographies on dozens of topics, including alcoholism in specific minority groups.

Hazelden Foundation, Box 176. Center City, MN 55012 (800) 328-9000. A generalized chemical dependency services organization that offers residential assessment and treatment, interventions, consultation and training, and prevention support services. Also makes available an extensive selection of books, pamphlets, films, and other audiovisual materials on alcoholism and drug abuse.

Minnesota Institute on Black Chemical Abuse, 2616 Nicollet Avenue South, Minneapolis, MN 55408 (612) 871-7878. Provides a range of services related to substance abuse, including referral and advocacy, community education, family counseling, diagnosis and treatment planning, adult aftercare management

*From: United States. National Institute on Alchohol Abuse and Alcoholism. "Alcohol and Black Americans," *Alcohol Resources: Update*, September, 1985: 5-7.

and support groups, prevention, and internship opportunities. Also consults nationwide on program design, offers workshops on the above topics, and develops written materials pertaining to alcoholism and drug abuse among blacks.

Multi-Cultural Prevention Work Group, c/o Annette Green, Allegheny County MHMR/DA Program, 429 Forbest Avenue, 9th Floor, Pittsburgh, PA 15219 (412) 355-4291. A network of prevention organizations and individuals offering training and consultation in prevention issues and programming, organizing, and resource mobilization.

National Black Alcoholism Council, 417 South Dearborn Street, Chicago, IL 60605 (312) 663-5780. NBAC's 1,000 members in 20 chapters throughout the United States work to raise the consciousness of the black community about the impact of alcoholism and to represent black concerns in national alcoholism organizations. NBAC also publishes a semiannual newsletter, sponsors or co-sponsors workshops and conferences (including the annual Black Alcoholism Institute), and supervises a national speaker's bureau.

National Clearinghouse for Alcohol Information, (NCALI) P.O. Box 2345, Rockville, MD 20852 (301) 468-2600. The information service of the National Institute on Alcohol Abuse and Alcoholism (NIAAA). Collects information on studies and programs pertaining to prevention, training, treatment, and research aspects of alcohol abuse and alcoholism. Shares this knowledge with interested professional audiences as well as with the general public. Free publications and services are available. For further details, contact NCALI and request "An Introduction to NCALI" (MS219) and/or "Publications Order Form" (ENCAS 7304).

National Clearinghouse for Drug Abuse Information (NCDAI), P.O. Box 416, Kensington, MD 20795 (301) 443-6500. The Clearinghouse is an information service of the National Institute on Drug Abuse. NCDAI collects, classifies, stores, and disseminates scientific information on drug abuse; answers information requests, develops resource materials; and operates a Resource Center and Communications Network.

National Council on Alcoholism, Inc. (NCA), 12 West 21st Street, 7th Floor, New York, NY 10010 (212) 206-6770. A voluntary health agency with over 200 State and local affiliates whose purposes include educating the public about alcoholism, promoting the development of effective and accessible prevention and treatment programs, acting as an advocate for the alcoholism community before government groups, and stimulating research on alcoholism. Publishes or distributes an extensive collection of books and pamphlets on various alcohol-related topics, including materials pertaining to blacks and other minorities.

National Federation of Parents for Drug-Free Youth, 1820 Franwall Avenue, Suite 16, Silver Spring, MD 20902 (301) 649-7100. A national parent network organized to combat drug and alcohol use and abuse by adolescents. Publishes newsletter; brochures for parents and children; and manuals for trainers, speakers, and organizers. Operates the Nancy Reagan Speakers Bureau, which provides community awareness presentations, workshops, and training sessions as well as programs for young people. Maintains toll-free "Help Line" for parents: 1-800-554-5437 (K-I-D-S).

The Links, Inc. National Headquarters, 1522 K Street, NW, Washington, DC 20005 (202) 783-3888. Through its network of approximately 200 chapters and 6,000 members. The Links promotes educational, civic, and cultural activities to enrich the lives of its members and their communities. The Services to Youth division has worked with the National Institute on Drug Abuse and NIAAA to train Links national program personnel. This division has recently adopted substance abuse among black youth as a national program thrust. Local chapters will aid communities in alcohol and drug abuse program efforts through contributions of expertise and volunteer time.

In addition to the organizations described above, each State or territory operates an alcoholism program charged with planning and funding alcohol abuse treatment and prevention services. Representatives from the State programs also collaborate with NIAAA, the National Institute on Drug Abuse, and the National Association of State Alcohol and Drug Abuse Directors in operating the National Prevention Network (NPN). NPN works to promote prevention standards, to encourage the development of prevention constituency groups, and to exchange information on current prevention research, techniques, and policies.

Community groups and interested individuals can contact the State programs or NPN members for general information, technical assistance, and the names of local alcoholism programs. Lists of State program directors and NPN members are available at no charge from the National Clearinghouse for Alcohol Information, P.O. Box 2345, Rockville, MD 20852, (301)

468-2600. Request MS260 (State program directors) or MS310 (NPN members).

## DIRECTORY OF STATE AND TERRITORIAL ALCOHOLISM PROGRAM DIRECTORS

This directory of State and Territorial Alcoholism Program Directors is intended as a communication aid. Because names, addresses, and telephone numbers may change, periodic updates are made. For further information, contact:

National Clearinghouse for Alcohol Information
P. O. Box 2345
Rockville, Maryland 20852
(301) 468-2600

ALABAMA

Department of Mental Health and Mental Retardation
Ken Wallis, Acting Commissioner
200 Interstate Park Drive
P. O. Box 3710
Montgomery, AL 36193
(205) 271-9209

ALASKA

Department of Health and Social Services
Office of Alcoholism and Drug Abuse
Matthew Felix, Coordinator
Pouch H-05F, 114 Second Street
Juneau, AK 99811
(907) 586-6201

ARIZONA

Arizona Department of Health Services
Alcohol Abuse and Alcoholism Section
Gwen G. Smith, Program Representative
Office of Community Behavioral Health
1740 W. Adams, Room 001
Phoenix, AZ 85007
(602) 255-1152

ARKANSAS

Arkansas Office on Alcohol and Drug Abuse Prevention
Paul T. Behnke, Director
1515 W. 7th Avenue, Suite 310
Little Rock, AR 72201
(501) 371-2603

CALIFORNIA

Department of Alcohol and Drug Programs
Chauncey Veatch III, Esq., Director
111 Capitol Mall, Suite 450
Sacramento, CA 95814
(916) 445-0834

COLORADO

Alcohol and Drug Abuse Division
Colorado Dept. of Health
Robert B. Aukerman, Director
4210 East 11th Avenue
Denver, CO 80220
(303) 331- 8201

CONNECTICUT

Connecticut Alcohol and Drug Abuse Commission
Donald J. McConnell, Executive Director
999 Asylum Avenue, 3rd Floor
Hartford, CT 06105
(203) 566-4145

DELAWARE

Division of Alcoholism, Drug Abuse and Mental Health
Bureau of Alcoholism and Drug Abuse
Sally Allshouse, Chief
1901 North Dupont Highway
New Castle, DE 19720
(302) 421-6101

DISTRICT OF COLUMBIA

Office of Health Planning and Development
Simon Holliday, Chief
1875 Connecticut Avenue, N.W., Suite 836A
Washington, DC 20009
(202) 673-7481

FLORIDA

Alcohol and Drug Abuse Program
Department of Health and Rehabilitation Services
Linda Lewis, Director
1317 Winewood Boulevard, Room 157A
Tallahassee, FL 32301
(904) 488-0900

GEORGIA

Division of Mental Health, Mental Retardation and Substance Abuse
Georgia Department of Human Resources
Patricia A. Redmond, Director
878 Peachtree Street, N.E., 3rd Floor
Atlanta, GA 30309
(404) 894-6352

GUAM

Territory of Guam
Department of Mental Health and Substance Abuse
Dr. David L. G. Shimizu, Director
P. O. Box 8896
Tamuning, GU 96911
011-671-646-9260-9

HAWAII

Alcohol and Drug Abuse Branch
Mental Health Division
Department of Health
Joyce Ingram-Chinn, Branch Chief
P. O. Box 3378
Honolulu, HI 96801
(808) 548-4280

IDAHO

Substance Abuse Section
Department of Health & Welfare
Charles E. Burns, Supervisor
450 West State Street, 4th Floor
Boise, ID 83720
(208) 334-4368

ILLINOIS

Department of Alcoholism and Substance Abuse
Edward T. Duffy, Director
State of Illinois Center
100 W. Randolph Street, Suite 5-600
Chicago, IL 60610
(312) 917-3840

INDIANA

Division of Addiction Services
Department of Mental Health
Joseph E. Mills, III, Director
117 East Washington Street
Indianapolis, IN 46204
(317) 232-7816

IOWA

Department of Substance Abuse
Mary L. Ellis, Director
Colony Building
507 10th Street, Suite 500
Des Moines, IA 50319
(515) 281-3641

KANSAS

Alcohol and Drug Abuse Services
James A. McHenry, Jr., Ph.D.
Commissioner
Biddle Building
2700 West Sixth Street, 2nd Floor

Topeka, KS 66606
(913) 296-3925

KENTUCKY

Cabinet for Human Resources
Michael Townsend, Director
Division of Substance Abuse
Department for Mental Health and Mental Retardation
275 East Main Street
Frankfort, KY 40621
(502) 564-2880

LOUISIANA

Office of Prevention and Recovery from Alcohol and Drug Abuse
Vern Ridgeway, Assistant Secretary
P. O. Box 53129
2744-B Wooddale Boulevard
Baton Rouge, LA 70892
(504) 922-0728

MAINE

Office of Alcoholism and Drug Abuse Prevention
Neill Miner, Director
State House Station #11
Augusta, ME 04333
(207) 289-2781

MARYLAND

Alcoholism Control Administration
John Bland, Director
201 West Preston Street, 4th Floor
Baltimore, MD 21201
(301) 225-6541, 6542

MASSACHUSETTS

Division of Alcoholism

Edward Blacker, Ph.D., Director
150 Tremont Street
Boston, MA 02111
(617) 727-1960

MICHIGAN

Office of Substance Abuse Services
Robert Brook, Administrator
3500 North Logan Street
P. O. Box 30035
Lansing, MI 48909
(517) 373-8603

MINNESOTA

Chemical Dependency Program Div.
Cynthia Turnure, Ph.D., Executive Director
Department of Human Services
Space Center
444 Lafayette Road
St. Paul, MN 55101
(612) 296-3991

MISSISSIPPI

Division of Alcohol and Drug Abuse
Ann D. Robertson, M.S.W., Director
1102 Robert E. Lee Office Building
Jackson, MS 39201
(601) 359-1297

MISSOURI

Division of Alcohol and Drug Abuse
R. B. Wilson, Director
2002 Missouri Boulevard
P. O. Box 687
Jefferson City, MO 65101
(314) 751-4942

MONTANA

Alcohol and Drug Abuse Division
State of Montana
Department of Institutions
Robert Anderson, Administrator
1539 Eleventh Avenue
Helena, MT 59620
(406) 444-2827

NEBRASKA

Division of Alcoholism and Drug Abuse
Cecilia Willis, Ph.D., Director
Box 94728
Lincoln, NE 68509
(402) 471-2851, ext. 5583

NEVADA

Bureau of Alcohol and Drug Abuse
Department of Human Resources
Richard Ham, Chief
505 East King Street
Carson City, NV 89710
(702) 885-4790

NEW HAMPSHIRE

Office of Alcohol and Drug Abuse Prevention
Geraldine Sylvester, Director
Health and Welfare Building
Hazen Drive
Concord, NH 03301
(603) 271-4627, 271-4630

NEW JERSEY

Division of Alcoholism
New Jersey Department of Health
Riley Regan, Director
129 East Hanover Street
Trenton, NJ 08608
(609) 292-8949

NEW MEXICO

Alcoholism Bureau
Joe Gallegos, Acting Chief
Behavioral Health Services Division
Crown Building
P. O. Box 968
Santa Fe, NM 87504-0968
(505) 984-0020, ext. 493

NEW YORK

New York State Division of Alcoholism and Alcohol Abuse
Robert V. Shear, Director
194 Washington Avenue
Albany, NY 12210
(518) 474-5417

NORTH CAROLINA

Division of Mental Health, Mental Retardation and Substance Abuse Services
Alcohol and Drug Abuse Section
Thomas F. Miriello, Deputy Director
325 North Salisbury Street
Raleigh, NC 27611
(919) 733-4670

NORTH DAKOTA

State Department of Human Services
Division of Alcoholism and Drug Abuse
Tom R. Hedin, Director
State Capitol
Bismarck, ND 58505
(701) 224-2769

NORTH MARIANA ISLANDS

Dr. Torres Hospital
Ben Kaipat, Medical Officer
Saipan, Mariana Islands 96950
6112, 6222 (through International Operator 0-160691)

## OHIO

Ohio Department of Health
Bureau of Alcohol Abuse and Alcoholism Recovery
Wayne Lindstrom, Chief
170 North High Street, 3rd Floor
Columbus, OH 43215
(614) 466-3445

## OKLAHOMA

Programs Division
Thomas Stanitis, M.A., M.H.S., Chief of Programs
P. O. Box 53277, Capitol Station
Oklahoma City, OK 73152
(405) 521-0044

## OREGON

Program Office for Alcohol and Drug Abuse
Department of Human Resources
Jeffrey N. Kushner
Assistant Director
301 Public Service Building
Salem, OR 97310
(503) 378-2163

## PENNSYLVANIA

Office of Drug and Alcohol Programs
Luceille Fleming, Deputy Secretary for Drug and Alcohol Programs
P. O. Box 90, Department of Health
Health and Welfare Building, 8th Floor
Harrisburg, PA 17108
(717) 787-9857

## PUERTO RICO

Puerto Rico Department of Addiction Control Services
Alejandrina S. deLugo
Assistant Secretariat of Alcoholism
P. O. Box 21414, Rio Piedras Station

Rio Piedras, PR 00928
(809) 763-5014 or 763-7575

RHODE ISLAND

Department of Mental Health, Mental Retardation and Hospitals
Division of Substance Abuse
William H. Pimental, Assistance Director
Substance Abuse Administration Building
Cranston, RI 02920
(401) 464-2091

AMERICAN SAMOA

Human Services Clinic
Alcohol and Drug Program
Fualaau Hanipale, Director
LBJ Tropical Medical Center
Pago, Pago, American Samoa 96799
011-684-633-5139

SOUTH CAROLINA

South Carolina Commission on Alcohol and Drug Abuse
William J. McCord, Director
3700 Forest Drive, Suite 300
Columbia, SC 29204
(803) 758-2521

SOUTH DAKOTA

Division of Alcohol and Drug Abuse
Lois Olson, Director
Joe Foss Building
523 East Capitol
Pierre, SD 57501-3182
(605) 773-3123

TENNESSEE

Tennessee Department of Mental Health and Mental Retardation

Robert Currie, Assistant Commissioner
Division of Alcohol and Drug Abuse Services
James K. Polk Building
505 Deaderick Street, 4th Floor
Nashville, TN 37219
(615) 741-1921

## TEXAS

Texas Commission on Alcohol and Drug Abuse
Ross Newby, Executive Director
1705 Guadalupe Street
Austin, TX 78701
(512) 475-2577

## TRUST TERRITORY OF THE PACIFIC ISLANDS

Masao Kumangai, M.D., Director
Health Services
Office of the High Commissioner
Saipan, Mariana Islands 96950
Trust Territory of the Pacific Islands
9854, 9355 (through International Operator 0-160691)

## UTAH

Division of Alcoholism and Drugs
F. Leon PoVey, Director
150 West North Temple
P. O. Box 45500
Salt Lake City, UT 84145
(801) 533-6532

## VERMONT

Office of Alcohol and Drug Programs
Richard Powell II, Director
103 South Main Street
Osgood Building
Waterbury, VT 05676
(802) 241-2170

## VIRGIN ISLANDS

Division of Mental Health, Alcoholism
and Drug Dependency Services
Patricia Todman-Rhymer, Director
P. O. Box 7309
St. Thomas, US VI 00801
(809) 774-4888

VIRGINIA

Department of Mental Health/Mental Retardation
Wayne Thacker, Director
Office of Substance Abuse Services
P. O. Box 1797
109 Governor Street
Richmond, VA 23214
(804) 786-3906

WASHINGTON

Bureau of Alcoholism & Substance Abuse
Glen Miller, Director
Mailstop OB-44W
Olympia, WA 98504
(206) 752-5866

WEST VIRGINIA

Division of Alcoholism and Drug Abuse
Office of Behavioral Health Services
Jack Clohan, Jr., Director
State Capitol
1800 Washington Street East
Charleston, WV 25305
(304) 348-2276

WISCONSIN

Wisconsin Office of Alcohol and Other Drug Abuse
Larry W. Monson, Director
1 West Wilson Street, Room 441
P. O. Box 7851
Madison, WI 53702
(608) 266-3442

WYOMING

Division of Community Programs
Jean DeFratis, Substance Abuse Program Manager
Hathaway Building, 3rd Floor
Cheyenne, WY 82002
(307) 777-7115, ext. 7118

INDEX*


Aborigines (Australia), 352
Acker, J., 52
Adickes, E., 312
Africa, 111
African Beer Gardens of Bulawayo, 95
Agarwal, D., 313
Aguirre, M., 190
Albrecht, G., 168
Albuquerque, N.M., 93
Alcohol, Drug Abuse and Mental Health Administration, 283, 304, 305
Alcohol Rehabilitation Centers (US Navy), 109
Alcoholics Anonymous, 50, 96, 222, 326, and Appendix
Alexis, R., 491
Alksne, H., 199
Allen, B., 4
Allen, C., 116, 191
Allen, D., 437
Allen, L., 300
Alsikafi, M., 164, 280
Alston, J., 74
Alterman, A., 429
Ames, G., 494, 505, 513
Amin, R., 491
Anderson, R., 414, 448
Anderson, S., 392
Andrews, T., 153, 314
Appalachian(s), 3, 308
Arevalo, R., 316
Argeriou, M., 117, 140
Arkansas Office on Alcohol and Drug Abuse Prevention, 260, 492
Arnold, S., 220, 242
Aronson, B., 21
Aronson, S., 21
Asians, 122, 123, 236, 386, 479, 534
Asian-Americans, 194, 275, 370, 464
Athanail, S., 288
Atlanta, Ga., 64, 83, 132, 168
Atlanta University School of Social Work, 97
Audie Murphy Memorial Veterans Hospital, San Antonio, Tx., 227
Austin, D., 415
Austin, G., 188, 468
Austin, Texas, 310
Australia (aborigines), 352
Avery, R., 492

Bachman, J., 317
Bailey, M., 9
Baillargeon, J., 227
Balter, M., 404
Baltimore, Md., 87, 308, 343, 404
Baptist Hospital of Southeast Texas (Beaumont, Texas), 369


*This index contains a listing of all authors, and as well the names of cities mentioned, minority populations (Hispanics, Native Americans, etc.) agencies, tests or measurements employed, etc. This is not a subject index, per se, but this index should be expansive enough, along with the chronological listing in the index itself, to provide the reader with significant access to many facets of information on black alcoholism and related subject areas.

Barnes, G., 318, 387
Barsky, S., 192
Barton, J., 267
Baskin, D., 319
Baton Rouge, Louisiana, 509
Battle, C., 469
Bauman, K., 261
Beaubrun, M., 470
Beaumont, Texas, 369
Beck, A., 183, 214
Beck Depression Inventory, 183
Beckman, L., 479
Bedrosian, R., 214
Belcastro, P., 388
-Belcastro Sexual Behavior Inventory (BSBI), 388
Bell, C., 493
Bell, P., pp. xiv, xvi, xvii, 221, 262, 320, 321, 416
Belmont, H., 262
Bender, S., 298
Bentler, P., 236
Benin City, Nigeria, 487
Benjamin, M., 322
Benjamin, R., 118, 244, 322
Bennett, D., 336
Bennett, G., 457
Bennett, L., 494, 505, 513
Berberian, R., 78
Berman, R., 263
Bernstein, B., 296
Berry, G., 475, 506
Bertolucci, D., 495
Beschner, G., 225
Bessen, G., 54
Best, J., 222
Beverly, C., 98, 119, 323, 417, 496, 552
Beverly, S., 541, 552
Bhatia, P., 293
Biever, P., 227
Bigge, R., 89
Bingol, M., 277
Black Drinking Practices Study Project, 349
Blacker, E., 10
Bland, J., 324
Blassingame, J., xix
Blot, W., 364, 384
Bluestone, H., 49, 319, 504
Blumberg, L., 192
Blume, S., 219
Bobo, S., 223
Bohtemps, P., 325
Borinski, E., 8
Borker, R., 278
Bosron, W., 418
Boston City Hospital, 23
Bourne, P., 65, 80, 120, 224
Bowman, P., 265
Bramstom, B., 185
Braxton, E., 146
Brill, L., 481, 499, 515
Brisbane, F. L., xii, 121, 497, 498
British, 209
Brock, R., 41
Bronx Municipal Hospital Center, New York City, 298
Brotherhood Club, 50
Broward County, Florida Alcohol and Drug Abuse Services Division Outreach Program, 329
Brown, J., 254
Brown, R., 99, 387
Browne, P., 65, 88, 120, 224
Brozovic, M., 209
Brunswick, A., 27, 66, 79, 154, 225
Bryan, E., 261
Buckalew, L., 226
Bucky, S., 109
Burgos, W., 231, 232
Burke, A., 471
Burtle, V., 238
Butler, M., 1
Byram, O., 472

Caetano, R., 473, 474
Cahalan, D., 28, 34, 100, 122, 123, 155
Caldwell, F., vii, ix, 326, 419
California, 122, 155, 170, 453, 467, 473
Camey, F., 101
Cancer Institute, National, 553
Cancer Survey, Third National, 291
Career Maturity Inventory Attitude Component Scale, 482
Caribbean, 28, 34, 99, 174, 175, 407
Carlisi, J., 343
Carroll, E., 188
Carroll, J., 327, 389
Carson, J., 29
Carter, J., 156, 157, 328, 390
Carter, R., 329
Catholics, 155
Caution, G., 391
Center for Minority Group Programs, 59
Center for Multicultural Awareness, 256
Chafetz, M., 80
Chakrabarti, R., 209
Chambers, C., 113, 499
Charay, A., 159
Charles, H., 362
Charlotte Drug Education Center, 420
Chatham, L., 330
Chaucer, N., 50
Cherokees of Oklahoma (Native Americans), 250
Chicago, Ill., 290
Chicanos, 72, 107, 114, 122, 174, 175, 177, 238, 316
China, 455
Chit Chat Residential Treatment Center, 84
Christmas, J., 193
Cincinnati General Hospital, 235
Cincinnati, Ohio, 289, 308, 343
Cisin, I., 28, 100, 404
Clain, D., 185, 189
Clance, R., 102
Clark, L., 194
Clark, W., 67
Cleveland, Ohio, 132, 293
Cloninger, C., 445
Coakley, J., 266
Cohen, 477
Colby, J., 526
Coleman, S., 469
Combs-Orme, T., 500
Coney, J., 103, 158, 195
Connecticut Commission on Alcoholism, 5
Conrad, M., 267
Cooper, A., 340
Cooper, M., 87
Corrigan, E., 392
Costello, R., 227
Cousin, W., 50
CPI, 447
Crawford, G., 268
Crawford, P., 331
Crisp, A., 269, 270
Crossley, H., 28
Crow, J., ix

D'Amico, D., 200
Dandoy, S., 104
Darity, W., 228
Darvish, H., 309
Davies, J. E., 52
Davis, C., ix
Davis, E., 48
Davis, Jr., F., 41, 51, 68, 81, 124
Davis, L., xv, xvii
Davis, W., 69, 82, 332

Dawkins, M., xvi, 125, 126, 137, 166, 271, 272, 333, 421-424
Day, W.,
Del-Villano, B., 229, 273, 274
DeLuca, J., 230
Dembo, J., 230
Dembo, R., 232
Demone, H., 10
Dennis, R., 334
Department of Health, Education and Welfare, 306
Department of Health and Human Services Task Force on Black and Minority Health, 476
DeRisi, W., 425
Desjarlais, D., 231
Detroit, Mi., 192, 308, 343
Diagnostic Interview Schedule, 546
Diehl, A., 501
Dimock Community Health Center Alcoholism Program, Roxbury, Ma., 158
Do It Now Foundation, 159
Dohrenwend, B., 30
Dominican Republic, 202
Douglass, F., xix, 59
Downey, Ill., 69
Downstate Medical Center, 53
DuBois, W., 486
Dufour, M., 495
Dupree, D., 159
Durant, A., 335

Eagleville Hospital and Rehabilitation Center, 327, 389
East Indians, 259
Edmundson, W. F., 52
Edwards, D., 393, 502
Einstein, S., 503
Ellington, J., 233
Employee Assistance Programs (EAP), 534
Engler, R., 83
Ensminger, M., 290
Estes, N., 275
Evans, J., xiv, xvi, xvii, 320, 321, 416
Everette, L., 336
Eversmeyer, W., 196
Expand Associates, 197

Faulkinberry, R., 303
Faupel, C., 399
Fautimi, E., 198
Feagins, J., 84
Feazell, C., 530, 552
Federal Correctional Institute, Tallahassee, Fl., 353
Federal Revenue Act, 1
Felice, M., 484
Ferguson, L., 337
Fernandez-Pol, B., 504
Fialkov, M., 160
Fine, E., 161, 247
Firland Tuberculous Sanatorium, 14
Fisher, R., 15
Fleetwood, M., 276
Florida, 329, 353, 399
Floyd, L., 338
Fly, J., 472
Fox, R., 65
Framingham, Ma., 465
Frazier, 4
Freedman's Hospital, Howard University, 146
Freeman, D., 199
Freeman, H., 10
Friedberg, B., 33
Friedman, A., 225
Friedman, G., 170, 442
Fuchs, M., 277

Gadsen, R., 361
Gaines, A., 278, 505
Gaines, J., 104.5, 127
Galanter, M., 247, 298
Galchus, D., 162
Galchus, K., 162
Galizio, M., 427
Gardena, Ca., 369
Garrett, G., 42
Garris, A., 288
Gary, Indiana, 64, 83
Gary, L., 279, 394, 395, 428, 475, 506
Gay, J., 339
Gearing, F., 200
Genovese, E., 128
Georgia, 169
Georgian Clinic, 74
German, 313, 343
Gibson, D., 201
Gillis, L., 70, 163
Gillum, R., 396
Glasgow, xix
Globetti, G., 7, 13, 17, 18, 35, 36, 164, 280
Goddard, L., 480
Goldsmith, R., 235
Goldstein, G., 429
Gomberg, E., 397
Goodwin, D., 71, 398
Goodwin, F., 72
Goolkasian, P., 233
Gordon, A., 202
Gorwitz, K., 29
Grant, C., 396
Green, R., 463
Greenway, C., 343
Gregory, D., 105
Gross, M., 53
Gunderson, E., 109
Gutsch, K., 402
Guze, S., 39

Haberman, P., 9
Halikas, J., 309
Hall, W., 542
Halstead-Reitan Test, 429
Halverson, D., 14
Hanenson, I., 235
Hanisch, R., 467
Hanson, B., 508
Harada, S., 313
Hardesty, A., 213
Harford, T., 446, 509, 510, 552
Harlem Hospital Center, 41, 48 96, 219
Harper, F., 85, 118, 119, 120, 124, 125, 126, 127, 129, 130-137, 142, 145, 149, 152, 165, 166, 203, 234, 281, 424, 431, 432, 441
Harrison, D., 37
Hartford, Connecticut, 50
Harvey, W., 511
Harwood, E., 33
Hazelden Foundation, Appendix
Headlam, H., 235
Heath, D., 340
Heilbrun, A., 167
Heilbrun, K., 167
Heinemann, M., 275
Heller, J., 296
Helmer, J., 106
Helrich, A., 54
Henderson, B., 467
Henderson, P., 383, 433, 466
Henry, N. L., xv, xvii
Herd, D., 434, 435, 474, 476, 477, 512-515
Hermann Hospital, Houston, Texas, 369
Herrera, C., 86
Higgins, P. 168
Hillsman, J., 254

Hispanics, 27, 113, 123, 143, 190, 194, 202, 213, 215, 216, 236, 256, 258, 262, 277, 288, 302, 306, 318, 319, 345, 363, 370, 386, 438, 442, 457, 464, 473, 479, 484, 485, 534, 553
Hoban, C., 266
Hodges, E., 56
Hodges, H., 169
Holliday, B., 282, 341, 436
Horowitz, B., 342
Hospital for Joint Diseases, Harlem, New York City,
Houston, Texas, 369
Howard, J., 33
Howell, R., 177
Huba, G., 236
Hudson, H., 90
_Human Behavior_, 73
Humphrey, J., 437
Hunt, J., 210
Hyman, M., 54

Iiyama, P., 138
Illes, R., 516
Inciardi, J., 399
India, 455
Indianapolis, Indiana, 313
Indians (in South Africa), 461
Inge, R., 139
Institute for the Study of Drug Misuse (ISDM), 503, 517
_International Journal of the Addictions_, 517
Iosub, S., 277
Iran, 455
Irish Americans, 101
Isaacson, C., 204
Isralowitz, R., 438, 443
Italian, 343
Ivens, P., 284
Iverson, D., 285

Jackson, J., (Rev)., 187
Jackson, N., 343
Jackson, R., 205
Jacobs, R., 107
Jamaica Ginger extract, 144
Japanese, 289, 313, 442
Jarvis, E., 206
Jeffrey, T., 463
Jews, 155, 391, 464
Jim Crow legislation, 435
Job Corps, 174
Johnson, B., 138, 188
Johnson, R., 6, 518
Johnston, L., 317
Jones, L., 286
Jones, M., 69, 82
_Journal of Studies on Alcohol_, 140
_Journal of the National Medical Association_, 31

Kachrv, R., 287
Kaelber, C., 446
Kail, B., 478, 519, 552
Kalish, H., 344
Kaiser-Permanente Medical Center, Oakland, Ca., 442, 453
Kalow, W., 400
Kamar, N., 254
Kandel, D., 212
Kane, G., 288, 345
Karasawa, T., 289
Kaufman, E., 199, 398
Keenan, T., 207
Kellam, S., 290, 439
Keller, A., 291, 346
Kelly, J., 520
Kent, 3
Kentucky School of Alcohol Studies, 179
Kentucky Task Force on Minority Alcohol Concerns, 179, 245
Kidane, A., 347
Kilty, K., 440

King, L., 32, 108, 141, 401, 441, 521
King, S., 522, 552
Kirsch, R., 523
Kittrell, R., 348
Klatsky, A., 170, 442
Klerman, G., 292
Kline, R., 524
Kolb, D., 109
Korzis, J., 491
Kruzich, D., 463
Kuller, L., 15, 87
Kurpiel, R., 237
Kushida, T., 289

Labaw, P., 112
Landy, C., 442
Larkins, J., 11, 142
Latin-American, 28, 34
Law Enforcement Assistance Administration, 266
Leach, B., 80
League of Nations, 111
Leashore, B., 395
Lecca, P., xiv, xviii
Lee, L., 443
Leland, J., 479
Lescault, B., 296
Letman, S., 383
Lettieri, D., 188
Leunes, A., 148
Lewis, C., 444
Lewis, C. E., 445, 525
Lewis, E., 53
Lewis, H., 3
Lewis, J., 70
Lexington, Ky., 179
Li, T., 418
Liebow, E., 19
Light, E., 224
Lilienfeld, A., 15
Lincoln Community Health Center, Durham, North Carolina, 157

The Links, Inc., Appendix
Linsky, A., 526
Lipscomb, H., 48
Lipscomb, W., 43, 349, 350, 480, 481, 527
Lipson, A., A., 23
The Liquor Handbook 1980, 264
Littlejohn, Roy, Assocs., 51, 77, 83,
Littles, R., 351
Livingston, I., 528
Loon, N., 185
Louisiana, 509
Louisville, Ky., 179
Lopez, R., 108, 141
Lopez-Lee, D., 238
Los Angeles, Ca., 236, 467
Lowe, G., 56, 74, 169
Lowenthal, M., 239
Lowman, C., 446
Ludmar, J., 208
Ludwig, M., 462
Lukoff, I., 478

MacAndrew Alcoholism Scale (see Minnesota Multiphasic Personality Inventory).
MacDonald, D., 233
MacLachlan, S., 88
MacPhail, A., 240
McAdoo, H., 403
McBride,D., 258
McBride, W., 533
McCalep, S., 482
McClain, J., 449
McClean, V., 483
McClellan, K., 534
McCord, W., 33
McCreary, C., 171
McGrath, W., 89
McMillen, M., 242
McNeil, J., 535, 552
McReynolds, M., 7, 13
Mack, T., 467
Maddox, G., 4, 8, 22, 38
Magnes, L., 418

Majumdar, M., 293
Malcolm Bliss Mental Health Center, 94
Malezer, L., 352
Malin, H., 266
Malloy, T., 327, 389
Manhattan Alcoholism Rehabilitation Unit, 208
Marshall, E., 241, 254
Marshall, H., 57
Marshall, M., 259
Martin, C., 529
Martin Luther King, Jr., Health Center Alcoholism Unit, 288
Martinez, J., 143
Maryland, 266, 404
Massachusetts, 158, 202, 465
Massachusetts Youth Reception Center, 10
Mathews, R., 447
Mayers, R., 530, 552
Mayet, F., 531
Mayo, M., 532
Maypole, D., 414, 448
Meade, T., 209
Megargee, E., 353
Meier-Tackmann, D., 313
Mello, N., 39
Memorial Hospital (Gardena, California), 369
Mendelson, j., 39
Mercy Hospital Outreach Clinic, 84
Messolonghites, L., 243, 255
Mettlin, C., 294
Mexican-American, 171, 227
Miami, Florida, 132, 399
Michigan, 357
Milgram, G., 110, 295
Mill, W., 516
Miller, K., 296
Miller, L., 348
Miller, R., 210
Miller, S., 273, 274
Minneapolis, Minnesota, 113
Minnesota Institute on Black Chemical Abuse, 172, 354, and Appendix.
Minnesota Multiphasic Personality Inventory (MMPI), 167, 208, 353, 360, 362, 405, 463, 524, 532
Minor, M., 316
Miranda, V., 355, 356, 450
Mississippi, 7, 13, 17, 18, 35, 37, 64, 83, 118, 244, 377, 413, 447
Missouri, 445
Missouri, C., 504
Mizruchi, S., 504
Monroe-Scott, B., 356
Morales, G., 504
Morehouse, E., 211
Morgan, J., 144
Morgan, M., 484
Morgan, P., 451
Morris, L., 364
Morris, V., 469
Morse, R., 164, 280
Multicultural Drug Abuse Prevention Center, 173
Multicultural Prevention Work Group, Appendix.
Murphy, G., 32
Murray Thematic Apperception Test, 8
Myers, H., F., xv, xvii
Myers, V., 174, 175

Nace, E., 485
Nathan, P., 23
National Alcoholism Program Information System (NAPIS), 337
National Black Alcoholism Council, 357, 454, and Appendix.

National Center for Alcohol Education, 176
National Center for Urban Ethnic Affairs, 308
National Council on Alcoholism, 297, and Appendix
National Federation of Parents for Drug-Free Youth, Appendix.
National Institute for Community Development, 58, 63
National Institute on Alcohol Abuse and Alcoholism, vii, xiii, xiv, xvii, 55, 58, 59, 63, 68, 92, 117, 129, 140, 151, 152, 186, 187, 215, 234, 252-254, 307, 316, 323, 325, 326, 329, 330-332, 334, 336-338, 341 347, 351, 355, 356, 365, 369, 373-375, 377, 378, 383, 385, 409, 413, 458, 459, 460, 462, 489, 509, 512, 521, 539, 540, 543-546, 551, 552, 553, and Appendix.
_National Leader_, 452
National Youth Polydrug Study, 308
Native Americans, 72, 113, 114, 194, 216, 218, 238, 250, 256, 262, 275, 302, 306, 312, 343, 363, 370, 386, 391, 457, 464, 479, 534, 553
Nebraska Division on Alcoholism, 358
Nelson, M., 319
New Haven, 2
New York City, 40, 47, 49, 64, 83, 115, 190, 200, 208, 219, 225, 231, 319, 367
-Task Force on Women and Alcoholism, 359
-Veteran's Administration Hospital, 86
-Women's Emergency Shelter, 42
New York State, 212, 318
Newman, R., xv, xvii, 486
Newton, Ma., 202
Nicholson, T., 388
Nigeria, 487
Nishi, S., 138
Noble, J., 495
Nobles, J., 360
North Carolina, 1, 26, 156, 157, 261, 384
-Council on Alcoholism, Black Task Force, 408
Novick, L., 90
Novy, C., 361
Nurco, D., 404

Ohio, 293
Oklahoma, 218
Oldroyd, R., 177
O'Malley, P., 317
Oriental, 318, 442, 484, 553
Oshodin, O., 487
Owen, V., 89

Pachon, P., ix
Pacific Island minorities, 386
Padilla, E., 171
Pagan, G., 536
Pais, J., 445
Pan, L., 111
Panepinto, W., 298
Paredes, A., 218
Paterson, A., 537
Paton, S., 212
Patterson, B., 145
Patterson, E., 362
Pattison, E., 398
Payton, C., 262
Pelton, L., 342
Penk, W., 405
Perper, J., 87
Perrine, G., 267
Personality Research Form (PRF), 327
Peteroy, E., 299
Peters, R., 467
Petersen, D., 113
Petitti, D., 453
Petrarulo, E., 459
Phelps, D., 77
Philadelphia, Pa., 192, 247
Philadelphia Community Mental Health Center, 161
Philadelphia Psychiatric Center, 308
Piedmont, 3
Pike, M., 467
Pittman, D., 61, 149, 406
Pittsburgh, Pa., 84
Polish, 343
Pollack, M., 60
Pomeroy, G., 36
Porche, M., 363
Porter, D., xiv, xvii
Porter, R., 300
Pottern, L., 364
Pottiger, A., 399
Powell, B., 94, 115
Praeger, ix
Prendergast, M., 468
Primm, B., 178
Proskey, A., 287
Protestants, 8, 155
Providence, R.I., 308, 343
_Public Health Reports_, 283
Puerto Ricans, 30, 49, 50, 86, 90, 143, 202, 219, 231, 232, 504, 553
Purdy, R., 57

Quinn, L., 361

Raleigh Hills Hospital, Houston, Texas, 369
Ralston, L., 407
Rana, P. G., xv, xvii
Randolph, D., 402
Rao, V. N., 244
Rao, V. V., 244
Rappaport, M., 112
Ratcliff, K., 301
Rauh, J., 235
Rawson, J., 233
Redd, B., 365
Redd, M., 538
Reed, S., 366
Reichwein, J., 454
Reinach, S., 531
Research Triangle Institute, 446
Rice, J., 525
Richter, G., 533
Rivers, W., 367
Roberts, T., 455
Robey, F., 179, 245
Robins, L., 24, 32, 39, 44, 60, 62, 301, 500, 525, 539
Roebuck, J., 6

Roff, M., 60
Rogers, E., 300
Roizen, J., 246, 368
Roscioli, D., 327
Rosciolo, D., 389
Rosemon, W., 369
Rosenberg, D., 548
Rosenblatt, S., 53
Rosewood (in Austin, Texas), 310
Roy, T., 516
Royce, J., 370
Rubicon Black Alcoholism Research and Demonstration Program, 237, 336
Rubin, B., 439
Rubington, E., 45
Russel, M., 540
Russianoff, P., 372
Rutgers University Center of Alcohol Studies, 46, 302, 371, and Appendix

St. Louis Epidemiologic Catchment Area (ECA), 539
St. Louis, Mo., 25, 46, 61, 309
St. Paul, 113
Saleebey, D., xiv, xviii
Salt Lake City, Utah, 113
Sampson, C., 146
Samuels, F., 147
San Antonio, Texas, 227
San Francisco, Ca., 350, 474, 481
San Francisco General Hospital, 88
Saunders, E., 542
Schacter, L., 229, 273, 274
Schatzman, 4
Schecter, A., 366
Schick-Shadd Hospital, 75
Schmeidler, J., 231, 232
Schneider, B., 213
Schneider, E., 213
Schuckit, M., 180
Schutte, C., 531
Scoles, P., 247
Scott, B., 373
Seftel, H., 181
Seggie, J., 185
Seixas, F., 161
Senay, E., 268, 456
Shanks, P., 150
Shaw, B., 183
Sheinberg, J., 9
Shelly, C., 429
Sherman, M. J., 16
Shikata, T., 289
Shipley, T., 192
Shulman, N., 542
Shuman, R., 312
Shy, C., 384
Siegal, H., 40, 47, 113
Sieglaub, A., 170, 442, 453
Simmons, L., 374
Simon, M., 240, 290
Singer, M., 438, 443
Skolnick, J., 2
Slabbert, M., 70
Small, J., 408
Smith, D., 218
Smith, E., 375
Smith, W., 148
Smith-DiJulio, K., 275
Smith-Peterson, C., 457
Snyder, D., 524
Sobell, M., 410
Solomon, P., 23
South, 453
South Africa, 160, 163, 181, 204, 239, 240, 381, 461, 523, 531, 537
_South African Medical Journal_, 70
Southern Area Alcohol Education and Training Program, 182
Stanchfield, A., 248
Starland, V., 303
Starr, B., ix

State and Territorial
Alcoholism Program
Directors-Directory,
See Appendix.
Steeg, C., 249
Steele, R., 214
Steer, R., 161, 183
Stein, F., 427
Steinberg, A., 386
Stephens, V., 437
Stern, M., 20, 61, 149
Stevenson, D., 439
Stimmel, B., 488
Stone, G., 163
Stratton, R., 250
Straus, M., 526
Strauss, 4
Strayer, R., 5
Street, P., 150
Stroup, A., 62
Sullivan, N., 376
Swift, C., 91, 541, 552

Tallahassee, Florida, 353
Tally's Corner, 19
Tarica, C., 66, 79
Tarrter, R., 429
Taylor, J., 500
Telischi, M., 287
Tenery, J., ix
Texas, 184
Texas Commission on
Alcoholism, 184
Thematic Apperception Test,
4, 5
Thomas, G., 185, 189
Thomson, G., 542
Tinklenberg, J., 80
Tischfield, J., 229, 273
Tokyo, Japan, 289
Tongue, E., 406
Torrance, J., 240
Torres, J. 251
Toussie, S., 200
Treiman, B., 114, 123, 150
Trinidad, 259
Trocki, K., 350, 481
Tulloss, T., 144
Turner, D., ix

University of New Mexico,
Institute for Social
Research and Development,
93
University of Rhodesia, 189
The Utah State Prison, 177

Van-De-Merwe, T., 381
Van-der Burgh, C., 461
Varvel, W., 148
Vega, W., 415
Veterans Administration
Hospitals, 291
Veterans Administration
Hospital, Gulfport,
Mississippi, 447
Vettraino, A., 23
Viamontes, J., 94, 115
Victor, 80
Vietnam veterans, 390
Vitols, N., 26

Waite, B., 462
Wallace, J. 219
Walters, G., 463
Ward, D., 306
Warheit, G., 546
Warner, R., 257
Washington, D.C., 19, 132,
198, 364
Washington Heights Study of
Adolescent Health, 27
Washington, M., 268
Washington, V., 152
Watson, D., 410
Watts, C., 382
Watts, D., v
Watts, M. C., v
Watts, T., xiv, xv, xvii,
xviii, 464, 490,
496, 522, 535,
547, 552
Webb, L., 217
West Indians, 471

West Side Veterans Administration Hospital, 366
*Webster's Ninth New Collegiate Dictionary*, xiv
Wechsler Adult Intelligence Scale (WAIS), 299, 429
Weiss, K., 548
Weller, R., 309
Welte, J., 318
Wernersville, Pa., 84
Westermeyer, J., 411, 412
Westie, K., 258
Wicks, A., 185, 189
Williams, G., 310
Williams, J., 112
Williams, L., 311
Williams, M., 413, 549, 550, 551, 552
Willis, W., 483
Wilsnack, S., 479
Wilson, J., 12
Wilson, P., 465
Winbush, R., 383, 466
Wingard, D., 484
Wingard, J., 326
Winick, C., 481, 499, 515
Winn, D., 384
Winston, S., 1Wolcott, H., 95
Wolfe, 80
Wolock, I., 341
Womble, M., 469, 498
Woodward, W., 362
Wright, D., 223
Wright, E., v, 385
Wright, R., xiv, xv, xviii, 464, 490, 496, 522, 535, 547, 552
Wyandotte County, Kansas, 89
Wyandotte Mental Health Center, Kansas City, Kansas, 89

Yamamoto, J., 386
Yawney, C., 259
Young, J., 553
Yu, M., 467

Zager, L., 353
Zalesnick, M., 343
Zambrana-Shojaei, R., 190
Zeiner, A., 218
Ziegler, R., 364
Zimbabwe, 95
Zimberg, S., 48, 96, 219
Zinkowski, J., 117, 140